CYBORGS@CYBERSPACE?

CYBORGS@CYBERSPACE?

An Ethnographer

Looks to the Future

[DAVID HAKKEN]

Routledge
New York London

Published in 1999 by
Routledge
29 West 35th Street
New York, NY 10001

Published in Great Britain by
Routledge
11 New Fetter Lane
London EC4P 4EE

Printed in the United States of America on acid-free paper.

Library of Congress Cataloging-in-Publication Data

Hakken, David
Cyborgs@cyberspace? : an ethnographer looks at the future / by David Hakken.
p. cm.
Includes bibliographical references and index.
ISBN 0-415-91558-9 (hc.: alk. paper). — ISBN 0-415-91559-7 (pbk.: alk. paper)
1. Computers and civilization. 2. Computers—Social aspects. 3. Cyberspace. I. Title
QA76.9.C66H34 1999
303.48'34—dc21   98-38185
                                                                                      CIP

Table of Contents

Acknowledgments   ix

1   Introduction

What Are We to Make of Cyberspace?   1
Conceptual Presumptions   3
Key Issues in Cyberspace Ethnography   7
Structure of the Book   11
Cyberspace Research Narrative   12

2   An Alternative to "Computer Revolution" Thought

Has There Been a Computer Revolution?   15
Reasons for Being a Computer Revolution Skeptic   18
An Alternative Framework for Assessing AIT's Contribution
    to Social Change   23
An Evolutionary Approach to AIT and Social Change   25
Initial Empirical Data on AIT and Social Change   33
Conclusion   34

3   Doing Ethnography in Cyberspace

Introduction   37
Ethnographic and "Natural" Science Ways of Knowing   39
Doing Cyberspace Ethnography Anthropologically   43
Examples of Anthropological Cyberspace Ethnography   47
Hurdles Encountered in Anthropological Cyberspace Ethnography   55
Epistemological Challenges in Anthropological
    Cyberspace Ethnography   62
Conclusion: Issues in Classical and Cyberspace Ethnography   67

4   The Entity Problem: What Carries Culture in Cyberspace?

Introduction   69
The Entity Problem   70
Conceptualizing Culture-Bearing Entities   71
A Cyborgic Model of Human Mental Activity   72

Cyborgic Entities and Cultural Processes   78
An Alternative Cyborgic Model of Culture, Based on
    the Ethnography of Information System Development   80
Entities in Cyberspace: Actors, Creoles, Objects?   84
Self-Identity in Cyberspace   87
Conclusion: Embodied Imaginings   91

5   **The Ethnography of Mid-Range Social Relations
in Cyberspace:** Community, Region, Organization,
and Civil Society

Social Relations in Cyberspace   93
Contemporary Issues in Meso-Social Relations   94
The Ethnography of Cyberspace Communities and Regions   97
Computing and Workspace Cultures   108
The Ethnography of Organizational Culture in Cyberspace   115
The Recent Emergence of a Cyber-Culture-Facture Stage
    in the Labor Process   120
Conclusion: Virtual, or Virtually No Work/Community?   126

6   **Macro-Social Relations and Structure in Cyberspace**

Introduction   129
National/Cultural Aspects of Computing   134
Transnational CMC   140
Scandinavia and National/Cultural Differences in
    Constructing Cyberspace   142
Neo-Classical Approaches to Cyberspace in Economics   158
Alternative #1: Technicist Political Economies of Cyberspace   164
Alternative #2: Substantive Political Economies of Cyberspace   169
Conclusion   173

7   **Knowledge in Cyberspace and the Practice of Ethnography**

The Knowledge Question in Cyberspace   179
A Cyborg Anthropology Alternative:
    Realist Actor Network Theory   185
The Practice Question in Cyberspace Ethnography   191
Policy Implications of Applied Cyberspace Ethnography   203
Ethics   209

8   Conclusions

Empirical Results: What We Can Say about Cyberspace   213
Analytic Conclusions   216
On the Science Question, or Reconstructing
    Techno-Science Practice   220
Implications of a Cyberspace Ethnography-Based
    Reconstructed Techno-Science Practice   225

References Cited   229

Notes   245

Index   257

Acknowledgments

Cyborgs@cyberspace? began as a survey of anthropological research on computing and social change. It has been completed as a more narrowly focused reflection primarily on my personal research and practice. Even in a narrower form, writing such a book involves engagement with the thinking of many others; the work of only some is referred to in the main text and references section.

Research, practice, and writing are only possible because one is supported, and it is support that I wish to acknowledge here. The sponsorship of several institutions deserves recognition. Of great significance for a full-time teacher like me are institutions that provide financial support for various research, writing, and conference projects beyond normal academic duties. These include the US National Science Foundation Programs in Anthropology and Ethics and Value Studies (now Societal Dimensions of Engineering, Science and Technology), the Norwegian Fulbright Commission, The State University of New York Institute of Technology (SUNY-IT) at Utica/Rome and the SUNY Professional Development/Quality of Work Life Committee, and Routledge. Equally important are institutions hiring me on consulting projects, which enable me to "buy back" teaching time, including the Resource Center for Independent Living, The Oneida/Herkimer Human Needs Assessment, The Oneida County Department of Mental Health, and the Central New York Disability Service Office.

For me, at any rate, people's support is more important than institutions. Here I wish to thank all those individuals who have worked with me in especially humane ways; I apologize to those whose names I inadvertently fail to include below. At NSF, Rachelle Hollander and Stuart Plattner have been particularly helpful. At SUNY-IT, a number of students, colleagues and administrators have supported me, often through their challenges as well as their compliments. They include John Backman, Janice Brooks, Jackie and Reed Coughlan, Eileen Deckman, Joe deFrancisco, Pat Dorazio, Bill Jack Harrell, Maarten Heyboer, Dan Howard, Lisa McKinney, Dan Murphy, Russ Kahn, Bryan Phillips, Alphonse Sallett, Ron Sarner, Steve Schneider, Michael Spitzer, and Shirley Van Marter. At Routledge, Bill Germano, Gayatri Patnaik, and Brian Phillips have been helpful in winding up a long project.

My work within the American Anthropological Association and the Society for Applied Anthropology would not have been possible without Jack

Alexander, Jon Anderson, Myrdene Anderson, Meta Baba, Jeanette Blomberg, Bill Derman, Jim Dowd, Gary Downey, Joe Dumit, Maria Grosz-Ngate, Marvin Harris, David Hess, Carol Hill, Eve Hochwald, Lee Komito, Louise Lamphere, Karen Larsen, June Nash, James Nyce, Bryan Pfaffenberger, Julian Orr, Peggy Overby, Roy Rappaport, Pat Sachs, Artur Serra, Susi Skomal, Lucy Suchman, and Sharon Traweek.

The networks of scholars who share an interest in Science, Technology, and Society and have helped me immensely; they include Phil Agre, Paul Attewell, Jen Croissant, Carroll Purcell, Jim Rule, Susan Leigh Star, Randy Trigg, Langdon Winner, Steve Wolgar, and Eleanor Wynn. The same goes for scholars in Participatory Design, especially Joan Greenbaum, Tom Hassler, Sarah Kuhn, and Randy Trigg.

For over twenty years, various scholars and activists in Britain fostered my interest in computing and social change: Janet and Alan Baldwin, John Darwin, Mike Fitter, Les Levidow, Jenny Owen, and Robin Williams.

In the Nordic countries, the following have loomed large in my experience as well as my thinking: Karl Martin Allwood, Peter Boegh Andersen, Mats Benner, Anna Jorun Berg, Boel Berner, Gro Bjerknes, Joern Braa, Tone Bratteteig, Gudrun Dahl, Bo Dahlbom, Pelle Ehn, Niels Ole Finneman, Christina Garsten, Hans Glimmel, Marianne Gullestad, Gisle Hannemyr, Ulf Hannerz, Ole Hanseth, Bo Helgeson, Robin Jeffner, Oskar Juhlin, Karl Kautz, Galena Lindqvist, Marete Lie, Randi Markussen, Erling Maartmann-Moe, Erik Monteiro, Ingunn Moser, Ulf Maelstrom, Kristen Nygaard, Finn Olesen, Aake Sandberg, Francis Sejersted, Andreas Silow, Henrick Sinding-Larsen, Keith Smith, Ivar Solheim, Knut Soerensen, Yngve Sundblad, Ann Saetnan, Kari Thoresen, Tomas Timpka, Stefan Wellin, and Helena Wulff. (Here and in the main text I have followed the evolving cyberspace pattern of using the standard English character set in spelling their names, as well as Scandinavian place names, and words.)

Several people in Oneida County social service and activist circles have worked supportively with me on projects: Ken Abramczyk, Linda Allen, Frank Anechiarico, Isabel Arthur, Sunithi Bajakel, Paul Baker, Steve Darman, Burt Danovitz, Joan Davis, Ralph Eannace, Phil Endress, John Johnsen, Ken Mazlen, and Shannon Tilbe.

Of special importance has been a group of friends who helped Barbara and me remember that work and leisure are not antithetical: Anne Fausto-Sterling, Marlene and Bill Fried, David Gerber, Carolyn Korsmeyer, Judith Lieban, and Paula Vogel. Another group is composed of those who allowed me to treat them as "key informants," giving of themselves in that way which makes ethnographic work both possible and rewarding. Even in cyberspace, this role is as likely to include various forms of sponsorship, especially for group discussion of my work: I thank Alan and Janet, John, Phil, Burt, Francis, Ole, Kari, Gudrun, Bo, Boel, Andreas, Cristina, and Randi. A special impetus to believing that what one does is important has come from those who left us too early, especially Frank Dubinskas, Diana Forsythe, and Tomas Gerholm.

My boys Nate, Karl, and Luke have always had a special place in my work, and this continues as they themselves journey into cyberspace. One could not hope for a better co-conspirator, comrade, and interlocutor than Barbara Andrews.

What Are We to Make of Cyberspace?

Computer theorists use the term "cyberspace" to refer to the notional social arena we "enter" when using computers to communicate. "Cyberspace" can be used more generally to refer to the potential "lifeway" or general type of culture being created via Advanced Information Technology (AIT), the congeries of artifacts, practices, and relationships coming together around computing.

[1]

Introduction

What are we to make of this cyberspace emerging around AIT? Will it remain merely a "cool" curiosity, or will it become the dominant mode of human existence?

Cyborgs@cyberspace? is an attempt to answer these questions. Presenting what I have learned via studying this space through fieldwork, the book builds a discourse supportive of the ethnographic study of cyberspace.

Coming to terms with cyberspace is important. Multiple popular, policy, and academic discourses presume that new technologies *cause* social change. A by no means extreme statement of this conventional wisdom is that of historian Eric Hobsbawm:

> [W]hat can already be assessed with great confidence is the extraordinary scale and impact of the consequent economic, social, and cultural transformation, the greatest, most rapid and most fundamental in recorded history . . . [, t]he end of the seven or eight millennia of human history that began with the invention of agriculture in the stone age. . . . The world was filled with a revolutionary and constantly advancing technology, based on triumphs of natural science. . . . Perhaps the most dramatic practical consequence of these was a revolution in transport and communication which virtually annihilated time and distance (1995:8,9, 12).

Frequently, these ideas take the more specific form of talk about a "computer revolution" (CR).[1] Lifeways based on AIT are not only real and distinctly different; they are transformative. The transformative *potential* of AITs lies in the new *ways* they manipulate information. The new, computer-based ways of processing information seem to come with a new social formation;[2] or, in traditional anthropological parlance, cyberspace is a distinct type of culture.[3]

To what extent are these views justified? What dangers follow from acting on inappropriate or doubtful understandings of cyberspace? What possibilities for politics, or other interventions into social formation reproduction, emerge when we think consistently about cyberspace?

Indeed, how can one study such a vast, inchoate problem? *Cyborgs@cyberspace?* is based on the premise that careful fieldwork in current manifestations of cyberspace, its already existing "outpost" practices, processes, and arenas, is a good way. The results may be our best current indicators of what future, more complete cyberspaces might be like. Mark Dery, for example, captures this prefigurative sense in his argument that "flame wars," the periodic extravagant, often *ad hominem* linguistic performances in computer-mediated or "on-line" communication, merit serious study: "[T]hese subcultural practices offer a precognitive glimpse of mainstream culture a few years from now" (1994:6).

After fitful starts and some hesitation, anthropologists (Forsythe 1992; Pfaffenberger 1990; Suchman 1987) and ethnographers from other fields like sociology (Sproul and Kessler 1995; Leigh Star 1995) history (Haraway 1991; Traweek 1988) and computer science (Kling 1980; Pape and Thoresen 1983), now regularly do fieldwork in proto-cyberspace. I agreed to write *Cyborgs@cyberspace?* because I believe that this cyberspace ethnography is exciting and it's getting somewhere intellectually.

Cyberspace ethnography has a potential for contributing substantially to the cultural construction of this new social arena. Before this can be realized fully, however, cyberspace ethnographers need to make more explicit the general perspectives within which they work, and even strive to construct a shared intellectual problematic.

Through retrospective description primarily of my own work, I intend *Cyborgs@cyberspace?* to exemplify how to do cyberspace ethnography. In eighteen years of cyberspace research, I have been regularly forced to look beyond my own work, to create venues for more general discourses, initially primarily with colleagues inside anthropology, but then through networks and organizations of other scholars and cyberspace practitioners. As a result of this organizational entrepreneuring, I have a particularly broad view of Cyberspace Studies.

EXPLORING CYBERSPACE CULTURALLY

Anthropologists are commonly thought of, and socially justified as, cultural explorers. Emissaries from one culture, we go out deliberately to experience another. The new lifeways are typically both "other" and ones about which "we" are collectively unsure. The hesitation typically stems less from ignorance of the other than from the cacophony generated by multiple powerful describers of them, many of whose motives and interests are unknown and/or suspect.

Just as the nineteenth century West that produced anthropology had multiple discourses about the so-called "primitive" peoples that the new field was set up to encounter, so contemporary society has multiple, confusing discourses regarding cyberspace. The prime task of the cyberspace ethnographer is thus not to invent discourses about these new "natives"; there are arguably already too many. Rather—like Branislaw Malinowski (1922), the most effective promoter of anthropological fieldwork—she tries through extended participation in and observation of the new lifeways to bring some intellectual order into the talk.

Conceptual Presumptions

Perhaps the lesson about social theorizing won with the greatest recent effort is that intellectual practices cannot escape being affected by the concepts with and through which thought proceeds. Consequently, describers must be reflective, trying to be as clear about the work they intend their concepts to accomplish as they are about the picture they wish to paint.

In anthropology, these lessons are embodied in two related discourses. One, ethnography, is descriptive of specific cultures, while the other, ethnology, involves comparison of cultures and theorizing about culture in general. While ethnography is much better known, its practice is inevitably laced with ethnology, for most description uses terms that cross cultural frames. Good ethnography thus inevitably involves significant, reflective meta-discourse as opposed to only implicit theorizing.

As an analytic work, *Cyborgs@cyberspace?* is about the ethnology of one type of social formation, cyberspace. Because its ultimate cultural importance lies unclearly in the future, doing the ethnology of cyberspace is of more than usual difficulty. The phrase "cyborgs@cyberspace?" encapsulates how as of the time of writing I believe cyberspace stories are to be told. Perhaps most important is the interrogative, intended to suggest that there is good reason to withhold judgment about how ethnologically reliable the idea of cyberspace is; that is, how well the term captures what eventually will be.

GENERAL PROPOSITIONS

Following fieldwork, one typically writes an ethnography, a text which both describes the culture encountered and compares one's own experience ethnologically with that of other ethnographers.[4] Stylistically, ethnography's conclusions tend to emerge gradually through complexly woven narrative webs. While my full view of cyberspace is developed only in the detailed chapters to follow, I present here the general claims that *Cyborgs@cyberspace?* aims to establish:

1. That ethnography of current AIT-related practices—"proto-cyber-space" ethnography—is an effective way to study cyberspace;
2. That "cyborg" is an appropriate term for the entities who/which will carry whatever social formations are likely to come fully into existence soon (but not only these);
3. That while "cyberspace" is a useful term for at least one potential such future social formation type, its eventual dynamics remain obscure, and so at least for now we should refrain from presuming its eventual dominance or longevity, or even the stability of many of its current characteristics;
4. That the "@" symbol—the one contained in electronic mail addresses which indicates the electronic space or "domain" at which an individual can be contacted and therefore of which one is so-cially a part—successfully captures the likely-to-be-further-delo-calized-but-still-socially-significant kinds of relationships between cyborgs characteristic of cyberspace, if and when it comes into predominance;
5. That the form of ethnography best able to generate meaningful in-formation about cyberspace is the reflexive, anthropological vari-ant (which has, for example, the capacity to address questions empirically while at the same time retaining a critical stance in re-lation to the validity of the notions in which the questions are phrased);
6. That in order to do effective ethnography in cyberspace, we are compelled to rethink classical approaches to several aspects of so-cial thought; while
7. At the same time, ethnography in proto-cyberspace provides infor-mation both useful for such rethinking and for guiding the cul-tural construction of cyberspace.

HOW I CAME TO MAKE THESE CLAIMS

My first articulation of the phrase "cyborgs@cyberspace" was as a humorous variant on "pigs in space," a standard element of early *Muppet Show* episodes. The phrase was intended to evoke Miss Piggy's sense of travail as a space trav-eler, but its broader evocations are also appropriate.

Consider its components. Like "robot," the term "cyborg" was deliberately invented, the former in the 1920s, the latter in a period similarly techno-science enthusiastic after World War II (Gray 1995). An imagining of science fiction, robots are purely electro-mechanical, but cyborgs are partly biological as well. A shortening of "cybernetic organism," a "cyborg" was to be a life form enhanced by additional capabilities—for heightening the effective use of feed-back through manipulating and responding to information. Initially used less frequently than "robot," "cyborg" has recently gained more currency, perhaps because it captures contemporary concerns, such as the feeling that AIT use fuzzes the boundary between human and machine. Indeed, the meaning of the term has changed, from "enhanced life form" to "form that acts, more or less, as enhanced human, irrespective of whether it started out biologically."[5]

THE INTELLECTUAL PROBLEM AT THE CENTER OF CYBORGS@CYBERSPACE

Generally attributed to William Gibson's novel *Neuromancer* (1984), "cyberspace" first referred to an electronic communication notional space. Essentially a collection of spatial metaphors, like the notion "desktop" employed in explanations of how to use an Apple Macintosh computer, cyberspace is now regularly used to refer collectively to computer-related social fields.

"Cyberspace" now has even more popular currency than "cyborg"; "cyberspace" was used without explanation in the 1998 Presidential "State of the Union" address, for example. It is thus natural to assume that the interrogative onus of my title *Cyborgs@cyberspace?* falls more on "cyborg" than "cyberspace." This is the view of Robbie Davis-Floyd, for example, who asks us to consider whether, as we enter cyberspace, we wish to become more "cyborgic" and less "human" (1995). The notion that in cyberspace we do indeed become something so profoundly different that we cease to be persons in the normal sense is a common refrain or "trope" in cyberspace talk.

While I understand this perspective, I employ a different, more sweeping concept. Because they *have always been* technological and biological, and therefore cyborgic, unities, I use "cyborg" to refer to *all* the entities that carry human culture. (In homage to Bruno Latour's *We Have Never Been Modern* [1993], I considered calling this book *We Have Always Been Cyborgs*.) While of course cyberspace cyborgs are different from pre-cyberspace cyborgs—in, e.g., the increased complexity of some feedback loops—these differences do not justify drawing a cyborgic ring around cyberspace, identifying its borders as the *boundary* between social formations carried by humans and those carried by cyborgs.

Because of the importance of artifice to *every* way of being human, "cyborg" is a proper general term for the entities which carry culture in *all* types of human social formations, not just cyberspace. (As such entities are the truly proper scientific object of anthropology, the discipline could with justice, but not style, be called "cyborgology.") Such conclusions about humans and cyborgs are indicative of the kinds of rethinking of basic social issues driven by ethnographic examination of cyberspace.

PROBLEMS OF CYBERSPACE AGNOSTICISM

Confident that, if cyberspace comes, its chief entities will be cyborgic, the interogative of my title relates primarily to cyberspace, and the likelihood of its emergence as a full human lifeway. I am an ethnological agnostic about cyberspace, but my agnosticism has an active, inquisitive quality; it is not know-nothingism. It is quite different from the animus toward the "computer society" of those preoccupied with the negative characteristics of the new AIT-based social patterns, those called "compputropians" later. Whether good or bad, I question cyberspace's presumed inevitability. Moreover, my agnosticism is provisional; fuller, appropriate ethnographic information would lead to a different conclusion. The ultimate, long-term uniqueness of cyberspace patterns has yet to be demonstrated.

This agnosticism is a consequence of the personal ethnographic experiences in proto-cyberspace described in the following pages. I began fieldwork in 1980 on a set of questions about "our times": How are we to understand the contemporary era? To what should the widely shared sense of substantial social change be attributed? Is the sense that "things are changing rapidly and profoundly" valid or a misrepresentation? Just how actually important are science, technology, and computing to the changes taking place? How reasonable is it to strive to influence either the changes or perceptions of them? To which trends should we pay most attention in making decisions about the future? What new concepts do we need to answer questions like these?

My asking such big questions followed doubtless from training in anthropology. Several of the subfields of this discipline regularly focus on issues of macro-change: archaeology on cultural evolution; biological anthropology on the development of forms; applied anthropology on economic and social transition. Indeed, vast upheavals in current social formations give cultural anthropologists like myself an unusual opportunity to use our field methods, unlike our colleagues, to study change directly.

However, I soon found that common rhetorics—"Computer Revolution," "Information Society"—got in the way of the empirical study I intended. These terms were used in ways that presumed the reality of exactly those phenomena whose existence I wished to investigate.

As I read the work of others interested in cyberspace, I encountered multiple, diffuse, disconnected discourses. I hoped initially that coherence might emerge on its own, but this has not happened. Perhaps because too many cyberspace ethnographers use its rhetorics uncritically, the diffuseness of cyberspace ethnography mirrors the hype of popular cyberspace talk.

Ethnology compels us to strive after more self-consciously shared intellectual weavings. To do ethnography in cyberspace, one should first clear rhetorics like these from one's conceptual space by defining a more precise set of research questions. Which approach to the design of a general cyberspace problematic is best?

Cyberspace ethnographers grapple with a range of fascinating intellectual puzzles: The nature of spaces less tied to places, whether cyberspace will be more democratic or more authoritarian, the practical problem of differential access to AIT of individuals and groups—classes, peoples, genders, races, and nations—whether AITs have agency in the philosophical sense, etc. In the tradition of humanistic studies, one *could* design an account of cyberspace in terms of such topics. The problem with this approach is that these issues arise at multiple levels of analysis, and the dynamics at one level often cut against those at another.

Key Issues in Cyberspace Ethnography

In the following section, I outline an alternative, "levels" program for coherence in cyberspace research a general intellectual context for Cyberspace Studies. My map of cyberspace highlights different levels of analysis. The key levels are arranged in a continuum that roughly parallels those of biology; that is, from the sub-individual to the macro-structural:

1. The basic characteristics of the entities carrying (proto-)cyberspace;
2. The self-identities formed by such entities;
3. The micro, close social relations these entities construct (e.g., with intimates and friends);
4. Their meso, intermediate social relations (e.g., community, regional, and civic relations);
5. Their macro-social relations (e.g. national and transnational);
6. The political economic structures which cyberspace entities produce and reproduce and by which they are constrained.

THE "ENTITY" QUESTION

In what follows, I discuss some core questions raised in thinking about each of these levels. On the first level, we ask after the characteristics of the primary entities (both more active and more passive elements) carrying/who will carry cyberspace culture. To what extent does the cyborg image capture their characteristics? Given the characteristics common to entities in all technology actor networks, to what extent are cyberspace entities unique? Empirical discussion of these points among ethnographers has involved relating to concepts from fields such as informatics (object orientation, parallel processing), philosophy (critique of Modernism) math (chaos theory), and cognitive science.

THE SELF-IDENTITY ISSUE

Identity is a central theme in contemporary anthropology. Formation of self-identity—the practices through which individual entities develop and promulgate a sense of who they are—is an important aspect of identity in general. Just how do entities in proto-cyberspace construct themselves—for example, is there a shift from biological to mechanistic metaphors? What qualities do they attribute to other cyberspace individuals? How are these attributes and characteristics constructed culturally? How are processes of identity formation changed? Is there a more extensive disembedding of experience? Of what value are current notions of culturation, such as Creolization, to understanding these processes? The empirical locus of research on self-identity in cyberspace has primarily been new forms of communication. These include on-line Multi-User Domains (MUDs), especially their more sophistocated forms (e.g. object-oriented MUDs or MOOs); bulletin board services (BBS); computer clubs; the use of electronic communications systems in organizations (e.g., e-mail, intranets); and the general use of the Internet, a system linking computer systems around the globe.

THE MICRO, CLOSE LEVEL OF SOCIAL RELATIONS

I believe it is useful to break down discussion of cyberspace social relations into three distinct levels. On the level of close social relations, those involving direct interaction, ethnographers study whether cyberspace social relations are less group- and more network-oriented. What new kinds of intimate relationships are created, and how significant are they? To what extent does communication among intimates in cyberspace replicate preexisting communication patterns—for example, domination, hegemony, aggressiveness, or preoccupation with sex? What are the social correlates in friendship formation of less face-to-face and more screen-to-screen communication? How does on-line affect off-line activity? Empirical focuses include many of the same activities examined by those concerned with self-identity.

THE MESO, INTERMEDIATE LEVEL OF SOCIAL RELATIONS

At this level, cyberspace ethnographers study the dynamics of communities, geographic units, and regions. How does the accelerating decoupling of space from place characteristic of cyberspace affect the construction of community social relations and norms, at work and at home? To what extent does use of AIT, as in Internet use or civic computing, foster new forms of community and democracy? How does cyberspace affect the social reproduction of regions, the spaces within which we physically still spend most of our time and which provide most of us with our jobs? Does the region become less important? How tightly are regions' declining ability to influence their own reproduction connected to the dynamics of cyberspace creation? Empirical loci include:

- Information system development (ISD), especially the Scandinavian approach, user involvement in ISD, participatory design, and

  multi-disciplinary (systems developers and anthropologists) ISD;
- Computer Supported Cooperative Work, new disability technology, and professional communities, including scholarly communication;
- regional computing and regional economic development strategies;
- workplaces with new technology; and
- studies of other activities related to more elaborate information infrastructures.

THE LEVEL OF MACRO-SOCIAL RELATIONS

How does cyberspace mediate the imagination/reproduction of cultures? How are the declining abilities of nations to influence their own reproduction connected to cyberspace? Given globalization, does it even make sense to strive to create a national Information Infrastructure (II)? Are there alternative models to the top-down, technology-driven approach to IIs? What are the political correlates of IIs? How relevant are national differences in the culture construction of cyberspace? What are the correlates of the differential availability of different technologies (for example the Internet in the U.S. vs. cellular phones in Sweden)? Are there prospects for reconstructing the nation as a meaningful social formation through cyber-technologies? What are the relations between these efforts and the creation of AIT standards? Empirical foci include comparative study of the cultural construction of computing/cyberspace in various nations and cultures and studies of whether specific information technologies (such as on-line searching, development of the PC, Internet as a model of distributed governance) result in more or less democracy.

THE POLITICAL ECONOMY/STRUCTURE OF CYBERSPACE

Ethnography at this level steps back from analysis of the dynamics of actual social relations and addresses what can be said about the more structural features of cyberspace. Which if any of the differences in the structure of how contemporary social formations are reproduced can reasonably be viewed as harbingers of a really new way of life? Does the locus of reproduction shift, either its geographic focus (from the region to the globe) or its character—is it less about scarcity and more about allocation of wealth, or risk? What is the connection between cyberspace activity and the creation of social surplus? How does the emergence of cyberspace change the sources of political economic power and their reproduction? What does ethnography suggest about the relationship between cyberspace and some of the changes in spatiality already perceived by some to be underway—globalization, or the decoupling of space and place—and what are the likely longer term implications of such changes?

  Ethnographic discourse at this level is built around consideration of arguments popular in economics and political economics as distinct intellectual trends. Empirical data include Internet governance, European Cooperation on "information society," and transnational corporate information systems. Issues include commercialization of the Internet and other communication technologies, both past (TV) and present (cable).

SUMMARY OF LEVELS FRAMEWORK

Each of these levels is a key arena of discourse regarding possible futures. Thus, a "levels" frame facilitates:

- Locating specific ethnographic examples in relation to each other;
- Separating the important issues about future social formations from the more frivolous;
- Distinguishing best currently available perspectives on these issues from the tendentiousness unfortunately all too prevalent in "cybertalk"; and
- Illustrating the implications of recognizing these examples, issues, and perspectives.

On each level, cyberspace ethnographers have learned something, both about what is worth asking after and what is worth saying.

The framework as a whole is intended to help ethnographers focus on the next questions we should be asking about this possible new way of being human, the fundamental descriptive issues to which cyberspace ethnography should be oriented. My cyberspace fieldwork has concentrated on the construction of intermediate and macro social relations, and other cyberspace work has involved the entity and political economic levels. Consequently, *Cyborgs@cyberspace?* deals primarily with these four and not the individual or intimate levels, although I do comment on these in passing.

Whether one approaches Cyberspace Studies topically or in terms of level of analysis, as humanist or social scientist, is in part a matter of taste or training. For example, I personally find it somewhat easier to think about the pattern formed by the various developments at the community level than to try to link up all the developments relevant to democracy at all these levels. Nonetheless, the key point is the necessity of some design or framework that addresses the complexity of cyberspace. Any transition to a fundamentally new social formation not only takes place on several, relatively autonomous levels; it is (or is not) a summation of developments on these several levels. There is no single level that will have paramount importance over the others. Thus, we will be able to decide, for example, if there has been a Computer Revolution only when we can see the patterns emerging at all of these levels. In short, the transition to cyberspace is an empirical question.

My initial draft of this book was a summary of what I felt was the important work on all of these levels, but I was unable to complete this task satisfactorily. The current text is focused primarily on my own experiences, but I nonetheless hope that, by explicitly locating my studies in a framework, others will be convinced either to adopt it or offer an alternative.

Structure of the Book

The two following chapters of *Cyborgs@cyberspace?* explore in more detail conceptual issues introduced earlier:

- How to problematize the dominant way of talking about cyberspace, so that it become the object of study rather than being presumed; and
- Why ethnography in proto-cyberspace is an appropriate way to learn about cyberspace.

Chapter 2 addresses how to deal with Computer Revolution Thought and why its rhetorics, which implicitly infuse talk about things like "the Information Society," should be replaced by explicit inquiry into the character of cyberspace. The chapter proceeds through a series of social context/critique issues:

- What, culturally speaking, is AIT?
- Where did this notion come from and what interests are served by it?
- Is a particular AIT, like a national information infrastructure, just another technology, or must it be located within broader social developments to be apprehended culturally?

Chapter 3 addresses how to execute empirical study (in) cyberspace. It makes explicit the case for ethnography as a highly appropriate approach to the holistic studies called for in chapter 2. It also addresses:

- How technicism-based shortcomings—either ones similar to those affecting computing/technology studies more generally, or ones particular to anthropology, such as conceptions of "object of study" which marginalize technology—affect ethnography's ability to offer a viable alternative approach to those of other fields;
- What practical hurdles are typically encountered by cyberspace ethnographers;
- What works and what doesn't in overcoming them;
- What epistemological issues are raised in cyberspace research: for example, is there an "ethnographic referent," and, if so, how is it to be located?
- Whether ethnography can provide a strategy for techno-science

research, one which overcomes the divide between social and technological research.

The remaining chapters are distinctly more empirical. Chapter 4 constructs an answer to the entity question adequate to the exploration of cyberspace. The chapter illustrates this cyborg answer in relation to the self-identity issues that have been the preoccupation of ethnographers like Sherry Turkle.

Chapter 5 discusses further the reasons for dividing consideration of social relations in cyberspace among micro, meso, and macro levels. The bulk of the chapter focuses upon mesosocial relations research on community computing, AIT and work, AIT and change in working class culture in Sheffield, England, and my efforts to use participatory AIT development to reform the social welfare system in the Upper Mohawk Valley, New York.

Chapter 6 turns to consideration of macro-level structures and the political economy of cyberspace. The main cases are my comparative study of the cultural construction of computing in Norway and Sweden and recent efforts within the OECD to articulate a substantive or institutional economics relevant to contemporary technological change.

Chapter 7 addresses two more "topical" than "level" issues, the character of knowledge in cyberspace and the practice of cyberspace ethnography. Consideration of knowledge is prompted by discussion of cyberspace as a "knowledge society." The case for ethnographic participation in the construction of cyberspace, in addition to study of it, is presented, especially its ethical quandries.

Chapter 8 summarizes what I currently think we can reasonably say about cyberspace and its likely dynamics. I take this concluding moment as an opportunity to outline my view of the role of cyberspace ethnography and anthropology in general in the reconstruction of technoscience on non-Modernist presumptions.

Cyberspace Research Narrative

In the spirit of reflexivity, I offer one further comment on how I became a cyberspace ethnographer. In 1980, at the "request" of a Dean (who suggested that I would respond positively if I wanted tenure) and because of an already extensive exposure to AIT, I found myself teaching computer science "literacy" courses for nonmajors. The Dean explained that the regular faculty in our newly organized Computer Science (CS) Department "had to be used in the important courses." Out of self-defense but also ethnographic curiosity, I embarked on a one-person action research program into what this newly emerging discipline was all about. I buttonholed CS colleagues in the hall and ask them Columbo-style questions like, "What's scientific about Computer Science?" (Artur Serra has developed a very insightful analysis of the ways in which the "science" moniker has hobbled the field's development [1992].) The colleague would usually say something like:

> "Computer Science is about the theory of calculation."
>
> "I see—it's a branch of applied mathematics," I'd respond.
>
> "No, no, Computer Science is a field with distinct problems, as can be seen in things like research on Artificial Intelligence."
>
> "I see, so Computer Science is a subsidiary branch of psychology or biology, providing tools for modeling another science's analyses?"
>
> "No, no, no. We model these amazing new calculating machines, computers."
>
> "But wait, a biologist explores a life form precisely because he doesn't know how it works, but if I want to understand a machine, I can just ask the person who designed it. Aren't sciences built around the investigation of 'naturally' occurring, rather than 'artificial,' phenomena? Whatever their shortcomings, social sciences can at least claim a valid scientific object."

At this point, the colleagues usually blurted out something about making more money than I did and terminated the conversation. Later, I realized that I wished they had responded more snappily: "In what sense is the object of anthropology 'natural?' Is it not also what Herbert Simon called 'a science of the artificial,' like Computer Science?" (See also Dahlbom and Mathiessen 1993.)

While engaged in the intellectual project which has occupied the last eighteen or so years, I have often thought about how this imagined/invented dimension gives computer science and anthropology several commonalities. Each has one foot in the humanities and another in the sciences; both are simultaneously colonial and anticolonial, popular and marginal. They both burrow deeply inside techno-science while at the same time stand outside it, are in the here and now as well as the there and the to come. Do cyberspace ethnographers and students of informatics (the engineering-oriented label which I prefer to "Computer Science") share the same ultimate focus?

Cyborgs@cyberspace? is an attempt to come to terms with the unasked question, an effort to cast light on the ambiguities of ethnography, AIT machines, and their makers. I aim to present a more effective way to think about the unified natural/artificial entities or "cyborgs" which carry cyberspace "culture." This way builds on E.P. Thompson's paradoxical insight (1963) into the making of the English working class, that a social entity can be "a presence at its own creation." Applying Thompson's perspective to "humankind in space and time"—all of it—*Cyborgs@cyberspace?* aims to take seriously the claim that anthropology is about how "man [sic] makes himself [sic]." Through developing a complex discourse on culture in cyberspace by confronting technicist myths like the notion of technology as something "outside" us, anthropology can find and create more such alternative discourses and metaphors. On these new stories we can base the collective self-control necessary for survival in whatever future—whether "cyber" or some other "space"—our progeny experience, whatever the proportion of their biological to technological components.

In an important sense, computing is a central myth or story of our times; that is, narratives about AIT and what it implies for human life and society are central elements of the way those "colonizing" cyberspace think about the things important to them. What follows is a personal telling of cyberstories, enhanced by the existence of a growing body of actual research experience "in" cyberspace and shaped strongly by colleagues' struggles with and involvement in it.

Has There Been a Computer Revolution?

Few would question the enormous *potential* of AITs to foster social transformation. At the same time, the dominant way of talking about AITs and social change, Computer Revolution (CR) rhetorics, impedes cyberspace ethnography by presuming that the potential is already the reality. What way of thinking about cyberspace properly balances awareness of potential with insistance on evidence, promotes an empirically refutable skepticism about the dominant view of the future?

[2]

An Alternative to "Computer Revolution" Thought

Problematizing CR Thought is the task of this chapter. It begins with some illustrations of the broad array of discourse domains into which CR talk has penetrated. It then analyzes the ways this talk hampers thinking about cyberspace, such as its speculativeness and its simplistic and distorting assumptions about AIT. It describes alternative discourses which clear conceptual space to attain the desirable balance and some empirical studies which have begun to map this space. These alternatives build on research in Science, Technology, and Society (STS) and evolutionary perspectives from general anthropology. By focusing on the cultural *correlates* of computing—that is, establishing which social changes co-occur with computing, and which do not—these alternatives create an empirical program in which the CR presumptions become the object of research rather than its ideological framework. This program can differentiate out those changes which are truly transformative, whose character would justify concluding that the approaching cyberspace is indeed a new, distinct social formation, from those which are not.

THE ELEMENTS OF CR THOUGHT

Opinions expressed around the world take as given the notion that computing has changed/is changing our lives profoundly; that for individuals, institutions, and social policies, AIT is a primary adaptive imperative. While policy may marginally influence the course of change, there is little hope for controlling, let alone preventing, this Computer Revolution.

This CR view is definitely plausible. Contemporary social formations are changing along multiple dimensions, and these changes are temporally correlated with the rapid spread of computing. Moreover, computers are a frequent presence in our movies, television programs, and other forms of popular culture, capturing social attention and providing an arresting symbol of the other basic changes. This semiotic value, and the association of the spread of computers outside of scientific and defense research with the social instabilities identified with the 1960s, help explain why computers' "social impacts" became a major concern of political leaders, social activists, and policy analysts.

According to CR common sense, the profound social changes leading to cyberspace are caused by "computerization," the spread of new computer artifacts, first at work[1] and more recently in communication, transforming first these and then other social institutions. Formally, "computerization" can be defined as the process in which a domain of human activity becomes substantially mediated by electronic, programmable devices for rapidly storing and manipulating "data" in order to extract or transmit information.

The strong belief that computers more or less directly transform society is held in both overdeveloping and underdeveloping nations. The CR thesis takes curricular form in "Computers and Society" and other "technology preparation" or "computer literacy" courses, which focus on "how computers change society." That CR Thought is commonplace can be further established by reference to most contemporary educational, labor force, and policy planning documents. For example, a "career pathways" program, cooperatively developed by New York State government, teachers' unions, and the Business Council, was intended to refocus public education on the new computer-based job skills perceived as dominating future labor markets.

CR Thought is conventional wisdom among business theorists, like business process reengineers Michael Hammer and James Champy (1994). Creation of secure jobs is no longer an appropriate organizational goal. In order to compete in the global marketplace characteristic of cyberspace, organizations need to maximize their ability to hire and shed labor as quickly as possible. This extreme flexibility is necessitated, among other things, by the CR in the workplace: Because new processes massively transform the speed at which new products reach the marketplace, organizations tied to older processes are doomed.

Consider the similarity between these business conventionalities and the blurb on the dust cover promoting Richard Hernstein and Charles Murray's very influential *The Bell Curve* (1994): In the contemporary era, individuals will prosper primarily according to their capacity to handle information in the forms in which AIT makes it available. If some groups (for example, African Americans) lack such capabilities, policies like equal employment and educational opportunities are inappropriate, even a danger to national competitive survival.

These examples of CR-presuming arguments come from American business/rightwing rhetoric, but the liberal/radical left or other nations manifest them also. In his influential comments on the increasingly unequal experience of African Americans, William Julius Wilson gives workplace "technological change" a causal role comparable to that of Hernstein and Murray. The CR is central to case for the Postmodern sensibility articulated by Jean-François Lyotard (1984).

CR AS SOCIAL PROBLEM

Indeed, the CR emerged as a genuine "social issue" in the second half of the twentieth century—would computing enhance or disrupt the quality of life? Speculation about the consequences of computerization reached one peak in Europe during the late seventies and early eighties, when the cost of workplace computers declined rapidly due to the spread of microprocessors. Another peak developed in the early 1990s, when hopes for "information superhighways" grabbed public attention. Much talk about "cyberspace" is arguably the latest form of the CR problem.

One popular view of the CR as problem, the "computopian," is dismissive, holding computing's impacts to be positive. This is the dominant view in both the United States and in states historically connected to the Soviet Union. Borrowing from Raymond William's (1989) examinations of the degenerative or "putrefying" tendencies of modernity, an opposing position can be called "compputropian." On this reading, computerization has dire consequences, especially for already vulnerable social groups like the working class. Compputropian views were expressed strongly in, for example, the Nordic countries during the 1970s.

For computopians, general adoption of AIT improves people's lives through increasing their leisure time, stimulating economic activity, freeing them from drudgery on the job and at home, and providing better material objects. In contrast, compputropians fear that computers harm social life through disrupting existing work (via de-skilling and unemployment) or undercutting self-identity formation.[2]

DECONSTRUCTING CR THOUGHT

Because of their well-developed views of the CR, computopians and compputropians receive considerable public attention. My intent here is not to resolve this compputropian/computopian conflict. This will be impossible as long as both perspectives take as given that which cyberspace ethnography must first take up. If their rhetorics presume its existence, how can researchers hope to demonstrate whether or not there has been a computer-induced social revolution?

Reasons for Being a Computer Revolution Skeptic

As an early (born in 1946) baby boomer and an occasional member of some institutions central to AIT (including Stanford University, the University of Chicago, the State University of New York, and the U.S. National Science Foundation), I have had a chance to develop some perspective on this so-called "revolution." As a person and humanist, I object strongly to the adaptationism of CR Thought, whether from right or left. As a cyberspace ethnographer, my chief concern, however, is with the presumption justifying both forms of adaptationism, the inevitability of the CR. Despite its near-universal acceptance, I am skeptical of the CR, rejecting the taken-for-grantedness of both general and policy rhetorics. Such "givens" are overly speculative and too flaccid and are therefore serious impediments to effective study of the actual cultural construction of cyberspace. The flaccidity is rooted in CR mythification, facile acceptance of the notion that we are living through a social transformation induced by computing technology rather than demanding that this idea be examined empirically and its validity demonstrated.

CR conventional wisdom needs to be, at least for a time, bracketed as "myth" in the anthropological sense; that is, approached as narrative so often performed that its validity is seldom open to question, but for this reason alone great effort should be expended. My skepticism has several roots.

THE SOURCE IN ADVERTISING OF MOST CR RHETORIC

The cultural site of CR Thought's most vigorous performances is advertising, a practice whose rhetorics, detached from the normal mechanisms by which people make sense of their world, are contemptuous of validity standards. While CR-related advertising taps into strong currents of desire and imagination, its imaginings promote "mythinformation" (Winner 1984) and discourage reflective thinking.

ECHOES OF AMERICAN TECHNICISM

CR tellings usually equate technology with artifacts—with the computer as a machine. CR Thought strongly echoes the naive technological determinism which is a standard pattern or "trope" of American discourse, the long history of which is explicated in, for example, Leo Marx's *The Machine in the Garden* (1964). Attributing causative power to machines means Americans can avoid taking individual responsibility for social developments, which instead are viewed as something compelled by the nature of the artifacts and therefore beyond influence. Indeed, technology is a particularly appealing locus of disempowering transcendence, what Langdon Winner calls "technological somnambulism."

The most general name for the "explaining social change by technology" trope is "technicism." Most early futurists (c. 1970–80), whether computopians or compputropians, worked from the technicist premise that the computer was such a powerful machine that massive social change was inevitable. However, the very ebb and flow of stridency in futurist speculation are themselves indications that the popular sense of massive, computer-caused social change may be to some extent a consequence of a habitual way of speaking and therefore suspect.

Technicist reasoning is fallacious in that it presumes that social processes get their character from technology rather than demonstrating that this is the case. Thus, it is technicist habit which leads some to presume that, simply because there are so many computers around, they must be the cause of the social changes we are experiencing. When CR technicism is justified discursively, it is usually by simplistic technicist analogy—such as the idea that the steam engine unilaterally caused the industrial revolution (e.g., Frates and Molderup 1983), or the archaeological contention that irrigation caused social stratification (Pfeiffer 1987).

Technicism assumes that technologies develop asocially; or that technology is created in laboratories and acts upon, but is not acted upon by, social process. The CR view is technicist in that it only can see social changes as consequences, not causes, of technological change.

ABSENCE OF EMPIRICAL STUDY

An even stronger source of my suspicion of CR talk is the relative dirth of concerted discussion, either popular or scholarly, over how one might rigorously establish the effects attributed to the CR. With regard to politicized, knotty issues like welfare reform, gun control, and abortion, Americans manage to foster a modicum of talk about research relevant to claims made publicly. In contrast, the ratio of computer revolution claims to disciplined efforts to establish let alone critique them is huge. This itself justifies framing CR Thought as myth, as to-be-taken-for-granted nostrum so "good to think" that its relationship to actual experience can be ignored. The absence of an interest in the impact of social process on AIT, a possibility hidden by one-way rhetorics which presume AIT's massive impacts on society, is a related consequence.

RHETORICAL INFLATION

Much "Computer Revolution" talk is inflated. Most users of the label "postindustrial," for example, are really only referring to a change in the relative proportions of labor in goods production and in service, not to the replacement of the labor form of work by some other form. Empirically, the number of people "in employment" in Western Europe, like the population in general, is more or less stable, while in the United States, like the population, it continues to rise.

Some computer futurists (Lenk 1982) use "Information Society" as their label for the new social formation. Again, the inflated phrasing turns out to refer to the purported emergence of a distinct "information" sector of the economy. Sometimes this sector is operationalized so broadly as to be meaningless; e.g., to include any economic activity in which a computer is present, however marginally. However, a demonstration of the fact that existing activities can be relabeled after remediation in no way proves that a social revolution has taken place. Sometimes the "information" sector is conceived more narrowly, as the rough equivalent of "high tech." Even if, contrary to most current empirical evidence, social relations in this sector turned out eventually to be mediated by some nonemployment social form, one new sector does not a new society make.

The economic reproduction of contemporary capitalistic social formations, especially the United States, is greatly dependent upon the "high tech" economic sector—such as the economic centrality of products like "Windows 95." However, the production of "high tech" equipment often takes place inside wage relations very similar to those of preexisting sectors, evidence of social continuity. Again, the existence of a profoundly different social dynamic must be demonstrated, not just asserted.

ETHNOCENTRISM

Use of CR terms like "Information Society" to distinguish ours from other social formations can be profoundly ethnocentric as well as misleading. Information relationships are significant characteristics of all human social formations, not simply computerized ones. Such terminology is as appalling to anthropology as describing our era as "technological," legitimate only if previous eras lacked technology, rather than had different forms of it. If the intention were merely to indicate such a difference, to call others "nontechnological" is illiterate. That technology is implicated profoundly in all human eras is a key point of cyborg anthropology.

Arguably, "information" is more general than technology; all life forms depend upon "information," in the sense that, in order to survive, they must respond effectively to change in their environment. This responsiveness is itself the core element of a minimal "information cycle": Any message obtained from the environment which has a demonstrable impact on what the organism does is "information."

Any nonethnocentric (ethnological) perspective on information would have to take into account the distinctive way in which humans relate to information. To a substantially greater extent in humans than among other life forms,

1. Environmental data becomes semiotic—that is, data are "cultured" in the process of being perceived; and
2. This semiotic information is often "processed" again—compared

further to complex symbol systems and evaluated according to existing "knowledge."

Thus human information is different in being doubly cultured, and the difference between human and nonhuman information circuits is greater than that
among human social formation types.

Most definitions of information place in it the center of a progressivist linguistic chain—from "mere data" to "processed data" (information) to "verified
information" (knowledge) to, perhaps, "existentially validated information"
(wisdom?). This progression was employed implicitly in the previous para-
graph, as well as in my definition of computing. In their account of information system development in the Scandinavian tradition, Dahlbom and
Mathiessen (1993) further problematize as ethnocentric such standard presumptions about information. They do this by inverting the standard hierarchy. In Dahlbom and Mathiessen's view, the kinds of things which usually get
thought of as "data" are anything but isolated, raw, "bits" of something. Rather,
they exist primarily in already constituted practices and flows, the kind of thing
which the Scandinavians call "tacit knowledge." To become information, such
knowledge must be shorn of context, thereby transformed into something abstract. "Information" is thus deconcretized knowledge, not processed raw data.
Through further manipulation, perhaps according to formal rules (algorithms)
in a computer, this information may also find itself represented as free-floating
"factoids" or "data." While it is true that reprocessing these abstract formalizations constitute the privileged form of "knowledge" in the modern era,
Dahlbom and Mathiessen caution us against presuming that it is only such abstraction in search of "the one best way" which constitutes validity.

LOGICAL FLAWS

Much CR Thought commits the fallacy of presuming that processes which co-
vary are ipso facto causally related and, moreover, related in only one way. Logically, however, CR Thought would only be true if all of the following
empirical conditions held:

- There were extensive computerization of numerous diverse activities;
- Work and communication had changed substantially;
- The extent of general social change were also significant;
- The connection between these changes and computing were direct,
  not substantially mediated by other social forces. For example, the
  kinds of changes most recently characteristic of North Atlantic enterprises (downsizing) and most manifest in the experience of workers (the increase in the length of the working day and labor market

casualization) are explained as elegantly by shifts in the balance of power between labor and capital and/or the nation state and capital (related processes often masked by superficial notions of "globalism") as by a CR. On such alternative readings, the changes in technology could be accounted for by how they aid and abet the reproduction of capital, just as many other social changes contribute functionally to the same process. (Harry Braverman created an extremely influential explanation for the degradation of work along such lines in *Labor and Monopoly Capital* [1974].);

- Both such other social changes and computerization were not consequences of some third process—for example, a new, primarily ideological or economic commitment to "high technology," or vigorous public or private policy initiatives pushing adoption of AIT in worksites and homes, either of which could also "cause" the spread of computer-based systems; and
- Changes in other social dynamics had had demonstrably less impact on the development of computers than computers had had on these other social processes (a reversed view of the direction of causality).

"Computerization road to cyberspace" tellings effectively block disciplined examination of such logically possible alternatives. Rather than taking all of these presumptions for granted, we should encourage examination of multiple, alternative accounts of computing, change, and the connections between them. We should then go on to consider whether any of these alternative views of cyberspace are more appropriate than the CR.

Substantively, I am *not* claiming that there is *no* relationship between computing and social change. To the extent that "the times are achangin'," many of the changes are temporally associated with computerization. Computing clearly has the potential to be transformative. Indeed, AIT may at some point prove to be so intimately connected to fundamental social change that we would be justified in labeling it "revolutionary." What I question is:

1. the idea that computing is so self-evidently the cause of substantial current change that we can take its revolutionary consequences for granted, and
2. the embarrassing willingness of so many otherwise apparently intelligent people to act as if this potential alone ensures its reality.

In sum, the important work of the CR in influential political rhetorics, its powerful performance in advertising, its echoing of largely unexamined technicist tropes, the failure of scholars to examine it critically, and its logical vulnerabilities are all grounds for skepticism.

An Alternative Framework for Assessing AIT's Contribution to Social Change

The issue of whether any causation arguments make sense is a highly contested one in contemporary social science. Many forms of Postmodernism raise radical doubts about the value of causative talk altogether because of its tendency to become hegemonic "master" discourse.

The preceding critique of the causative logics only implicit in CR Thought indirectly rejects this aspect of Postmodernism. By invoking notions like "holistic causality" and deconstructing "mastery" tellings of causality into components and arranging them into the chains typical of open systems (social systems), philosopher Roy Bhasker (1989) articulates a socially defensible theory of causation. Basing his argument on Bhasker's and others' recent developments of realist philosophy, Sayer (1984) offers a paradigm for argument over social causation: If, in a wide variety of circumstances, one social process or structure (structuration) is accompanied systematically by others (in other words, there is a high degree of multivariant correlation), some causal-like relationship is strongly suggested. The task of research is to illuminate what characteristics might account for the correlates observed by identifying the conditions necessary for each of them to exist, to be reproduced, and to produce the observed effects in the others. For a realist-inclined ethnographic as opposed to positivist study of cyberspace, the important analytic step is the development of categories adequate to identify the structurations of interest and devoid of ethnocentric presumptions about them.

Barbara Andrews and I used these recently articulated social science epistemologies as the basis for our Sheffield and Nordic researches. One further presumption of our research addresses the "one-way causation" problem, studies which address the "social impacts" of computers but ignore the "computer impacts" of social process. My personal empirical research on computerization (1990, 1991, 1993, 1994) has been framed instead in terms of "the interdependence of computers and society." This approach prompts the analyst to consider the impacts of social process on technology as well.

SOCIO-TECHNICAL AGENCY: THE TECHNOLOGY ACTOR NETWORK

Another important causal perspective on AIT/social change is the proposition that computing constitutes a significant new type of technology actor network (TAN[3]), one with potentially transformative implications. TANs are part of the framework used in social studies of technology by Michel Callon (1986). They invoke the idea that, rather than being seen as artifacts alone, technologies are best conceived of as networks of interacting human, organizational, and artifactual entities and practices. Particular elements both constitute and are constituted by the networks in which they participate.

[23]

In any particular TAN, the more passive elements are "actants," the more active "actors." New TANs are created through interaction and negotiation among entities with differing and often conflicting forms of agency; consequently, they are more or less unstable. Periodically, however, particular new TANs attain enough stability—one can speak of TAN "hegemony"—to become "takeable as 'for granted.'" Such stable TANs constitute a significant source of momentum in the reproduction of social formations. Periodically, a newly stablized TAN becomes so important that it is reasonable to describe the reproductive dynamics of the social formation of which it is a part as having been altered through its hegemony.

Phrased in TAN terms, untestable CR Thought becomes the testable proposition that a computing actor network has become hegemonic, that "cyberspace" will have a computing TAN-related distinctly new general social dynamic. This conception is less vulnerable to the critiques of CR Thought outlined here because it allows us conceptually to disentangle several distinct, empirically testable propositions:

1. Do the artifacts, in this case computers, actually have the capacity to do what they are conceptualized as doing?
2. Are the potentials for new forms of activity implicit in the new networks actually realized?
3. Is the new TAN associated with new forms of social agency?
4. Is it characterized by social alliances substantially different from its immediate predecessors?
5. Do groups and organizations with significant social power, whether new or preexisting, actually frame their activities in terms of the concepts embodied in the TAN?
6. Are the individual "systems" of the new TAN, and the TAN as a whole, stable?

The more often one answers "yes" to these questions, the greater the likelihood that one is dealing with a hegemonic TAN and that therefore one can legitimately speak of a technology-related social transformation. For example, effective computing machines, and technological systems based on them, have been developed only recently. Because it is new, the computing TAN is likely to be noticed, even striking, but novelty is not itself evidence of significance. Moreover, the highly contingent nature of TANs severely limit their value at explaining social change. If one wishes to derive implications from the social study of computing and associated systems, in regard to educational policy or redesigned work processes, one must be able to say something substantial about the characteristics of the TAN itself, and its sources of stability.

An Evolutionary Approach to AIT and Social Change

Another obvious limitation of CR Thought is its binary quality: A revolution either has or has not taken place. However, the potential relationships between computing and social change are clearly matters of degree. We need to be able to talk about them more developmentally, to have a more explicit, sequenced continuum which reflects the multiple dimensions of underlying forces for social change. This continuum must reflect the importance of both new world views (Postmodernism) and material relationships (the new spatial arrangement in the so-called "Information Society"). If one had such a continuum, one on which empirical data could be successfully mapped (Hakken 1990), one would be better able to argue persuasively that the computing TAN was revolutionary, not "just another technology."

Such continua are susceptible to distortion when constructed out of the "accepted" categories of current social formations, because such categories are likely to be ethnocentric. The computerization/social change connection should be approached ethnologically, comparing study of the basic dynamics of the general forms of human social life, and therefore incorporate an explicitly general anthropological approach. This may seem odd to the reader who thinks of anthropology as the study of "primitives," confusing the field with an earlier conception of it as the comparative study of less complex social formations. Contemporary anthropology has a broader compass, as an integrative, holistic study of the biological, linguistic, archaeological, and contemporary practices characteristic of all human groups.

This General Anthropology can help differentiate out truly remarkable from "everyday" computer-related phenomena. Current thinking about cultural evolution is particularly relevant to discussion of the alleged CR. (In taking up evolutionary theory, I am rejecting the "antievolutionism" of much cultural studies work in contemporary anthropology.[4]) Understandings of what changes have in the past meant fundamental transformation for humans provide more concrete ideas about how to draw meaningful pictures of the transitions between various current or future stages, images which enhance our ability to recognize the implications of any particular innovation like computerization.

Just how fundamental, in comparison to other anthropological changes, is the change we have in mind when we use the phrase "Computer Revolution?" Few words in the English language carry as much complex symbolic baggage as "revolution." In order to decide if there has been a CR, we need a clear standard: How extensive and of what kind must a change be in order to qualify as "revolutionary?"

The computerization literature contains a variety of different standards, often used in confused and uncritical ways. However, these standards can be arranged into an evolutionary sequence helpful to answering whether the social changes associated with computerization deserve description as "revolutionary." CR Thought can be arrayed into the following propositions, that

1. At the most expansive level, computerization will result in the End of the Human Age, the marginalization or even total transcendence of human society altogether;
2. Somewhat less cosmically, computerization will mean the End of the Job, the creation of a fundamentally new type of human social formation;
3. Even more soberly, computerization will only mean the End of Machinofacture, passage to a new stage within the same basic type of social formation; or
4. Anticlimactically, computerization implies the End of Nothing Really Significant. The attraction of revolutionary language is primarily rhetorical, and computerization is best seen as merely another development within the same stage of the current social formation.

These four possible conclusions constitute a continuum of degrees of transformation, the first being an extreme form of evolution and therefore most justifiably labeled "revolutionary," the last involving more continuity than change and thus justifying such a label least.

STAGE #1: THE END OF THE AGE OF THE HUMANS, OR THE COMPUTER REVOLUTION AS A SPECIES REVOLUTION

Is a transition to cyberspace so profoundly fundamental that it constitutes a biological revolution, perhaps even the disappearance of the human species? As an unemployed or "labor-free" informant in South Yorkshire put this question, "Will computers make people redundant?" In his English, the phrase "to make redundant" communicates the same message as the American English phrase "to lay off," but "redundant" also continues to mean "unnecessary" or "superfluous." This person, who had been unable to find paid work for more than two years after the strike-related closing of the coal mine in his pit village, was thus asking a question with a double meaning. On one level, he was wondering if he and his comrades would ever find work again, still be necessary for "machine fodder," as wage laborers. At the same time, he casts doubt on the general future of humanity.

If our future as a life form is in doubt because of computerization, we are talking about a change so momentous that "species revolution" is more appropriate than "social revolution." It is the potential for such a transformation which is portrayed in much advanced technology-related science fiction. That intimations of change at this scale have popular currency is to be inferred from the popularity of whole genres of film (for example *Alien* or *War Games*). A similar sensitivity is at the root of much of the way in which the cyborg image is currently evoked: Davis-Floyd (1995) treats the cyborg implicitly as a new species, something profoundly alien to human experience.

What kinds of standards would have to be met to establish this degree of change? A species revolution implies more than the standard biological notion of speciation, the developmental separation of a new life form from a "parent" species. Speciation has taken place quite frequently, but only rarely does the new species marginalize or eliminate the parent, let alone a parent that, like humans, has dominance in such a broad range of econiches. The End of the Age of the Dinosaurs, which paleontologists estimate to have occurred quite rapidly some 65 million years Before the Present (BP), is somewhat analogous. However, new, quite different mammalian species likely achieved dominance after, rather than over, dinosaurs, so this transformation was likely the result of a profound disruption of general life processes consequent to disturbance of basic ecological relationships. There surely are contemporary ecological disruptions with potentially catastrophic consequences, such as global warming. While computing can be linked to them, one would need much more conclusive evidence of direct links to prove a computing-induced general threat to life.

Besides, as the generic conventions of the films mentioned above attest, visions of cyborg transcendence are more about direct interspecies "survival of the fittest" conflicts than general catastrophy. Cyborg anthropology holds that, from the beginning, humans have constructed themselves substantially in relation to technology and that therefore "we have always been cyborgs." From this perspective a "new cyborg"/computer vs. human conflict is as frameable in intraspecies as interspecies terms.

In short, it is difficult to specify concretely the implications of a "species revolution" reading of the CR. Such talk is perhaps best understood as a manifestation of various popular misapprehensions of Darwinism connected with (Christian?) milinarianism than as a serious, empirically studiable notion.

STAGE #2: THE END OF THE JOB, OR THE CR AS A SOCIAL REVOLUTION

Other variants of the CR present computerization as a "very fundamentally" new social formation, one "based on" computers in a sense comparable to the idea that gathering and hunting is "based on" digging sticks and spears. While profoundly different, it is still fundamentally a human social formation.

General anthropologists explore the differences between such fundamental types of social formations and debate theories intended to specify the scale of and identify the conditions under which such fundamental changes in basic social formation take place (Harris 1980; Ruyle 1987; White 1949). Many accept the idea that roughly four million years BP, a set of changes resulted in the first human social formation. Systematically, people began living in cooperative groups, obtaining their means of survival in a more communal structure dependent upon the capacity to use shared symbols and communicate through them about the material world around them, and using tools like digging sticks and spears. Anthropologists call this first human pattern of existence gathering and hunting.

The second great human transition, the development of more settled social formations dependent upon the cultivation of domesticated plants and/or the husbandry of animals (horticulture and pastoralism), began about 10,000 BP. A third great transition—about 5000 BP—was the development of complex, large-scale state level societies, or agriculture.

The commonly acknowledged fourth transition is quite recent; it involves the development of social formations dependent on the large-scale creation of commodities. The predominant activity through which subsistence is obtained is labor, the exchange of one's capacity to execute directed activity for money, so the job is the primary social relationship. Thus, it makes sense to identify this fourth social formation as the labor social formation, a term descriptively accurate that avoids the complications associated with terms like "industrial."[5]

As in this typology of stages, General Anthropology often labels each type of social formation in terms of the typical social relationship, the activity through which the means of human physical subsistence is typically obtained: In a word, its work (Hakken 1987). In order to claim that computerization means a truly new, fifth social transition, one would have to show how its work dynamics are as different from those of the fourth stage as each of the four transitions were from their predecessors. This implies identifying the new form of work mediation that replaces labor, as well as the general characteristics of a "post-labor" social formation. Identifying such basic relationships is not easy, but General Anthropology shows that it is possible. It is necessary if we are to speak meaningfully about a fundamental change in human social formation type.

An Information-linked Concept of a "Cyberspace" Social Formation Type

By thinking about "information" not as a product label or an economic sector but as a social processes which changes with each social formation type, we can recast "Information Society" discourses. We can construct an information-based "basic social relation" conception, as different from labor as gathering and hunting are from chimpanzee foraging, or labor is from peasant subsistence production. In *Modernity and Self-Identity* (1991), for example, Anthony Giddens describe changes in "informational" activity—from a reliance on custom and authority to consultation of independent "experts" and individual construction of narratives of self-invention—as important in the transition to "high modernity."

Given the extent of the dependence of all human social forms on information circuits, a substantial change in human information processes might, as argued by Giddens, have extensive implications. Many information circuits have been altered through the inclusion within them of computers. Computers' unique capabilities for speed and breadth in the manipulation of at least some kinds of "data," and therefore the production of what we agree to treat as "information" in at least some senses, are certainly impressive. Shoshona Zuboff (1988) uses "informated" to characterize the greater extent to which computer-mediated production processes are saturated by abstractions. Similarly, Norwegian anthropologist Henrik Sinding-Larsen (1991) foresees a greater formalization of human thinking with computing. He compares computing's impact on thinking to the impact on musical practice of the development of formalized systems of notation.

Still, it is important to keep in mind that computers are not the first technology to mediate the human information circuit—tools for food production and books are other examples. Instead of a simple "information" label for the new social formation, we minimally require a more exact information-related label ("neo-" or hyper-informating). Use of this label would only be justified if we could specify empirically:

1. the new techniques of handling information which were significantly different;
2. the actual, not just potential, correlates in general human activities of these techniques; and
3. the new social relationship (gatherer/hunter to band, gardener to village; peasant to lord; worker to boss) at the center of this new social formation type.

While computers may mean we have more information, in terms of volume, or that we have it in a different forms than we used to, it's not, yet, obvious anthropologically that we are now dependent upon information in some way as profoundly different as is in these previous cases of fundamental social transformations. Still, the possibility of such a profound transformation is real.

STAGE #3: THE COMPUTER REVOLUTION AS A NEW SOCIOLOGY OF LABOR

Some analysts characterize the computer age still more narrowly, as one in which already important machine-based technology is used in new ways—such as in the "technotronic" label of Levitan and Johnson (1982). This brings us to CR interpretation #3, as a new stage of the existing labor social formation, the implicit position of those who refer to the CR as a "second" or "third" industrial revolution. To investigate empirically whether the new stage is profoundly different from/"more" technological than previous stages, we need a theory of the general relationship between technology and work within labor social formations.

Recent historical sociology of work[6] suggests that we can conceive of the labor process as following a distinct pattern of social evolution. An initial "craft" stage of production, in which individual craftspeople carry out all steps in the typical production process, is generally associated with small cities and towns in a largely rural social formation. A second "manufacture" stage, beginning in the late eighteenth century English North, involves the introduction of a detailed division of labor and the dividing up of craft labor processes into distinct jobs, as well as much unskilled repetitive labor and a smaller but strategic group of skilled, directing workers. The manufacture stage is associated with the development of large production units and a flow of population into industrial cities, which rapidly achieve social preeminence. Worker living standards are typically low, with many unable to buy the things they produce. A third "machinofacture" stage involves the large-scale introduction of quite autonomous mechanical devices, fixed or so-called "Detroit" automation, into the labor process, especially to replace skilled workers. Various authors, following Gramsci (1971), have identified the social pattern associated with machinofacture as "Fordism," a mass production, mass consumption society. In it, factory workers themselves, in part as a consequence of their self-organization into unions and political parties, are among the most important consumers of the commodities they produce. The working class suburb is perhaps the distinctive new feature of the social landscape. In sum, what one sees with each stage of the employment social formation is both a new characteristic form of the labor process and a new general social pattern, one involving significantly different class cultures.[7]

Cyber-facture?

Close analogs of the idea that computing correlates with a significantly new society can be found in contemporary social thought, as in "Post-Fordism." For David Harvey (1989), postmodern, post-Fordist society "was in part accomplished through the rapid deployment of new organizational forms and new technologies in production. Though the latter may have originated in the pursuit of military superiority, their application had everything to do with bypassing the rigidities of Fordism" (p. 284).

Similarly, Manual Castells (1989) presents new technology and change in political economy as the dual sources of the Information City, the characteristic new spatial form. His view of work technology echoes the influential ideas of Michael Piore and Charles Sabel (1984).

In order to speak meaningfully of a new "cyberfacture"[8] stage of labor-mediated work, we would have to demonstrate:

1. substantial change in the labor process, attributable to particular, computer-incorporating types of machines and in scale and form comparable to those in previous changes;
2. an associated new kind of basic social pattern, especially in the experience of working people; while, as opposed to Stage #3,
3. stability in the underlying basic social relationship, i.e., that of selling and buying labor.

If so, it would be reasonable to describe "cyberfacture" as a fourth stage in the evolution of the labor social formation.

STAGE #4: COMPUTER REVOLUTION AS "JUST ANOTHER TECHNOLOGY"

Conversely, if we couldn't specify both a new labor process and a new social pattern, we would have to choose Stage #4, to conclude that computerization is anthropologically quotidian or "everyday," "just another technology" (King 1982).

Forms of Technology

Humans have used technologies throughout their history (Adams 1996). To decide how different computing TANs are from others, we need a theory of the evolution of TAN types. The first important type of TAN was productive technology, the social patterns developed to provide the first humans more adequately with material necessities like food, health care, clothing, shelter, and energy. This TAN was central to the emergence of the human species.

The next significant TAN, the horticultural/pastoral type, involved dependence upon domesticated life forms and included the development of abstract technology. This term refers to broad conceptual approaches to human processes, including the kind which domestication involved. The abstraction-dependent capabilities or "informating," which Zuboff identifies with computerization, developed first in productive technology with plant and/or animal breeding. The deliberate development and transmission of human cultural constructs implied by these capabilities was rapidly generalized into other aspects of human existence, including those which we in the West associate with "science."

The use of instruments and techniques, both physical and social, which enhance the power of elite social groups, first those who created and dominated the new agricultural state structures of 5000 BP, involves a third TAN form, repressive technology. As described in regard to Stage #3, a fourth type, machine technology, replaced skilled labor in the machinofacture stage of labor process evolution.

In anthropological perspective, then, new TANs have appeared in conjunc-

tion with diverse changes in social life: new species, new types of social formations, and new stages of the same social formation type. Computing is of such
potential significance because it can so easily integrate all four preexisting general TAN types—productive, abstract, repressive, and machine. Arguments
against the fourth view of the CR, that computers "are just another technology," usually draw attention to this polyvalent characteristic: It is difficult for
us to imagine such a broadly usable instrument not leading to great change.
Still, interpenetration among the various TAN forms has a long history. Further, even though case studies of the computerization of particular labor
processes often document significant short term change, the long term consequences are not as clear. The picture is even less clear when we try to take com-
positional shifts in entire economies or the global system into account. One
can perhaps differentiate between the dynamics of the machine-monitoring of
a human worker on a transfer line—that is, an assembly line which includes
both humans and robots—and those of the machine-operating work labeled
"semiskilled" characteristic of machinofacture. I find it difficult to do so.

In some informated organizations, the outlines of a new stage in the evolution of the labor process may be emerging. The eventual result of matrix structures, or networked virtual organizations, may indeed be a historic reversal of
the individuation at the core of previous labor process evolution and especially
visible in Taylorism. Were we to hold this version of CR view #3, in my view
the empirically most likely case for the CR, we would reject view #4.

Yet how signficant this initial "resocialing" of work will be in the long run
remains to be seen. Not only are its basic characteristics or eventual scope unclear; the associated new patterns of social life or "cyberculture," comparable in
newness to the difference between nineteenth century urbanism and Fordism,
are even murkier. "Resocialing of work" is the focus of my current research.

STAGES #5, 6, AND 7: COMPUTERIZATION AS DEVOLUTION

Developing an evolutionary approach to the CR has clarified the different degrees of change implicated in its diverse forms. These different claims have to
then be transferred into a more specific, graded continuum.

However, social change need not be progressive. This continuum must be
completed before we can identify which point on it most accurately represents
the range of actual computing/social change connections. For example, an "information rich, information poor" (see Bjorn-Andersen et al. 1982) line of argument suggests that computerization might result in a social structure with a
small new elite, knowledgeable about computers and with access to resources,
and a vast underclass of information resource poor computer illiterates. Were
this social structure still dominated by the labor form, it might be more reasonable to view it as a devolved form of Stage #3, a regression back from Fordism
toward nineteenth century manufacture-based labor urbanism, than as some-

thing new and progressive. That this is a real possiblity is suggested by the extent to which much current computing ignores the way noncomputered information is cultured. Thus, much computered information is misrepresented, and computing is as likely to promote mass ignorance as a "Knowledge Society."

Further, if it were the case that the computer illiterates found themselves having no paid labor, we might wish to label the computer era "neo-feudal," a devolved form of Stage #2. This label emphasizes similarity with the prelabor, agricultural social formation. Were substantial numbers of humans to perish because of computer-induced changes which blocked their access to necessary physical resources—or were we all to disappear through some computer-related techno-holocaust—we might be justified in viewing computerization, in a negative analogy to Stage #1, as a devolution to a preanthropic, in contrast to a transanthropic, condition. The Stage #4 "just another technology" position, then, really represents a midpoint on the CR continuum:

1. A species revolution involving the End of the Age of the Humans;
2. A new human social formation, the End of Labor;
3. A new stage of the existing labor social formation, the End of Fordism;
4. Just another example of the machinofacture/Fordist stage of the labor social formation;
5. A regressive stage, something like manufactory urbanism, in the labor social formation;
6. A neo-feudalist regression to something like a pre-labor social formation; and
7. A regression to a prehuman bioformation.

Initial Empirical Data on AIT and Social Change

The kind of argumentation initiated in the preceeding section shows that it is possible to say something empirical about whether computing constitutes a significant, stable TAN and of what sort. This can be done despite the huge public discourse stake in acting like we already know that computers cause massive social change and despite the suspicion that knowledge to the contrary is not all that welcome. Of course, it is difficult to use much of the by now vast literature regarding computing and social "impacts" because it presumes an "undeconstructed" CR. This literature of course remains of value to those who wish to study how people talk about computing, an important issue in its own right, but a different one.

Some scholars have persevered and analyzed computerization empirically in ways which can be arrayed on the continuum described above. Attewell and Rule (1985), for example, provide a helpful guide to earlier empirical research on computerization as well as some important arguments about its likely future direction. Andrew Friedman (1989) and Joan Greenbaum (1995) provide compelling explanations of the failure of AIT itself to experience the social transformation that it is so widely presumed to induce in other labor processes. David Noble's work (1984) on the evolution of computer-based technologies in the machine tool industry is an eloquent empirical inversion of typical CR rhetorical practice, one which highlights the role of social conditions, ideologies, and power relations, rather than some internal technological imperative, in shaping AIT. Numerous other examples (for example, Pfaffenberger's [1988] explanation of "Why the PC Revolution Was No Revolution") erode the simple CR. (See, e.g., Hakken [1993] for a summary of such data.)

"Computing Studies" (CS) is a useful term with which to label this work, which rejects technicist presumptions and attempts to grapple with computing and its causal correlates. This discourse has roots in various academic disciplines and national scholarships. Bijker, Hughes, and Pinch's attempt (1987) to ground a sociology of technology features Noble's history of computing technology. The workplace implications of computing are a key illustration in Harry Braverman's work (1974), as they are in the important work of Braverman epigone like Philip Kraft (1977), Andy Zimbalist (1979), and Evelyn Glenn and Ros Feldberg (1979). Equally important is work in computer science, particularly the research of Rob Kling (1980) and others active in Computer Professionals for Social Responsibility. Nordic computer science is noteworthy for its attempts to develop a "sociotechnical" perspective on information system development; perhaps the applied work of Pelle Ehn (1988) is known best.

In the mid-1980s, CS reached a level of methodological sophistication. For example, both Attewell's and Rule's (1985) research on workplace computerization near New York City and mine with Barbara Andrews (1993) in Sheffield, England were attempts to bridge the gap between case studies of particular firms and national aggregate data. This was done through regionally integrated studies. Given the tendency of compputropians to focus primarily on case studies, while computopians tend to use data in aggregate, such studies were strategically necessary. While discourse is too frequently truncated at discipline boundaries, CS is a viable research field, a legitimately empirical consideration of cyberspace. The rest of *Cyborgs@cyberspace?* demonstrates further the viability of this research program.

Conclusion

This chapter has explored systematically the intellectual shortcomings of a major discourse about the connection between computing and social change, the CR way of talking about cyberspace. The presumption that AIT causes social change, while firmly grounded in popular discourse, is as yet not established and is logically suspect. Suspicion is further justified by the absence of much meaningful empirical examination, outside of a few important studies whose influence has seldom reached outside academic circles. In addition to indicating some of CR talk's social functions, the chapter linked its shortcomings to technicism. One might argue that empirical study of this relationship is so difficult that it can only be confronted in ideological/rhetorical rather than research terms. Here, STS and anthropological perspectives were used to outline a framework for serious empirical analysis of the implications of the changes in human informational activity associated with computing.

Indeed, there is a growing body of relevant research: Social scientists, business scholars, information systems developers, and reflective practitioners have studied what actually happens when the computers come. It recognizes the co-occurrence of the spread of new information technology and social change, but it rejects the specific form in which this connection is typically cast, that of the CR. It is the main object of *Cyborgs@cyberspace?* to show how, shorn of mythologies like CR, this ethnography of cyberspace can provide useful analysis in several different arenas.

Introduction

While the pervasiveness of CR Thought complicates Cyberspace Studies, the benefits of attaining a better understanding of the connections between computing and social change would be significant. This chapter makes the case for ethnography as a key path to understanding cyberspace.

[3]

Doing Ethnography in Cyberspace

Topics addressed herein include:
- What ethnography is;
- Its potential contribution to cyberspace studies;
- Some hurdles encountered in transferring the ethnographic approach into empirical studies in proto-cyberspace; and
- The relationship of cyberspace-specific problems to the general problems of ethnography which have greatly exercised anthropologists in recent years, such as ethnography as a way of knowing or the "ethnographic referent."

Also addressed are issues more particular to the community of anthropologists pursuing cyberspace ethnography. These include how implicit CR presumptions have limited some ethnographers' ability to provide good data on cyberspace and more useful alternative presumptions—including a conception of anthropology's "object of study" which does not marginalize technology.

While any ethnography is methodologically risky, cyberspace ethnography is vulnerable to unique disruptions. For example, my research on Nordic computing included participation in transnational computing listservs, a form of electronic discussion. Because we could "meet" in cyberspace, such participation meant that potential informants would be more likely to know what I was about when I contacted them.

When I turned on my computer at the Norwegian Computing Center in the winter of 1993–94, I was faced with an immediate threat to my research: a private email from an ex-"colleague" at the State University of New York whose tenure had been in question before he left voluntarily. After stalking me privately across the net for some time, he was expressing his decision finally to denounce me publicly. The next message, on the SCI-TECH-STUDIES listserv, indeed did "flame" me, alleging heinous acts and involvement in dastardly conspiracies, including membership in the Ku Klux Klan!

During my 1976 fieldwork in Sheffield, an informant had become suspicious that I was a CIA agent. I was able to recover from the situation by continuing gradually to build informants' confidence in me through working together in meetings, teaching, and in dealing with industrial hazards. In Norway, I made a quick check with the "owner" of this list, and with a few other colleagues, to see if there was anything comparable I could do to contain the damage. They had little to suggest. They argued that the charges were on their face so ludicrous that those who didn't know me would not likely be disturbed, and that further intervention by me would only draw more attention to the incident.

I did nothing further. However, several months later I learned of at least one person who was put off from further contact with me by the message. I don't know how many other Nordic researchers distanced themselves from my work, and therefore I can't specify the extent to which my data were distorted by this intervention. I do know that my opportunity to do this field project, as well as the quality of data gathered, were both affected to some extent. The "shared place" means I had used in Sheffield were not available in this cyberspace less tied to a specific location.

Besides such vulnerabilities, cyberspace ethnography has to deal with anti-STS natural scientists like Paul Gross who attack ethnographers and their methods and results generally. Quoting me in an exchange on an Internet discussion group, Gross argued, "Attempts to 'develop a persuasive account of the cultural construction of techno-science' have been in full career for at least two decades: these have had, well, a mixed success. Is there an intellectually urgent reason to keep trying?" (SCI-TECH-STUDIES 1996) Gross' case against ethnography rests on general epistemological or "theory of knowledge" grounds.

There are reasons to be critical of some current ethnographic practices in cyberspace. Yet Gross' comments are indicative of the number of scholars whose understanding of ethnography, let alone acceptance of it, is limited. For all these reasons, we begin with a general discussion of ethnography.

ETHNOGRAPHY AS A WAY OF KNOWING

"Ethnography" refers both to study of the distinctive practices of particular human groupings and representations—*pictures* of a *people*—based on such study.[1] The idea behind ethnography is that one can learn something worth knowing by doing more intensively something typically human: making sense out of the new situations in which we find ourselves. To find my way in a new city, for example, I look at the buildings and streets, try to read the signs, maybe ask some questions of the "natives." If staying, I construct a mental "map" of the place, and I increase the interpretability of my actions by modeling them on what those around me do. Ethnographic fieldwork involves doing these kinds of things more reflectively, more systematically, and for a longer time than the ordinary visitor.

Moreover, unlike a tourist, the ethnographer visits primarily to communicate about the new to those left behind "at home." Selecting a proper site, one in which understanding is likely to be fostered, and finding a way to participate in and observe practices of interest are some of the many tasks which an ethnographer must successfully complete on the way to a serviceable understanding of a culture.

There are many similarities between good journalism and good ethnography—such as a desire to understand what people say in their own terms and a commitment to reporting back. Some journalists (and ethnographers) purport to be only interested in description. Good journalists, like good ethnographers, however, are also interested in developing convincing accounts for the practices examined. What primarily separates ethnographers from journalists, in addition to average length of stay, is breadth of method, the array of ways information is obtained. In addition to interviewing, ethnographers also:

1. Search for ways to observe directly and meaningfully the practices of interest, not just talk about them with the participants; and, even more importantly,
2. Find ways to participate actively in the practices.

This latter is based on the notion of embodied understanding, or the idea that, if I can actually do something (perform a practice), chances are greater that I understand it more fully than if I have only observed it or heard another person describe it.

Ethnographic and "Natural" Science Ways of Knowing

Like others who think of themselves as scientists, ethnographers are motivated by the desire to explain, to account for the practices observed. Both also share a commitment to empirical work and recognize as problematic the many ways in which the situation and characteristics of the observer can affect what is observed.

A good way to begin locating differences between ethnographers and other scientists is in their contrasting responses to this observer effect. The typical nonethnographic scientist is committed to a Modernist program, one with empiricist (as opposed to empirical), positivist, hypothesis-testing, laboratory, "natural" orientations (Toulmin 1990; Whitehead 1925). This program means one sees the observer effect as an unfortunate problem to be overcome. One attempts to do this through procedures like double-bind protocols, creation of artificial situations in controlled circumstances (labs), or translation of observation into rigid abstract systems (mathematics). One seeks a double alienation of the relationship of interest from its context, and of the practice of science from its base in human activity.

While some ethnographers share this Modernist program, the typical ethnographic explanatory move is to highlight rather than to try to banish context, to pervade description/explanation of the patterns identified with attention to the human dimensions of their co-discovery by the ethnographer and her informants. One wallows in, rather than alienates oneself from, the observer effect. Which response is better depends upon circumstance and objective. An ethnographic approach makes sense in general because of the doubly culturized character of human information. While natural science deals with the "culturization" of knowing by trying to avoid it, an equally legitimate response is actively to compensate for it. Through anthropological education, for example, one aims at awareness of how one's culture of origin may shape one's response to events in another culture. A critical awareness of this process means one is better able to "bracket out," through anticipation of its likely effects, at least some of the biasing cultural construction of one's knowledge.

Indeed, ethnography uses culturalization: Awarenesses of likely ethnocentrisms improve one's sensitivities to how cultural construction might take place in diverse situations. The ethnographer's reflexive observation of her own response and behavior while trying to embody her understanding of the new culture becomes another important source of data, in something like the desired impact of a Brechtian "alienation effect."

Rather than trying to banish culture from science, as in the Modernist approach, the ethnographer tries to keep it in the frame, takes an "experiential" rather than an experimental approach. That is, the ethnographer pays attention systematically to both what is being studied and the way the studied is being co-constructed by the situation, one's informants, and one's self. What anthropologists refer to as holism, the "emic/etic" approach, means adding to awareness of co-construction

1. The testing of one's model of the situation by acting on it and seeing what happens (participation), and
2. Attendance to material and other more structural—political economic—processes which set limits on cultural construction.

As part of a general questioning of the place of Modernism in science, the ethnographic, experiential gaze is currently attracting increased general interest. As an ethnographer, I often find the hypothesis testing efforts of other social scientists of considerable interest, just as technoscientists like my colleagues at the Norwegian Computing Center or biologists like Richard Levins and Richard Lewontin (1985) and Steven Rose (1992) find value in ethnographies of techno-science.

While I integrate their ideas into my ethnographically derived models, my models do not thereby become equivalent to theirs. Experimental and experiential science are related, but the relationship is "orthogonal," perhaps complementary but different enough to justify characterizing them as evoking different theories or existing in different "arenas" of knowing. They are based on different epistemologies, or at least what Foucault referred to as distinct "epistemes." *Pace* Paul Gross, one need not, in any definitive sense, choose between experimental and experiential approaches.

The claim of the ethnographer to be heard is fundamentally a different claim from that of the experimentalist. In essence, the ethnographer claims that "you should listen to me precisely because I am an outsider, someone with sensitivity to how human practices are always culturally constructed and with the capacity to comprehend in some detail both the mechanisms of this constructing and the material relations within which it takes place. Unlike the experimentalist, I make no general claim that my understanding transcends its conditions of production, but I am correspondingly less subject to making premature or unwarranted assumptions that this is the case." The risk of ethnography is that any knowledge remains tied tightly to its space of production.

The experimentalist is making the opposite claim to be heard, that general knowledge is approachable through rigorous attempts to banish context. To do so is to increase the risk of creating "mythinformation," knowledge only apparently free of context (Winner 1984).

THE ROOTS AND FORMS OF CYBERSPACE ETHNOGRAPHY

As a scientific way of knowing, ethnography has a history complementary and subordinate to the more dominant Modernist Program. Cyberspace ethnography has a similar relationship to the dominant trends in the study of computing. Among the first to be concerned about the social dimensions of AIT were some professionals identified with the developing academic field which in the United States came to be known as Computer Science. This field has something of a schizoid nature; while its U.S. name implies identification with mathematics/natural science, its practice often looks like engineering. (The appellation "Informatics," more popular in Europe, reflects this practice more accurately.)

In the 1950s and 1960s, computing moved outside of military ballistics into scientific research and automated handling of large databases (as in commercial banking). Some computer scientists began to be interested in the broader implications of these developments. Prompted partly by general criticisms of technology, these concerns were institutionalized in "Computers and Society" courses as an early option in CS curricula. These courses tended to combine a number of functions: as "computer literacy" for those unfamiliar with the new machines, as a brief exposure to "real world" applications before moving professionally to the math-like programming more central to CS's academic institutionalization, and as an introduction to the philosophical issues confronted by projects like "artificial intelligence."

While there were noticeable individual exceptions (see Kling 1980; Winograd 1986; Trigg 1994), "Computers and Society" courses generally failed to foster a distinct research tradition of serious inquiry into the central relationship of computing to more general social processes (Kiel-Slawik 1995). Its texts continue to focus on "the impact of computers on society" and ignore the impact of society on computing. They repeat the popular rhetorics of the "machine in the garden" or "technological sublime" rather than developing new analyses based on empirical work. (This was due in part to the low rewards to "soft" topics within an academic discipline attempting to professionalize along the lines of a "hard" science. Also, computers were introduced into workplaces as part of a broader program of automation, the ability of these virtual machines to replace less reliable human labor altogether being their prototypic actual legitimation. Such contexts are not supportive of long term attention to the human dimension.)

A parallel nascent sociological discourse over computing typically adopted a similarly rationalistic "modernizing" rhetoric from pre-sixties industrial sociology. This discourse accepted workplace technology as the worksite manifestation of science, and thus tended to characterize any complications of worksite transformation as a "by-product" of "irrational" human "tradition." While constructing an applied role, those (mostly psychologists) able to assist individuals having a hard time making "the transition" again produced no substantial independent research tradition.

Harry Braverman's *Labor and Monopoly Capital* (1974) directly contradicted this mainstream industrial social science. Following his intervention, sociology of work reemerged. It was his thesis that, rather than improving as it became more dominated by science, the secular tendency was for the quality of work to decline (his subtitle was *The Degradation of Work in the Twentieth Century*). By arguing that one cause of degradation was the tendency of owners of capital to select technologies that systematically undermine worker power at the point of production, Braverman reopened the social dimensions of both work and technology to serious social research. His prescient study of office computing was an important prod to cyber-work ethnography.

Rob Kling championed a comparable minority trend in Computer Science. Philosophical (Weizenbaum 1976) and practical (Weinberg 1971) concerns were combined by Kling with more overtly political ones drawn from the Braverman revolution. Especially in the Nordic countries (Ehn 1988), this sociology of work-informed CS tradition problematized the social and cultural dimensions of AIT.

In their attempts to come to terms with Braverman's argument, the new computing/work sociologists drew heavily on ethnographic research on how work was experienced by workers (see Lamphere and Shapiro-Perl in the second Bravermanite *Urtext,* Zimbalist's *Case Studies on the Labor Process* [1979]). At the same time, ethnography was becoming a preferred approach in the developing field of STS (Latour and Woolgar 1979).

Today, ethnographic, culturally informed research constitutes a substantial proportion of Computing Studies. Ethnography helped "open up the black box" closed by the rationalist presumptions of Modernist Computer Science. One can identify several streams of contemporary ethnography relevant to cyberspace:

1. A Braverman-influenced hybrid of critical computer science combined with ethnographically informed sociology, interested especially in the political correlates of computing (see Bjerknes et al. 1987);

2. A practice of ethnographic study integrated into some forms of contemporary information systems development and social psychologically oriented "field" studies of human–computer interaction (described in Allwood and Hakken n.d.);

3. That sociology of techno-science as interested in the day-to-day reproduction of actual technology actor networks as in their historical development (see Latour and Woolgar 1979);

4. More general popular, postmodernism-influenced, approaches to cyber-issues like Computer Mediated Communication (CMC), developing especially in Communications and Cultural Studies (see the various authors in Jones 1995); and

5. An anthropologically oriented tradition based on transferring older models of fieldwork into new venues, like computerized workplaces, occupational and community groups, MUDS and MOOS, and larger cyberspace communities like on-line chat groups.

Doing Cyberspace Ethnography Anthropologically

While informed by all these trends, *Cyborgs@cyberspace?* is based primarily in this last, cultural anthropological one. Eleanor Wynn (1988), Gary Chick and John Roberts (1987), Bryan Pfaffenberger (1988), and Lucy Suchman (1987) contributed a pioneering, distinctively anthropological tone to cyberspace ethnography. To hear the tone, however, one's reading must range broadly. One must also distinguish anthropologists who study computing as a cultural process (anthropology of computing) from those who are mostly interested in computers as a tool or method, computing *in* anthropology,[2] to differentiate a research interest in cyberspace culture itself from an interest in computing as a source of new data recording and analysis techniques. Legitimating cyberspace as an anthropological object of inquiry has been difficult enough to justify repeating here the reasons for doing so (Hakken 1993):

- AITs really are capable of mediating cultural reproduction in profoundly different ways from previous ITs (e.g., interpersonal conversation or the book);
- AITs have come to mediate so heavily the lives of so many of the peoples whom anthropologists study that we can no longer ignore them;
- So many people are convinced that contemporary societies are currently experiencing a "Computer Revolution" that, despite difficulties in documenting it, the perception itself is worth studying;
- As representational devices, computers raise fascinating questions about how culture is generated and reproduced;
- Since a great deal of anthropology is about cultural change, understanding computerization is at the center of anthropology's interest in contemporary social formation reproduction; and
- Field studies of AIT in use, like Rathje's "garbology" (*Anthropology Newsletter* 1981), provide an opportunity to evaluate methods for analyzing other cultural transformations that can only be studied indirectly—such as through archaeological field study, linguistic reconstruction, or studying the current residue of changes which first occurred long ago (diffusion of industrialism/capitalism).

Gratifying to the anthropological cyberspace ethnographer are the many people in AIT-mediated organizations who see that computing's correlates depend on broader sociocultural milieus. This awareness is manifest in an explosion of interest in practices like Computer Supported Cooperative Work, Participatory Design, Joint Application Design, and so forth, practices that demand social as well as technical knowledge bases to be effective.

ANTHROPOLOGICAL AND OTHER ETHNOGRAPHIES

A serious ethnography of cyberspace would include intense discussion among all these scholars aiming to create meaningful accounts for cyberspace dynamics. Several factors inhibit appreciation of anthropological cyberethnography's contribution, however.

As indicated earlier, holistic ethnography strives to explain as well as describe, contextualizing the results of participant observation in relation to broader structural dynamics. However, several influential intellectuals treat ethnography as one method among many, ignoring its broader epistemology. For example, writers in cultural studies (Raymond Williams 1989), literature (the multiculturalists), science studies (Bruno Latour and Steve Woolgar 1979), sociology and organizational studies (John van Maanen 1983), and even philosophy (Bernard Williams 1985; Daniel Dennett 1991) often speak of the need for a cultural—indeed an anthropological—perspective. Using phrases like, "anthropologists have shown that. . . ," or "confronted with such phenomena, an anthropologist would. . . ," they assume an anthropological standpoint. Yet they seldom pay detailed attention to the discussions of relevant empirical dynamics within anthropology. Anthropological concepts (culture, ethnography, ritual) are appropriated with little regard for their current analytic provenance within the discipline. Donning the mantel of an anthropology of the contemporary but wearing it loosely, they make references to an imaginary anthropological ethnography rather than the existing one.

There is admittedly something satisfying in seeing a profession which, having spoken so much for others, now finds itself spoken for; I have over the years offered my own critique of facile anthropologies of the contemporary (Hakken 1987). Anthropologists' accelerating disintegration into disconnected specialties, as well as their doubts regarding ethnography's epistemological validity, make them less inclined to defend disciplinary territory. Loss of academic and governmental positions as "anthropological" peoples acculturated further lessened our capacities to fight misappropriations of ethnography more vigorously. Yet non-anthropologists use ethnography less effectively than they might were they also to attend to the rich, continuing discipline-based discourse about this intellectual approach. Misappropriation of ethnography is one reason intellectuals find it hard to construct a convincing account of culture in cyberspace.

THE DISTINCTIVE FEATURES OF ANTHROPOLOGICAL ETHNOGRAPHY

Since the Malinowskian fieldwork "revolution" (Jarvie 1964) in anthropology, taking an ethnographic approach has meant long-term participant observation, in a "real" field situation, and in a culture distinctively different from one's own. Stated in idealized programmatic form, the anthropological ethnographer

1. Identifies an intellectual problem in cultural anthropology of theoretical interest (such as the cultural dynamics of cyberspace);
2. Learns as much about this problem as she can;

3. Organizes her thoughts about it into as coherent as possible a sense of problem;

4. Selects a field site in which there is good reason to believe that the dynamics of interest would be accessible to her through participant observation;

5. Familiarizes herself with the general cultural dynamics of the field site before she enters it;

6. Once in the field, participates in as broad a range of relevant activities as is practicable;

7. Pays particular attention to the discursive accounts of her informants, those with whom she interacts regularly while in the field;

8. Analyzes the relationship between what informants say and what they do, aiming to strike a balance between respecting the rationality, in the broadest sense, behind informants' actions and a sensitivity to the indeterminancy of action;

9. Develops models of the relevant cultural dynamics based on all of the above;

10. Finds ways both to feed her models back to informants for criticism and to act as if her model were accurate (participation); and

11. Once back from the field, attempts to communicate both what she has experienced and her account of why the dynamics are they way they are, typically by writing a type of monograph also called an "ethnography."

Its simultaneous commitment to "real" situations and grasping the understandings of informants separates ethnography in this anthropological tradition from Modernist science. In its commitment to problem identification, thoroughness of preparation, and construction of analytic models, anthroethnography is also different from relativist, textualist postmodernism (Grint 1991). Methodologically, its commitment to long-term participating exposure also separates anthropological ethnography from some appropriations of ethnography in information system development, where ethnography tends to be shorter term, possibly involving attendance at some meetings and doing some interviews. Anthropological ethnography is not mere description of practices, as it seems to be for some in the human–computer interaction (HCI) tradition in informatics (see Nyce and Loewgren 1995; Shapiro 1994). In its commitment to developing broad ranges of data sources in the field, and use of equally broad ranges of both quantitative and qualitative data in analysis, neither is anthroethnography just qualitative methods or methodology.

Finally, anthroethnography involves a "going out" to the field and a "coming back" from it, a prior experiential differentiation between the ethnographer and her field site. Our claims to be heard thus derive at least in part from the notion of being more or less outsiders, "marginal natives." In this regard, ethnography is rooted in an Occidental discourse of alterity or otherness. Unlike so-called "nativist" ethnography, it is ambivalent about and does not privilege an unmediated "insider" perspective as such.

Examples of Anthropological Cyberspace Ethnography

AIT AND THE REPRODUCTION OF CULTURE IN SOUTH YORKSHIRE

In 1986–87, Barbara Andrews and I returned to the region around Sheffield in the north of England for a second ethnographic study. The basic empirical problem we addressed was the relationship between forms of computerization and changes in regional working class culture, changes in social relationships, symboling, and patterns of action. The "working class" are those in a labor social formation whose access to necessities depends primarily on selling their capacity to do work. By the mid-1980s in Sheffield, this included many who, while not themselves "working" (more accurately, "laboring") in the sense of being in paid employment, were nonetheless extremely dependent on the reproduction of labor markets.

The lives of working class people are insecure precisely because of their dependence on the successful reproduction of often erratic commodity systems. People in other social positions (professionals) tend to have more effective mechanisms to protect themselves and their families from such vagaries. Working class people are also in a profoundly different structural position than capitalists or even many rural agriculturists, whose access to the means of physical survival are not as directly mediated by a market in labor; they come instead through ownership of profit-generating organizations, or property or patron/client relationships, respectively.

It was this vulnerability which accounts for the general consensus in the mid-1980s that working class lives were most likely to be changed by computerization. In addition to its heavy industrial character, Sheffield was a good site because its political leaders developed a proactive social policy on AIT: There were several coordinated initiatives intended both to counteract negative AIT effects (unemployment and de-skilling) and to shape technology socially, what I call "culture-centered computing" (1991). Because the impact of such policies was of political interest, regional data about the relationship of AIT and culture change were available, and such data would help us build a bridge between case study and national aggregate data.

Although real, material process must often be taken into account when it is created, human information is semiotic, or meaning-impregnated. If it is important, computerization changes both what working people do and what they perceive themselves as doing, the ways they make sense of their world. The Sheffield data on these matters were compared with previously gathered, similar data from the Upper Mohawk Valley region of upstate New York around the city of Utica.

Methodology

One task in Sheffield was to identify specific co-occurrences of computerization and changes in the lives of working class people. We also needed to analyze in detail practices that seemed like they might illuminate the changes observed and how closely related they were to computerization. Finally, we had to identify specific conditions, including particular forms of computerization, which appeared to enhance or impede particular changes. In the field, then, our National Science Foundation–supported activities included:

- Executing case studies of worksite computerization;
- Discussing similar case studies with other social scientists;
- Interviewing computer practitioners, working class organizers, and working class people in the region extensively; and
- Participating in a variety of computerization, education, and organizing initiatives involving working class people, both men and women, waged and unwaged, in both workplace and nonworkplace locations.

Results

The Sheffield data indicated that the social correlates of computerization were manifold and complex. While computerization was clearly not just an externality largely unaffected by local actions, neither was it a contentless process whose character was determined by nontechnological forces. The computerization/class culture relationship is complex and multisided, including both uses of computers that have a clearly positive connection to the lives of working people and other, more negative forms.

We found some important examples of progressive computerization. There was a worker co-op that used computers both to secure the income of its members and to cut the cost of the services it sold to local governments. An imaginative local state-supported projects helped working class people overcome personal anxieties about their futures and computers by finding ways to use computers in their community groups and projects. Unfortunately, worksite computerization in Sheffield was as frequently accompanied by de-skilling, disemploying, and the marginalization of women and minorities as by such progressive effects. In line with other integrative studies of computerization, however, the negatives were not as pronounced as many Sheffielders (and compputropians in general) feared they would be (Attewell and Rule 1985). The most positive and successful examples of the uses of computers were in areas of cooperative work where hierarchies were diminished in favor of shared skills, a finding which ran counter to the ideology of the macho, individualist image of the computer scientist or hacker.

ANOTHER "BASIC" ETHNOGRAPHY:
THE NORDIC NATIONAL COMPUTING PROJECT (NNCP)

In 1993–94, Barbara and I carried out another field study of culture and AIT, with individuals and in institutions active at the national level in the design and development of computing systems in Norway and Sweden. The extensive policy discourses on technology in the Nordic countries as well as the broadening of social participation in its creation were once again important reasons for siting the project there.

NNCP premises and objectives

The NNCP presumed that a controlled comparison[3] of Sweden and Norway, two nations similar in many ways but with distinct national discourses and histories, would contribute to general understanding of the relevance of cultural/national difference to computing TANs. As in Sheffield, a first objective was to identify the broad patterns of computing in the two nations, including general computing discourse, patterns of policy development, and the structural characteristics of the TAN—the people, institutions, and artifacts—most centrally involved in information system development. To gauge the social effectiveness of national technology policies, three application areas were studied in greater detail:

1. User participation in information system development, the practice cited most frequently by those who posit a distinctly Scandinavian approach to computing;
2. Use of advanced technology to increase the independence of people with disabilities, a group in relation to which Nordic social policies enjoy a positive international reputation; and
3. Programs to address the implications of AIT for gender dynamics, something which had also been a focus of both researchers and policy makers in Norden.

Methodologically, the project aimed to test the limits of ethnography as a means of studying structure. Epistemologically, it was based on a "soft" feminist standpoint perspective, one that recognizes that knowledges are situated but remains committed to striving after a (reconstructed) notion of objectivity. Analytically, the project sought holistic (etic and emic) analyses of social process in contemporary social formations, to show that technology is amenable to holistic as opposed to merely interpretivist constructivism. The

NNCP was supported by the U.S. National Science Foundation Anthropology Program and the Norway U.S. Fulbright Commission.

Course of work

Existing studies (Ferne 1989) suggest that in general, AIT (including computing) policy in the Nordic region is developed primarily within flexible, consensual networks of academic, industrial, and policy specialists. Ideas about work in a particular area lead to convening of a policy commission or study group, which draws on preexisting collegial relations and often crosses both disciplinary and national boundaries. Once consensus over the proper procedures for encouraging appropriate research is achieved, research is carried out and policy proscriptions are developed and promulgated, all through networking. Appropriate existing agencies are identified, or new ones created, and policy is implemented. Political bodies like parties, legislatures, and executive arms of states generally endorse the consensus policies, often because of their prior involvement in this policy process. The general prosperity of these small, geographically peripheral economies in the postwar world has been presented as evidence of the effectiveness of this consensual policy system. Based on this view of how AIT TANs were created, the ethnographic task was to enter, observe, and participate in these networks.

Field study in Norway

Fall 1993 to mid-February 1994. Through the kinds of international contacts encouraged in Scandinavian techno-scientific circles, we arranged an affiliation with Norsk Regnesentralen (NR, or The Norwegian Computing Center) in Oslo. NR has been the home of several important development projects and is hospitable to international scholars. We were at NR six months.

Upon arrival in Norway, we established working relationships with colleagues at NR and executed a series of locating interviews on current issues in national IT policy. Throughout the field period, we participated as much as we could in activities surrounding projects at NR on both the social and technical aspects of creating broadband information infrastructures, and we participated in conferences and other events relevant to the formation of more general technology policy. We operationalized our focal concerns by:

- Talking regularly with indigenous scholars whose work was relevant to participatory design
- In regard to gender policy, investigating the gradual abandonment of gender-related IT projects despite continuing evidence of a substantial IT gender effect; and
- With reference to disability technology, executing interviews with participants in and visiting a selection of relevant projects.

Field study in Sweden

Spring and Summer 1994. In Sweden, our institutional home was not located centrally within the computing TAN. We had intended this to be the case, but changes in national policy created a more complex, differentiated, and sometimes conflictual institutional structure, marginalizing the position of the institution at which we had intended to work. We accepted instead an invitation to locate at the Department of Social Anthropology at Stockholm University, where an interest in the anthropology of technology has recently developed.

Initially, we concentrated on a set of placement interviews and searched for projects like the ones we had encountered in Norway. While the Stockholm location provided access to top level government and national capital operatives, as well as the staff of the once activist Arbetslivscentrum (Center for Working Life) and other institutions, we also made site visits, often involving presentations on our research, to several other locations. On balance, participatory access to the field was more difficult in Sweden than in Norway.

Procedures executed

Field activities in both sites followed this general plan:

1. Assembly of information regarding the individuals, institutions, practices, and artifacts that constitute the relevant national computing actor network;
2. Execution of open-ended interviews with at least ten key individuals in the relevant networks, including policy administrators, politicians, trade unionists, and disability and women's activists, regarding the policy formation and implementation process;
3. Identification of projects, especially those relevant to participatory design, technology for people with disabilities, and gender, in which further observation was likely to be fruitful;
4. Initiation of participant observation in a selection of these activities;
5. Creation of a support network of key individuals who shared an interest in the cultural construction of computing;
6. Collection of written documents, including committee/commission minutes, legislative studies, policy memos, and scholarly documents relevant to the national computing process; and
7. Preliminary analysis of data collected in the field in terms of general computing patterns and actor network models and feedback of these analyses to key informants for their reaction; this included several presentations on the project in both sites and circulation of paper drafts for comment, delivered to academic and practitioner audiences in both countries and in Finnland.

THE PRACTICE-ORIENTED PROJECT: RECONSTRUCTING SOCIAL SERVICE THROUGH ADVANCED INFORMATION TECHNOLOGY (RSSAIT)

While the two projects described above are similar in style if not in siting to traditional anthropological ethnography, RSSAIT was much more practice oriented. (Chapter 7 develops a justification for such practice-oriented cyberspace ethnography, despite its frequent violation of anthropological ethnography's orientation toward the "other.") This project developed in 1995 out of my desire to promote uses of AIT that achieve socially transformative objectives. RSSAIT aimed to assist the Department of Mental Health (DMH) and the Community Services Board in Oneida County, New York (where Utica and SUNY Institute of Technology are located). Our objective was to use AIT to meet new public policy objectives and to do so in a manner that both improved services to individuals and met the objectives identified in a community needs assessment that I had recently led. (Funded by the local United Ways and executed by the SUNY Institute of Technology Policy Center that I coordinate, this Assessment [1991] had identified innovation in social service infrastructure to promote integrated service delivery as the key local objective, resulting in the creation of a new Human Services Board.) The project was motivated out of fear for the potential consequences of uncoordinated change (for example, a large "die off" of deinstitutionalized patients during a severe upstate winter cold snap) and hope to demonstrate the positive contribution of AIT to community-based decision-making, along the lines of Participatory Design.

The DMH has primary local responsibility for "mental hygiene/behavioral health" public programs—that is, those for individuals with mental illnesses, alcohol/substance abuse problems, or mental retardation/developmental disability. With a staff of over 130 until the 1990s, the Department provided many of these services itself. By 1994, there were fewer than ten staff left, the bulk of previously public employees now working for local not-for-profit agencies (NFPs) which on public contract provided similar service to the same clients.

The Community Services Board (CSB) exists to advise the Commissioner of Mental Health, prepare statute-mandated plans for mental hygiene services, and evaluate the proposed certificates of need prepared by agencies whenever they wished to pursue new publicly funded activities. Perhaps the historical factor with greatest impact on the mental hygiene situation in the county was the decision, beginning in the late 1960s, to deinstitutionalize into the local community the patients at two facilities, one a 6000 bed state psychiatric hospital and the other a comparably sized facility for the developmentally disabled. The result was in a network of community-based services for a disproportionately large service population.

Major challenges faced this system in 1995. At the state and federal level, new Republican Party initiatives strongly endorsed managed care, which meant movement of publicly funded programs from a "contract for needed service" to a "capitation" or "payment for actual individual services rendered" system, to be administered by private health maintenance organizations (HMOs) but delivered through the same local agencies. The same political forces supported allocation of all public social service funds as a single block, first from federal to state then from state to county government, rather than mandating specific services. Managed care and block granting were justified as prompters of improved quality and individuation via greater client choice and as ways to save money, since the block total would be significantly less than the contract total under the mandated service system. Impending passage of federal Welfare reform (which occurred in 1996) seemed to make these trends irreversible.

Initial RSSAIT Plan of Work

During the work on the Needs Assessment, the DMH had emerged as the most advanced county government user of AIT, its commissioner being an enthusiastic proponent. At privatization, the Department had instituted a wide-area network of computers in all of the NFPs contracted with, which was to provide an integrated database, updated nightly, on all transactions involving recipients of county-funded services. In early 1995, the county, the Institute of Technology, and the Rome Air Development Center, a research laboratory operated by the U.S. Air Force, announced a major technology transfer initiative: the location on my campus of several work stations to run PROSCLE, an integrated suite of software to support business process reengineering developed for the lab at a cost of over $20 million in taxes. The intent of the transfer initiative was to make PROSLCE available to support planning and implementation of reconfiguration efforts within county government, especially those endorsed by the shared services initiative of the county executive.

I assembled a team of people from the Lab, the Institute, and the county that proposed to put DMH at the head of the PROSLCE line. My plan was for us to contract with the county to plan and implement reconfiguration of first mental health and later general social services in the county. The project was to have several phases, including:

1. Refining the DMH wide area network to make the database more relational and therefore more useful for manipulation by PROSLCE-type software;
2. Work with DMH, CSB, local service providers, HMOs, Behavioral Health Care Organizations, politicians, and community representatives to establish local priorities for the reconfigured system;
3. Use of a PROSLCE model of client and financial data to simulate

alternative new network configurations compatible with the local priorities; and

4. Bringing together all the interested parties to select the optimal plan.

Actual Work Accomplished

I was appointed to the Community Services Board and later nominated to chair it. Initial work on the DMH data was completed, and I did considerable participant observation in regard to new system creation, while using my position on the CSB to promote awareness of the need for system-wide planning and a commitment to more active intervention.

During this period, under the slogan, "reinventing government outside of government," the commissioner of DMH actively explored new conceptions of his agency's role. His basic approach was to function as a contractually mandated liaison between the HMOs, on the one hand, and the network of local providers on the other. In conjunction with the CSB, such a DMH could protect a broad community interest. This approach was endorsed by several of his counterparts in other counties and the state Commissioner of Mental Health. Funds were obtained from the Robert Wood Johnson Foundation to support creation of a network to provide integrated child and family mental health services. The commissioner and I presented the RSSAIT plan to a statewide conference on AIT and organizational change in mental hygiene.

Results

Nonetheless, little of the proposed work plan was completed. Unable to entice more than one SUNY colleague into the project, we settled for a much scaled-back project based on consultant rather than contractor roles. The individual primarily responsible for PROSLCE at the military lab gradually revealed to us the severe limitations of the instrument, including

- Its inability to handle quantitative data like that in our database; indeed, this individual indicated that it would be necessary for us to be able to develop "paper and pencil" models of alternative system configurations before we could run them on the software!
- The lack of support from the prime contractor, which was more interested in providing Business Process Reengineering services itself than in supporting PROSLCE; thus, our approach made us competitors.

In the meantime, the state insurance commission indicated that it was likely that only for-profit organizations could link HMOs to service providers. At the federal and state level, block grant programs were announced then abandoned, and governments adopted budgets late. The federal welfare reform plan was only slowly implemented. The state announced that oversight responsibility of publicly funded mental hygiene was to be transferred under managed care to the state Department of Health, leaving the CSB as well as state Office of Mental Health in limbo. Several dates for beginning mandatory enrollment of Medicaid-eligible service recipients were announced and then rescinded.

Locally, the rump state hospital unilaterally announced its own HMO for its large number of outpatients. The county approved six private HMOs, all but one of which had withdrawn from the market within a year, and the County Executive announced he was running for state senate and promptly stopped signing contracts (including the one for my and my colleague's consulting fees!). While two of the three big local hospitals formed one service-provision network, six of the big local NFPs talked about forming a joint corporation. These networking initiatives (one of which would involve extensive electronic information sharing among agencies and the one hospital not included in the hospital network) introduced new forms of competition among local NFPs, many of which were also competing to be included individually on the panels of approved HMO service providers.

The Community Services Board and RSSAIT responded by convening a one-day conference on interorganizational networking in behavioral health care (the new term for mental hygiene services). In addition to discussion of national and local networking initiatives, a workshop at the conference dealt with using computerized information for organizational and network planning purposes. Hopes for using AIT to promote community and client participation have shifted from Participatory Design to post hoc participation, through the CSB, in selecting outcomes to measure system performance and publicizing evaluative judgments based on them. Even this limited objective has been stymied by the decision of the current CSB chair to fight my appointment, the job still being his by rights because he "had paid political dues" as a local Republican committeeman.

Hurdles Encountered in Anthropological Cyberspace Ethnography

These three projects represent two different types of cyberspace ethnography. The Sheffield Project and the NNCP investigated the "pure," basic issue of the relevance of regional and national factors to reproduction of AIT TANs, while RSSAIT, which uses ethnographic techniques to bring about a particular policy objective, is primarily practice. This differentiation should not be essentialized; NNCP involved some intervention (with regard to discourses on "use") into the practice of information systems developers (Allwood and Hakken n.d.). Conversely, RSSAIT provided a chance to observe directly a very "basic" phenomenon: the important symbolic terrain provided by AIT for otherwise unlikely transorganizational integrations.

The projects also illustrate how actual ethnography normally falls somewhat short of the ideal outlined earlier. To fit NNCP into the one year sabbatical frame, field stays had to be limited to only six months in each site (albeit one year in Scandinavia), and English was the primary mode of verbal communication, energy for language study being put into mastering written forms. Similarly, in RSSAIT I am an "outsider" in a limited sense, although, for example, not being a Republican is very relevant.

Ethnography was developed for the intensive study of small-scale societies, often conceived of as "simple" if not "primitive." Not surprisingly, the more specific, recurring problems in transporting ethnography into cyberspace cluster around the terms of the relationship to a very different kind of "field" in which to work.

"PROBLEMING"

Among anthropologists who study computing culturally, some, such as Pfaffenberger (1988) and Hakken (1990, 1991) reject CR Thought. Some anthropologists (Wynn 1988; Jules-Rosette 1990) take the computer revolution as a central presumption of their argument. Michael Evans and H. Russell Bernard (1987) assert the notion in spite of the fact that their data appear to erode it. In making a pro forma nod in the CR direction, often in an introductory comment on how computers are changing things radically, but marginalizing the notion in cultural analysis, these ethnographers are typical of too much anthropological cyberspace ethnography. Appearing to accept the Computer Revolution by adopting its rhetoric, while implicitly rejecting its importance analytically, stressing other, nontechnological mediators, produces an equivocal, difficult to understand position.

Thus, there is a basic issue concerning the intellectual framing of research, or operationalizing one's problem identification. Much of the leading anthropological work in STS, as well as in STS based in other disciplines, is framed in ethnomethodological and/or textualist problematics. These approaches provide an immediate answer to the question of what shall I study—the minutiae of the constitution of everyday life, in ethnomethodology, or conceptualized-as-text behavior in textualism. Each of these orientations also contains a strong implicit analytic program: the mystery of how social order emerges from these minutiae, and the radical equality of all readings.

As argued in Hakken (1993), many difficulties in developing a serviceable sense of field problem derive from trying to operationalize fieldwork within these orientations. By reinforcing predilections popular in this postmodernist moment, ethnomethodological and textualist problematics marginalize attention to, for example, the impact of CR Thought. A "serviceable sense of field problem" provides a dense awareness of the kinds of things one needs to learn about in the field, an indispensable tool if one is to respond effectively to the vagaries of the unfamiliar. "Unfamiliarity" is inevitable given the centrality of "being from the outside" to the anthropological enterprise.

These difficulties in field probleming are connected to the related adoption of frames (postmodernism) which radically critique the very idea of cumulative knowledge. How much cumulation should one strive for in an intellectual practice like ethnography? My contention is that, practically speaking, one needs a strong sense of how one's work relates to that of others if one is to "get somewhere" in cyberspace ethnography.

MASTERING

A second problem in doing good anthropological ethnography in cyberspace is the extent to which one must/should master and/or identify with the professional field(s) relevant to her research. Cyberspace ethnographers often differentiate between those who are "into" the technology they study and those less involved or experienced.

Cyberspace anthropologists share with other ethnographers doing field-based studies of technology-related activities the problems of penetrating the strong barriers of language, social relationship, and access to information erected by apprenticeship, professionalization, claims to proprietary rights, and ambitious personal programs of self-promotion. To gain the cooperation of both U.S. and Nordic IT system developers during the NNCP, I found myself increasingly making personal competence claims relevant to their professional turf.

I believe that this was necessary in this project if informants were to take me seriously, but such a judgment should not be elevated to methodological principle. Indeed, while such claims led to my being treated as more of an insider, they also made me a competitor. Claims of mastery can have "Hawthorne effects," given that informants read (and even professionally evaluate) my ethnography of them. Equally problematic is how the terms on which one constructs one's field entry narrative can dominate interpretation. As brilliantly explicated by Sharon Traweek (1988), at the novice or intermediate level in techno-science, true belief is demanded more than mastery of issue. The critique of scientism and the rejection of science as a master narrative at the core of the Postmodern critique of science (Hakken 1995) further complicates the "mastery" problem.

In the NNCP, my competence claims were a contingent consequence of my experience—having been introduced to computers as an undergraduate in the sixties and having had regular recourse to them since. There are other ways field workers can overcome cyberdefenses against "professional strangers" like ethnographers. A second approach is to enter technological practice not as a competence-claiming "colleague" but nearer the bottom of these generally hierarchical activities: to "study up" in the service department (Garsten 1994), as a tour guide (Traweek 1988), or as a lab technician (Heath 1994). Unsurprisingly, younger and female cybernauts adopt this second approach more frequently than older, male ones. Such entrees are less likely to pollute ethnographic sensibility with promotional personal narrative, but they may also mean that participation in some "high" technological activities cannot be arranged. Both strategies are legitimate.

SITING

Related to mastery/identification is the problem of finding field sites analogous to the geographic "thereness" of Malinowskian field work, in which the site both grounded the fieldwork and bounded it, making it manageable. In cyberspace, the site problem is as much conceptual as "geographic." If one of the important consequences of cyberspace is significantly more separation of space from place, what constitutes an acceptable answer to the question: "Where is your field site?" How does one even begin looking?

One solution is to identify the cyberspace site as itself a virtual space, like that evoked metaphorically in computer-mediated communication (CMC). This solution presumes that on-line activities constitute a sufficient social analogy to the field site, that this is a "where" which, while "nowhere" in the geographic sense, can safely be presumed to be sufficiently "where-like" in some relevant cultural sense.

Alternatively, while cyberspace may not yet exist as such, certain practices (such as computer-mediated work) can be simply presumed to be prototypically "there-ish" enough. These two alternatives involve presumptions about what cyberspace, alternatively, "really is" or "really will be." Such presumptions, for ethnographers like everyone else, are drawn from the cultures in which they live and thus may reflect ethnocentric blindnesses. This is especially the case if their veracity is presented as self-evident and/or if no effort is made to investigate their justness as sites.

When Oscar Lewis (1960) wanted to follow Tepoztecan villagers into the city, he faced a similar problem. He decided to focus more narrowly on single families and individuals. Within STS, advocates of the Social Construction of Technology (SCOT) and similarly narrow methodological approaches, like Bruno Latour and Steve Woolgar (1979), focus on practices in individual labs. Their decision is one source of the tendency to equate ethnography with micro-level studies.

I have chosen sites differently. In my 1986–87 study of computing and reproduction of working class culture in Sheffield, England, I tried to study an entire region. This was a way to bridge the gap I perceived between the results of micro and macro level studies of the social correlates of computing. In the

NNCP, I was interested in cultural dynamics at the national level, and so I chose to do fieldwork in the national networks of those creating computing professions, artifacts, and policies. In my current research in cyberspace, I consciously aim to transcend national effects. Like Traweek (1988) and Dubinskas (1993), I have also developed a comparative research practice. There is no "natural" type of site for cyber-research, nor a single appropriate way to enter the field. We need diverse initiatives, especially those which transcend the more rigid notion of appropriateness now associated with ethnography in STS.

SURFING THE INTERNET VS. SITING

Alternatively, one can rethink the idea of a specific "site" altogether. George Marcus (1993) applauds recent attempts to address anthropology's crisis of representation by pursuing "multi-sited" ethnography, because such approaches reject "closed . . . systems narratives of macro-social processes." In some ways, Marcus' approach fits the way Barbara Andrews and I sited the NNCP: internationally, and in networks. Like Linda Layne (1997), however, I have a problem with "multi-sited" as a term. It implicitly retains the centrality of (admittedly several) localized sites, while analysis implies that any "siting" is suspect "for those . . . interested in placing their specific projects of research in the unfolding of new arrangements for which past historical narratives were not fully adequate, a firm sense of a world systems framework was replaced by various accounts of dissolution and fragmentation" (Marcus 1993:98).

Rather than something to be embraced, or glossed over with ambiguous phrasings, this frame fragmentation should be resisted. Instead, empirical study of cyberspace must develop frames for handling simultaneously the global and the national, the cultural and the local.

"Non-site bound" or "trans-sited" are more accurate descriptions of some cyberspace research, which "surfs" virtual space in a manner similar to the way one can navigate the World Wide Web. With system development colleagues, for example, I used the Internet to find qualified participants for a professional conference. Participating in talk about which individuals had appropriate standing within the international professional community helped me to identify the underlying criteria on which such judgments were collectivized. Indeed, I found myself engaged in hyper-reflexivity at the 1993 AAA meetings: commenting upon a paper some of whose content was composed of my own email messages!

Despite its attendant research vulnerabilities, the existence of the Net was extremely important to my attempts to get to the national level in "Norden." In some ways, a professional "community" in cyberspace is very metaphorical. In others, precisely because of technologically enforced abstracting from local conditions, it is culturally more analogous to the "primitive isolate" hypostetized by Malinowski than any "real" laboratory.

But can one really "participate" meaningfully in CMC practices that extend across continental and sensory, let alone national and language, boundaries? Colleagues at Stockholm University (Hannerz 1992) have for some time been arguing for ethnographers taking the methodological implications of globalization seriously. Partly their argument is theoretical: that older concepts of culture unnecessarily reinforce nationalist discourse. It is also practical, in that national and similar boundaries are increasingly of marginal relevance to the practices they wish to study, from mass media to professional arts and global education and business. After a year in Scandinavia, I more fully appreciate the practical advantages that follow from their surfing.

PROTECTING

The possibility of radically different discourse patterns justifies ethnography of CMCs (Internet, multimedia, even home shopping). Perhaps the special vulnerability of this fieldwork is related to a new kind of exposure, consequent to the speedy achievement of the apparent intimacy of the face-to-face connection in the absence of the normal interaction patterns through which humans learn to trust each other. The low return rates to cyberspace surveys is probably related, too. Indeed, the vulnerability of research to sabotage, and the immense difficulties of negotiating appropriate speech conventions, justify some skepticism about whether CMC really will be associated with changes in basic communication patterns. Nonetheless, American culture maven Miss Manners recently expressed great satisfaction with CMC precisely because of the large degree of explicit concern with "proper behavior" manifest in it.

In addition to finding ways to protect their individual access to the field, cyberspace ethnographers face a problem of collective "protection," the emergence among professional techno-scientists of a "backlash" against studies of them by non-techno-scientists like ethnographers. The backlash is more overt in the United Kingdom than in the United States, but it has spilled over into the pages of the *Chronicle of Higher Education,* sessions at professional association meetings, and publications like Gross and Levitt's *Higher Superstition* (1994). The backlash emerges in highly publicized events like the Sokal affair (and the less publicized scandal surrounding the denial of an academic appointment to Norton Wise). It is also implicated in U.S. congressional attempts to eliminate funding for social, economic, and behavioral research at the National Science Foundation, research constructed by Republican Congressmen as something NSF "wandered into" as part of trying to be "politically correct."

While presented to date primarily as a critique of analytic stances, the backlash against STS also targets ethnographic practices with feminist and similar sensibilities. Protecting involves projecting a clearer, more collective model of alternative ways to practice science, both within anthropology and more generally.

TALKING

My work on computing and social change led me to be skeptical of CR Thought. The dynamics of contemporary social formations remain more similar to their immediate predecessors than some new society. Still, I have recently become more willing to use terms like "cyberspace." I am convinced that that some AIT-related social changes may indeed be prefigurative, not of some inevitable cyberspace but of some radically different potential patterns of social reproduction. To participate in making choices about the future, it is important for anthropology to help focus attention on the alternative futures which confront us. Learning to talk "cybertalk" is one way to do this. Nonetheless, I am an uneasy "cybernaut," because the point at which "talking the talk" means reinforcing its constructions rather than illuminating them remains unclear.

THE REPRESENTATIVENESS OF DATA DERIVED FROM STUDY OF A "PROTO-" SOCIAL FORMATION

An additional challenge follows from the fact that, in current Cyberspace Studies, we pursue the ethnographic episteme in a social formation as yet unrealized and perhaps never to be. Ethnography involves identification of patterns, but how indicative of the future are patterns identified via fieldwork in proto-cyberspace? For example, most ethnographic analyses of computerized work, even those by ethnographers committed to the CR, emphasis continuity with preexisting work patterns rather than uniqueness (Hakken 1993). Of what relevance is this finding to a vision of a full cyberspace social formation?

Bound to the here-and-now, ethnography cannot be definitive about the ultimate parameters of future social formation types. Yet cyberspace ethnography can deal with this issue in a number of ways. One is to look for "best case" field spaces—why I chose Sweden and Norway as sites to study national, the Department of Mental Health for social, and Sheffield for local policy interventions regarding AIT. Similarly, the tradition in anthropological ethnography of cultivating critical awareness—both of your own and of the social formation in which you intend to participate—increases the fieldworker's ability to differentiate mere variation on existing pattern from the possibly unique. Our ultimate justification for ethnography in spaces at best "proto-" is that they are the only ones that we can access though our somewhat limited but still legitimate approach to investigating profound social issues.

Moreover, this limitation is also the source of cyberspace ethnographers' practical promise: As we develop fuller understandings, we can choose to ground imaginings and constructions of cyberspace on what we have learned through examining its early manifestations. Since we can choose to reinforce practices worthy of replication, while abjuring others, cyberspace ethnography can itself become an important tool in the creation of the future while further enhancing its predictive value.

Epistemological Challenges
in Anthropological Cyberspace Ethnography

While specifically linked above to cyberspace, these problems resonate strongly with issues relevant to all anthropological ethnography and are more about epistemology than method per se.

THE RELEVANCE OF CULTURE IN ANY COMPLEX SOCIAL FORMATION, NOT JUST CYBERSPACE

Many of the difficulties in analyzing cyberspace ethnographically derive from inadequately developed senses of culture. These difficulties parallel those encountered by an earlier generation of ethnographers, like Margaret Mead and Oscar Lewis. They were trying to use the notion of culture, developed in anthropological ethnography to analyze simpler social formations, to study more complex ones. One result of their efforts is the current popularity of anthropological notions in analysis of contemporary social problems, as witnessed by the widespread use of concepts like "organizational culture" or Lewis' "culture of poverty." Unfortunately, such concepts tend to be used in ways in which analytic breadth is sacrificed for facile echo.

For example, since the problem of U.S. poverty was "rediscovered" in the 1960s, both the political left and right have cast it in largely cultural, rather than psychological or social structural, terms. The right justify massive cuts in benefit spending as legitimate in the face of cultural patterns "chosen" by the poor which are highly resistant to change, while the left argues for transformed opportunity structures as the best way to counter behaviors "adaptive" in relation to existing reward systems.

Each appropriation is simplistic, but unfortunately both can be justified. In his original articulation (1966), Lewis did indeed talk of the culture of poverty in negative terms: "The chief characteristic of the culture of poverty is the poverty of culture," or "the ironclad lifeways of the poor." These rhetorics can be exploited to justify seeing poor people as responsible for their own plight, their lifestyle a cultural "choice." But Lewis also stressed how the poor could not generally be expected to change this lifestyle in the absence of sufficient resources: "The primary cause of the culture of poverty is lack of resources."

However, most anthropologists are uncomfortable with the way culture has been appropriated. The utility of "culture of poverty" has been drastically reduced by separating it from the particular research context in which it originated, such as Lewis' intellectual and methodological quest to develop an anthropology as relevant to peasants' experience in Mexico City as in their home village. The rich tradition of anthropological ethnography provides more complete, holistic accounts of human action, by combining attention to both distinctive choices and structural constraints.

CRITIQUE OF ETHNOGRAPHY WITHIN ANTHROPOLOGY

The richness of this tradition is in part a result of a history of an internal anthropological critique of ethnography. When I became an anthropologist thirty years ago, the strongest critique was external, on the purpose or use of anthropological knowledge—for example, whether it was a handmaiden of imperialism (Gough 1968). What critique of anthropological knowledge itself there was came primarily from formalists, arguing in the natural science mode for standardization of analytic constructs (Parsonian pattern variables, mathematical models) and/or approaches (more hypothesis testing).

Arguing that there is a "crisis of representation" in ethnography, James Clifford and George Marcus (1986), Marcus and Michael Fischer (1986), and John Van Maanen (1983) recently stimulated another critical wave. Their humanities-oriented critique questions the value of ethnography for any purpose other than telling nice stories. Fieldwork's most famous proponents like Clifford Geertz doubt the general value of its results and urge us to see ourselves as more capable of commenting on style than substance. (This radical relativizing thrust has spread from philosophy into literary criticism and thence to anthropology and the other social sciences. It has also made some inroads into technology, especially in more obviously socially dependent areas of technology like ISD.)

Several responses to this critique have been developed. One is to reduce ethnography to a set of supplementary methods. Sociologists tended to treat the new work anthropology of Lamphere (1979), Nash and Fernandez-Kelly (1983), and Sacks (1982) in this way, and computing anthropologists like Wynn (1988) and Sachs (1995) tend to present method as what is distinctive about computing anthropology. On this approach, ethnography is simply to be added to other disciplines' methodological armamentarium. It also unfortunately disconnects ethnography from anthropology's long search for a proper scientific object.

Strongly influenced by linguistic anthropology and sociological ethnomethodology during graduate study at the University of California at Berkeley, Suchman, Traweek, and Wynn, as well as technology anthropologist Carol MacLennan, tend to ground the ethnography of computing in a similarly strong methodological orientation. The result is a primary stress on interpretivist, semiotic rather than holistic analyses. This cast to computing anthropology's methodology is evident in the work of Jules-Rosette (1990), Dubinskas (1988), and Pfaffenberger (1992).

In contrast, *Cyborgs@cyberspace?* reaffirms the value of a more holistic commitment to both interpretivist and materialist moments, epistemology as opposed to mere method. Of course the limits of ethnography must be recognized: its ultimate dependence upon flawed data-gathering instruments (humans), it inevitably partial analytic results, its profound problems with generalization, and its dependence upon a stance of alterity. It is the ability of ethnography to produce knowledge anyway, through confronting squarely knotty tangles like the ones encountered in cyberspace, which provides its justification.

LOCATING CYBERSPACE ETHNOGRAPHY WITHIN ANTHROPOLOGY

I have recounted elsewhere (Hakken 1990; see also chapter 8) some of the "crisis of representation"-related difficulties encountered in founding an AAA group dedicated to ethnography of computing, as opposed to the use of AIT in anthropology. Two tendencies have marked the group (CASTC) finally organized. One perceives the primary task as the fostering of an anthropology of techno-science (including science, technology, and medicine), while the other wants to focus on cyberspace. Each sees its problematic as the more general, encompassing the other—computing/cyberspace as merely one example of trans-historical techno-science practices—techno-science as one of the several "fronts" on which a new, AIT social formation is battling to emerge.

In CASTC, this difference interacts with others—between those who cast their work in the tradition of "basic" research and those primarily concerned to apply knowledge in redirecting techno-science; optimistic computopians and pessimistic compputropians; those who feel it likely that anthropologists can influence techno-science and those who think it unlikely. Creating a shared view on the place of cyberspace ethnography within anthropology is further complicated by the different positions we occupy within the field; as basic researchers, practitioners, or, like me, people doing both basic, applied, and practice work. Several located in techno-science organizations (and/or working for private sector employers) are concerned to have their work perceived as basic rather than applied.

For all these reasons, a high degree of consensus on the place of cyberspace ethnography in anthropology is unlikely to emerge anytime soon. Further, given the popularity of CR Thought, any attempt to separate the anthropology of techno-science from the anthropology of imagining cyberspace would not be well understood. Constructing a common problematic is complicated by the dynamics of professionalism (careerism, the necessity of self-promotion) in a competitive capitalist political economy. While the advantage of the current situation is the sense of considerable activity to which it contributes, the disadvantage is the relative absence of a shared problematic, to help us feel like we're getting somewhere. *Cyborgs@cyberspace?* was written in part to address this problem.

ANTHROPOLOGISTS' TECHNOLOGICAL AMBIVALENCE

The difficulty in situating cyberspace ethnography within anthropology has a deeper root as well, which is the problem Americanist anthropologists have with technology. Rooted in fundamental analytic constructs, flawed notions about the technical inhibit anthropologists' collective ability to come to terms with a range of contemporary issues; when appropriated by others, as via notions of culture, they inhibit broader publics as well.

Among the manifestations of the difficulty is anthropologists' personal technophobia. Our difficulty may have something to do with our individual psychic histories, having perhaps picked this field because it wasn't science or math, perhaps reinforced by personal self-perceptions of ourselves as "people people," not "geeks."

Skitishness about technology makes anthropologists peculiarly subject to the technicism which permeates modern culture, itself arguably connected to the tendency of humans to distance themselves psychically from technological dependence; schizoid on technology, humans tend strongly to treat it as external. Anthro-practices also follow the technological determinism general to "industrial" culture. It is similar to industrial sociology prior to Braverman, where work organization was seen as essentially rational, determined by technology. The consequence is ambiguity regarding the place of technology in anthropology, an ambiguity that results in a particular kind of marginalization of the technical.

The claim that the practice of anthropology marginalizes technology is not obvious. In some ways, it is an overstatement, given, for example, the classic characterization of the field's object of study as "man (sic) the tool-maker." Indeed, certain segments of the field (as in archaeology) have overt interests in seeing technology as integral to culture. Moreover, the major evolutionary divisions of culture types described in chapter 2 are grounded on technologically based criteria, from "gathering and hunting," to "horticulture," and so on.

Further, a marginalization of technology is a paradox within a culture like our own, with its inclination toward "technological determinism," technology being typically taken as constituting the starting point of social causation. The paradox is even more peculiar, for, as in the broader public discourse, technology is used in anthropology as a fundamental framing device, as the basic explanator in most accounts of cultural evolution (for example, as the movement from gathering and hunting to horticultural/pastoral, then irrigation/agricultural, and then finally to commodity production social formations). How can technology be both marginal and fundamental?

Pfaffenberger (1994) helps us to understand how this can happen. Precisely because of its presumed universal characteristics, technology has been moved to the margins of anthropological interest, a context, rather than a central part, of culture. He and Ingold (1993) have argued that anthropologists do this at least in part because they have read their Durkheim too well, identifying technology with "the profane" and culture with "the sacred" (or more recently, "the symbolic," semiotics, and cultural constructs). The variations that matter, those which constitute cultural boundaries, are by definition located in the nontechnological. The marginalization of technology as a subject of anthropological interest has interfered with our understandings of cultural performance, whereas, as Pfaffenberger has argued, it is exactly in the technological that culture is most vividly embodied.

Consider the way anthropology's object of study is usually defined: "the cultural manifestations of humankind in space and time." This approach teaches young anthropologists that the entity properly taken as the carrier of culture is the human being—"man," as we used to say. Since the boundary of the human life form is the skin (even if this skin is conceived as the collective skins of a "people"), it follows that technology is part of the context of, and therefore peripheral to, culture. Since the early twentieth century, an antitechnological stance has increasingly pervaded the dominant theoretical orientations in the field, focusing instead on:

- Social structure (Radcliffe-Brown 1968);
- "Patterns of and for behavior" in the Parsonian social science division of labor (Parsons and Shils 1951);
- "Semiotic" or "symbols and meanings" (Schneider 1968; Geertz 1966); and
- "The linguistic, Postmodern turn" (Clifford and Marcus 1986).

Given this intellectual history, it is no wonder that anthropologists tend to see "culture" and "technology" as distinct, related in ad hoc fashion rather than parts of a single whole. Whatever the reason, issues of cyberspace come to be posed among most anthropologists, as among other intellectuals, as problems of the impact of technology on culture, while the impact of culture on technology is ignored. Yet science, for example, is arguably the most symbolic (and, in this sense, "cultural") of activities (think of theoretical math or physics), and it is at the same time deeply imbricated in (often inseparable from) technology. Techno-science is seldom subject to the kinds of intellectual activities of cultural criticism so much a part of our approach to painting, film, or language (see Winner 1994). Technicism-based shortcomings—in particular, a definition of its "object" of study which marginalizes technology—similar to those affecting computing studies more generally provide grounds for questioning whether mainstream anthropology offers an epistemological grounding sufficient to the exploration of cyberspace.

Although we have not generally recognized it, through evolution, both physical and cultural, technology has become functionally inseparable from our biologically based patterns of and for behavior and our ways of living, whether gathering and hunting or production of commodities. One of the points of the typology of technology types outlined in chapter 2 is that technologies gradually became as constitutive of us as we are of them.

The main difficulty in creating a syncretic science, one that encompasses both the "natural" and the artificial, is figuring out how to handle technology and humanity in a unified frame. This is not a matter of "contextualizing" technology with the human, or, conversely, setting the human in the context of the technology, for either of these moves decenters one at the expense of the other. One can accomplish the necessary syncretism by recasting anthropology's object of study, to no longer draw the boundary of the field's object at the human skin but treat humans and their technologies as unitary entities.

In sum, then, anthropology manifests multiple ambivalences about technology. In theory, technology is important, but in practice, anthropology generally treats technology as an exogenous variable, as part of the given context (Dobres 1995). When they do confront techno-science, they either treat it semiotically as "the symbolic" in talk of "scientific ritual," or they take its "truths" as given—for example, as in the willingness of my colleagues studying information technology to adopt CR Thought. In sum, they fail to problematize techno-science, to treat it as an important site of cultural reproduction. (This is another reason for failure to achieve the level of mastery required to do serious study of techno-science). Many of the specific problems of cyberethnography described here have roots in anthropology's technological ambivalence, for which the exploration of cyberspace is itself an important antidote.

Conclusion: Issues in Classical and Cyberspace Ethnography

Seven specific hurdles and four epistemological issues with particular salience to anthropological cyberspace ethnography have been listed. Yet the stories anthropologists are able to tell have always very much depended on

- The problems we choose,
- The points at which we enter the field,
- The ways we draw intellectual and social boundaries,
- The levels of our units of study,
- Our practices in the field, and
- The terms we employ to describe these experiences.

Hurdles and issues like these were problematic in the Malinowskian era as well; we just weren't as aware of it. Thus, cyberspace ethnography is no more (and no less) at risk of collapse under the critique of ethnography than is any other ethnographic practice.

There is at least one sense in which cyberspace ethnography is actually more defensible. After my year in Fenno-Scandia, I am more aware than ever of how the enterprise of anthropology is, in the words of Jean-Claude Gallie, a "round trip" (1993). We go out to "the other" in order to return to our "own." If done in a sufficiently self-conscious manner, we believe that our self-imposed, studiedly different outsider way of seeing things can legitimately be considered insight; informants often argue that this is the case.

In taking our field trips, we engage in Wittgensteinian "language games" of several sorts, but we needn't hide from this existential fact. Much of the political critique of anthropology stems from the fact that ethnography was largely practiced by Westerners on others whose relationship to the West included one or another important forms of dependence. We can turn our back and study "at home"—which I do—in response to this critique, but when we do so exclusively, we lose our ability to justify our perspective in "outsider" terms.

As a new terrain for social life, cyberspace is more or less equally "other" to everyone. Cybernauts thus avoid at least some of the "ethnographer at home" problem, although this is less true perhaps for those who enter it occupationally. It is professional cybernauts whose ability to see cyberspace clearly may be most constrained by the "taken for granted." The hype and self-delusion characteristic of capitalism triumphant—its pronounced occupational fetishism—is most developed in AIT. What I offer such informants is a different point of view on issues about which we both care. To the extent that my vision is informed by, but not bound institutionally to, their professional "conventional wisdom," we can engage. Our discourse, moreover, can be mutually satisfying and produce knowledge, of a relative sort, of value both to creating systems that work better and to an understanding of culture.

Benedict Anderson (1983) pointed out that much national discourse itself actively creates the nation. Similarly, E.P. Thompson (1963) referred to the working class as being a presence at its own birth. One of the most striking aspects of cybertalk is the extent to which its speakers are aware that their discourse about it is also creating cyberspace. While this awareness sometimes leads to tendentiousness and the shrillness of cyber-hype, it also means one wastes less energy grappling with at least some problems of misplaced concreteness. Johannes Fabian (1991) argues that ethnography is a viable project *because of,* not despite, its discourse-dependence. At the same time, this dependence *upon* discoursing to engage the field does not mean that we can *only* study discourse itself.

Introduction

Anthropologist Robbie Davis-Floyd has a very personal relationship to AIT. She began her 1995 paper to the American Anthropology Association's Symposium on "Cyborgs in Cyberspace or Humankind in Space and Time?" by describing the birth of her first child in 1979:

[4]

The Entity Problem:

What Carries Culture in Cyberspace?

A twenty-six-hour hospital labor that started out in the hospital's alternative birth center ended in Cesarean section. As I lay on the operating table, numb from my shoulders to my toes, I received graphic confirmation of the "reality" of the Cartesian mind–body dualism—for the first time in my life, I existed only as a disembodied head. I was a cyborg—my body and my experience of that body had been irrevocably altered by the deadly cold metal table on which I lay, by the green curtain that cut me off from even visual contact with my pregnant belly and my emerging child, by the epidural anesthesia that coursed through my veins. I wish I had known that then, because that concept has such power—cyborgs are often more than human and in those moments of disembodiment, I could have used the sense of transcendence which might have accompanied my cyborgification. I could have thought, well you know, here I am taking the next evolutionary step! But Donna Haraway had not yet written *The Cyborg Manifesto,* and so instead of transcendence, what I felt was a profound alienation from my body and from the experience of birth, an overwhelming loneliness, and a sense of helplessness and victimization from which it took me four years to recover.

Once I realized that contemporary obstetrics is a system that is co-created by obstetricians and women, each of whom have much to gain from deconstructing organic childbirth and reconstructing it as technological production, I was forced to look again at the human–machine interaction that characterizes this reconstructed technobirth—at the strong symbiosis between the woman and the technology; at the way in which it removes the chaos and fear from women's perceptions of birth and at its perfect expression of certain fundamentals of technocratic life. . . . The IV, for example, is the umbilical cord to the hospital, mirroring in microcosm the fact that we are all dependent on society and its institutions for our nurturance and our life. The fact that the baby's image on the ultrasound screen is often more real to the mother than its movements inside her reflects our cultural fixation on experience one-step removed on TV and computer screens. The electronic fetal monitor wires the women into the hospital's computer system, bringing birth into the Information Age. . . . I began to see the mutilation and prosthesis of technobirth as the fullest metaphoric expression of life in the technocracy, which I define as a society whose central organizing mythology constellates around a technological progress that will culminate in transcendence of all natural bounds, including both biological and planetary limitations. . . . The cyborg represents our increasing closeness to that goal, and so takes on a mythological significance that is extreme (pp. 1–2).

The Entity Problem

Ethnography is about understanding culture. Whatever else they disagree about, anthropologists generally believe culture to have a largely extra-somatic, nonbiological character. That is, to be reproduced, culture must be learned. Whatever continuity it has—indeed, the very patterned nature of culture itself—is the result of invention and thus necessarily compatible with characteristics of its inventors. Thus, individual entities capable of producing and reproducing culture extra-somatically are a necessary, although by no means sufficient, precondition to culturing.

Exuberant evocations of the distinctiveness of culture carrying entities in cyberspace, like those of Davis-Floyd, are a frequent trope in cyberspace talk. Whether held to be wonderful or horrible, as in the subgenre of science fiction exemplified by *Neuromancer* (Gibson 1984), "cyborgs in cyberspace" are presented as increasingly unlike those entities which populate ordinary space. As beings incorporate more AIT-based medical technology into their bodies, they cross some life form/hybrid-mechanism boundary and "become" cyborgs. Mark Dery (1994), for example, glosses this process with the cyber-slang notion, "Borged." Referencing a character in *Star Trek: The Next Generation,* to be "Borged" means to be "transformed into cyborgian hybrids of technology and biology through our ever-more-frequent interactions with machines, or with one another *through* technological interfaces" (emphasis in original, p. 6).[1]

As is often the case in ethnography, then, popular usage presents cyberspace ethnography with elemental empirical questions: Just how different are the entities that carry culture in cyberspace? What are the implications of the differences for the general dynamics of cyberspace culture? How reliable are accounts like Davis-Floyd's as guides to the ways we should perceive ourselves and construct our identities in the future?

Invoking the idea that cyberspace involves a "species revolution," such cyborg talk is a form of CR Thought. In this chapter, I describe the empirical grounds of my skepticism toward thinking of cyberspace as a space where "new creatures take over." Still, the popularity of the idea points toward a different impediment to thinking culturally about cyberspace: Popular conceptions of the *current* culture-bearing entities are inadequate. My efforts to think systematically about the entity question in cyberspace have led me to the apparently paradoxical position hinted at in the Introduction: Cyberspace entities are cyborgic, *but they are substantially the same* as the carriers of culture in other eras. For this to be true, precyberspace entities must also be/have been substantially cyborgic.

Two kinds of work are necessary in order to talk cogently about cyberspace culture bearers. One is empirical ethnography, the development of compelling accounts of "real" entities. First, however, we need to be ethnological, to develop concepts which clarify rather than obscure the characteristics of culture-bearing entities in general. We need an anthropology of cyborgs.

Conceptualizing Culture-Bearing Entities

To speak of a Cyborg Anthropology (CA) is catchy, but is it not perhaps a bit too hip, utilizing a discourse style associated with postmodern "disruptions" more intended to be disruptive than to be taken literally? (see Downey, Dumit, and Williams 1995) For me, CA must stress the cyborgic rather than the biologically bounded as the chief characteristic of the "human" entities which generally carry culture. Indeed, since this has long been the case, cyborgs are therefore the most proper object of study for anthropology. The cyborgs of which I speak have much in common with the "quasi-objects" whose characteristics constitute for Latour the most important evidence of the failure really to be modern. A properly cyborgic anthropology's concepts will promote adequate cultural attention to technology.

From my CA perspective, while Davis-Floyd accurately states the perceptual importance of the passage of medical devices from outside to inside, across the boundary of the skin, she overstates its *ethnological* importance. As evidenced by the normalcy of implanted heart pacemakers or artificial hips—really, any prosthesis (vs. an orthosis)—crossing this boundary has been common for some time and is not that new. My point is not simply that humans have been piercing their skin for a long time. The "cyborgs in cyberspace as species revolution" view treats as a dichotomy (human vs. cyborg) that which is at least a continuum—from all biological to all artificial. It may well be that, as we move along this continuum, the newer forms of cyborgification are so different from their predecessors that we are justified in developing a typology of cyborgs related to substantial differences in the ratio of biological to artificial "content." One such "among cyborg types" boundaries may be closely tied to the enhanced information processing characteristics of AIT, that in cyberspace we become cyborgs of a profoundly new type; that, as in Gouldian (1981) evolution, quantitative change achieves qualitative change. However, that any such typology is justified must be demonstrated empirically, not just affirmed based on potential.

Even if the justice of such a boundary were demonstrated, the contrast would be between one form of technologically mediated humanity/cyborg and another, not, as Davis-Floyd presents it, a contrast between a purely biological human and a highly technologically mediated cyborg. If not coinciding with entry into cyberspace, what in evolutionary time was the most significant cyborgification? This question is related to a central issue in anthropology, how to conceptualize in an evolutionarily consistent fashion the relationship between the carriers of culture and the biological world. Briefly, we know of nonhuman life forms who "use tools," for example, termites who use sticks, chimps who assemble a tower of boxes to reach bananas. What is distinctive of humans is the way they can also use tools inventively, rather than relying exclusively on "instinct" or developmentally learned coding. What separates gatherers and hunters from their proto-human ancestors is their capacity to invent not only new tools but also new uses for them, an extra-somatic learning or culture. One could indeed argue that we became a distinct species at the point where our reproduction became more than halfway dependent upon such creative tool use.

In sum, my Cyborg Anthropology stresses how humans have been quite "cyborgic" from early in the emergence of the species. Technology is so deeply implicated in human existence that it is a core aspect of our being. If we have probably almost always been cyborgs, the entity question in cyberspace becomes about the particular implications of AIT in comparison with other TANs rather than in contrast to some "non-TAN" period of human existence. How do the increased capabilities of AIT affect our already considerable cyborgic qualities?

A Cyborgic Model of Human Mental Activity

A more satisfactorily cyborgic approach to the entity question can be grounded on recent empirical work on the human brain. Research into neurophysiology and neurochemistry, on the one hand, and computer-based modeling of human thinking on the other, has particular implications for understanding human consciousness.

THE PROBLEM OF CONSCIOUSNESS

The capacity for consciousness has often also been taken as constituting a philosophical boundary between humans and other life forms, on the one hand, and machines, on the other. Like treating the body as bounded by the skin, conceiving of consciousness as a distinctive human activity also needs to be rethought as part of the process of cyborging anthropology. Developed as part of a broader effort to rid philosophy of its Cartesian baggage, this rethinking also has implications for how we understand culture as a collective activity. (In addition to their increasing use of data and perspectives from both natural and artificial science, the general projects of philosophy and anthropology have grown closer in recent times.[2])

The model of human consciousness developed in Daniel Dennett's *Consciousness Explained* (1991) is much more compatible with my sense of culture-carrying entities than is the standard Cartesian account of consciousness. As argued eventually later, however, the inadequacies of his account of culture shine a reverse spotlight on some important aspects of culture theory. Still, Dennett's account can be revised to provide a useful model of culture carriers in general, an extension that also allows us to be more specific about the cultural implications of the transition to cyberspace.

Dennett's account of mental processes uses empirical research from both neurology and artificial intelligence to reject Cartesian dualism (the mind/body split). In particular, Dennett displaces the metaphor for consciousness which has dominated philosophical thought since Descartes—that of some mental performance space in the mind or "Cartesian theater"—with a computing metaphor, the notion that consciousness is a "virtual machine software" "running" on brain "hardware." For Dennett, the functioning of this "consciousness machine" is roughly analogous to that of a distributed computing system built on a parallel processing architecture.

Dennett provides a nonmodern account of consciousness. His argument offers additional bases—the parallel processing metaphor being one—for thinking of humans as constitutionally cyborgs. In his adoption of a machine metaphor for consciousness, Dennett risks (as do I with my "cyborg" notion) falling victim to the dominant modernist conceit of technicism, nonreflective explanation of human phenomena through mechanistic metaphors. His description of the role of consciousness in humans/cyborgs *at the individual entity level* provides an important demonstration of an underlying human/cyborg continuity which is not technicist.

A NON-CARTESIAN APPROACH TO CONSCIOUSNESS

Dennett summaries his account of individual entities and their "consciousness" in the following way:

There is no single, definitive "stream of consciousness," because there is no central Headquarters, no Cartesian Theater, where "it all comes together" for the perusal of a Central Meaner. Instead of such a single stream (however wide), there are multiple channels in which specialist circuits try, in parallel pandemoniums, to do their various things, creating Multiple Drafts as they go. Most of these fragmentary drafts of "narrative" play short-lived roles in the modulation of current activity, but some get promoted to further functional roles, in swift succession, by the activity of a virtual machine in the brain. The seriality of this machine (its "von Neumanesque" character) is not a "hard-wired" design feature, but rather the upshot of a succession of coalitions of these specialists.

Dennett goes on to discuss these "coalitions" of "specialist circuits" in the following terms:

The basic specialists are part of our animal heritage. They were not developed to perform peculiarly human actions, such as reading and writing, but ducking, predator-avoiding, face-recognizing, grasping, throwing, berry-picking, and other essential tasks. They are often opportunistically enlisted in new roles, for which their native talents more or less suit them. The result is not bedlam only because the trends that are imposed on all this activity are themselves the product of design [sic]. Some of this design is innate, and is shared with other animals. But it is augmented, and sometimes even overwhelmed in importance, by micro habits of thought that are developed in the individual, partly idiosyncratic results of self-exploration and partly the pre-designed gifts of culture. Thousands of memes, mostly borne by language, but also by wordless "images" and other data structures, take up residence in an individual brain, shaping its tendencies and thereby turning it into a mind (pp. 253–54).

To make cyborgic sense of this evocative (partly through his use of "everyday" speech) but still somewhat opaque (partly because he puts everyday speech to new purposes) description, we begin with Dennett's critique of the Cartesian conception of consciousness. On his reading of Descartes, the notion "human consciousness" implies that there is some place in the brain associated with those points in mental acts where we become aware of or "see" what we are experiencing. This is what Dennett calls the metaphor of the Cartesian theater, a "place" "where" we perform "conscious acts." Like the audience at a performance, we look at the data provided by our senses and then decide what to do about them. In Modernist philosophy, it is precisely such acts of consciousness which distinguish us from other animals and which are taken to be a central element of intentionality, moral reckoning, and the other mental capabilities on which we construct notions of human culpability, responsibility, and agency. (In attacking such constructions of consciousness, cyborgic accounts raise serious problems for conceptions of agency and thereby for notions of ethics; see chapter 7.)

ACCOUNTING FOR OUR "FOLK" MODEL OF CONSCIOUSNESS

Dennett questions whether this model is an accurate description of actual human mental processes. First, he argues that there is no neurological evidence for such a central "clearing house." (A similar point is made in Damasio's *Descartes Error,* 1994.) Second, there is no compelling argument for keeping this model, only the tradition of Modernist discourse in philosophy and science already discredited for other reasons. Third, he argues that any machine designed along such "von Neuman" lines could not possibly handle the volume of sensory signal processing actually executed by even a young child, and certainly not at the speed at which a child does this. A von Neuman machine executes processes serially (assembling, judging, and operating upon one set of inputs, followed by another, followed by another). This is especially true of a life form (a human/cyborg) run on electro-chemical, and therefore comparatively slow, "hardware."

So if the Cartesian description is not even vaguely accurate, where does it come from? On Dennett's account, our "theater" sense of our consciousness corresponds to the after-the-event, non-real time reconstructions we make of our actual mental processes. These narratives are constructed to fulfill some other demand. Like Weizenbaum's ELIZA (1976), our sense of consciousness is an imaginative, serviceable "interface metaphor" "designed" (Dennett uses this term much too freely for my taste) to fit with a sense of ourselves and what we are like culturally constructed for other purposes. Like ELIZA's users, who found interacting with her to be cathartic despite her total insensitivity to the actual content of their communication, we find this image of consciousness "good to think." We are egged on in this regard, Dennett implies, by multiple Modernist narratives which dress up our myths in the garb of science.

Rather than a constant processing of all sensory input, moments of something like Cartesian consciousness, on Dennett's reading, are only occasional. Most of what goes on in our brains can be accounted for in terms of three other, non-Cartesian theater-like processes. One type of process, like the "duck" response to looming objects, or the "pay attention" response to patterns of vertical axis symmetry, is genetically based, adaptive responses following from natural selection. A second type is "learned" in much the same manner as are many bird songs or any arrangement conducive to the rapid execution of highly specifiable routines or "algorithms," like walking; that is, they are patterns which are learned very easily and which we are in a sense primed (metaphorically "designed") for. One might make a rough comparison here with resident ROM (read only memory) on a computer.

In describing the third type of nonconscious mental act, Dennett draws upon Richard Dawkins' notion of the "sememe," by which is meant a culturally conditioned, "artificially" created mental "habit," similar to Bourdieu's "habitus" (1978); in "computerize," like a macro or other user-programmed subroutine. Such nongenetic, nonpredisposed procedures are also things that an individual might invent herself, albeit probably under the supervision of a cultural "master programmer" or in close cooperation with other people. Like Dawkins, Dennett is in my view too willing to assume that this third type of activity is simply "copied" from others. In any case, individual development takes place in a manner that increases the likelihood that one's behaviors are compatible with others'. Again, in the computer parallel, a sufficient part of the programming must be compatible with networking, "runable" successfully on multiple "units" in the "culture."

DENNETT'S VIEW ILLUSTRATED

In Dennett's view of the individual brain, several of all three types of processes are going on simultaneously in each unit at any given time, even when we sleep, like so many processors linked in a parallel (non-von Neuman) rather than serial architecture. What happens when we walk through a room whose walls are covered by small reproductions of Andy Warhol's Marilyn Monroe painting, one of Dennett's examples? First, we might respond via hardware to the vertical symmetry of one image of the face and focus visual attention on it. Second, we might, as we have predisposedly learned to do, very rapidly "sample" several other locations on the walls and preconsciously "note" that it is the same image. Third, we might classify this image as a female human face and even, if we are American, given the many repetitions of this image in this national culture, fit the pattern to previously "stored" images and, in this sense, semiconsciously "recognize" it.

After we leave the room, were we asked to describe it, we might respond by saying something like, "Its walls are covered by reproductions of Warhol's painting of Marilyn Monroe." How should we account for this response? Dennett dismisses a strict empiricist account, on which we are held to have exhaustively examined each part of every wall and determined that all parts are covered by essentially the same image. Humans don't act like this; if they did, they'd seldom leave one room for another. He also rejects an interpretation based on a Cartesian "central information processor," taking in all the sensory input, examining it, and constructing the most coherent account of the data, then storing it for potential later retrieval under a hastily constructed index linking all appropriate prompts—thus, a query about what the room is like. His case is based on things like the failure of chess programs designed along such "data crunching" lines to compete with any but the rankest amateur.

On Dennett's reading, what has taken place is more like the following. Distributed throughout the human brain are mechanisms which relate sensory input to various compatible images of "what might be going on in a world which could produce such an input," images constructed out of hardwired-like, ROM-like, or sememic information processing. In his view, such associative activities are running more or less constantly in any human animal's brain. In the room, it is the hardwired vertical axis response that is most likely to respond to the images present. Results from stimulated "visual sampling" become associated with the "hypothesis" of complete coverage of the walls by this image, as well as perhaps some other compatible possible senses of "what is going on here." This (or these) association(s) is (are) stored in some kind of short-term memory. In the presence of an appropriate (and appropriately timed) query, it is this (they) which is (are) elicited, reconstructed in relation to (each other and to) other culturally-constructed information, and given nice, linear narrative, verbal form. Indeed, given the heavily cathected quality of this particular image, it is likely to be the object of a rather larger than average amount of pattern recognition activity, and thus the associated "interpretation" is likely to have a somewhat longer life than would associations with less cathected images (like the tiny tulips on the wallpaper in the room in which I write). This why a room covered by Marilyn Monroe images is more likely to be "remembered,"constructed as a "memory" at some date in the future, than most others.

Dennett would, I believe, also have us imagine a person, less familiar with the Warhol painting and more marginal to American culture, who, upon entering the room and noticing the repetitive image in the manner described above, stops and "wonders" what the image is. She might even say to herself something like, "Who is that woman, I know that face. Why, it's that film star, what was her name?" If she were to say this out loud, Dennett argues, it would increase the likelihood that she would "remember" who it is.

Were this latter set of events to take place, they would look a great deal like the conventional notion of consciousness, and could legitimately be considered so. This practice includes a capacity for periodic self-awareness, the ability to focus attention on the association-generating process itself, to slow it down or train it to generate associations in a more disciplined, deliberate, even rule-directed manner. This capacity would be of exceptional advantage to a creature dependent for survival upon learning symbols shared with other similar creatures.

SUMMARY OF DENNETT'S CYBORGIC ACCOUNT OF HUMAN CONSCIOUSNESS

Dennett's case, then, is not the total absence of the Cartesian *cogito*, but that this activity is a much less frequent and less regular part of normal mental process than is assumed in "modern" models of the mind. Consciousness in something like the "theater" sense—of substantially more self-reflection than is typical of the normal mental pattern—is a relatively rare, albeit still important, moment. He argues further that all mental processes—from far-reaching, nearly random association-making to nearly rigid, quite programmable matchings of narrative accounts—can at least in theory be run on a computer system, a "strong" claim.[3]

In my view, Dennett succeeds at the entity level; that is, in undermining any case which would draw a sharp dichotomy between individual human and other life or machine forms of "consciousness." (Dennett also makes the case that his model does not fatally undermine the case for human agency, and thus morality, although he does not completely persuade in this regard.)

Cyborgic Entities and Cultural Processes

More than British and much Continental anthropology, American anthropology is committed to a biocultural perspective—that is, to take seriously the problem of integrating biological and cultural construct-related accounts of human existence. Dennett's story qualifies as such a serious attempt. His attention to the way in which mental processes fit better to a "distributed processing" than "queuing" or von Neuman machine mode, for example, seems quite compatible with the conception of memory articulated in neurological researcher Steven Rose's recent book, *The Making of Memory: From Molecule to Mind* (1993). His account of entities as described here rings true for me also in relation to my own work in an independent living center with people who have experienced traumatic brain injury, especially the variable characteristics of their condition. Dennett is also quite committed to using evolution to account for the development of consciousness.

The "minding" Dennett describes would only have come into existence, let alone flourished, if it provided some selective advantage. Further, his model of consciousness at the individual entity level is valuable precisely because it reduces the amount of stability required to account for consciousness. It requires no Cartesian theater creating a high degree of order, only an incessant virtual narrative machine, generating stories bridging current sensory experience to previous activity. When needed, more complexity and coherence can be constructed, but reflexively, not in real time. In short, Dennett reduces the mental distances among human, other life form, and machine. By reducing the complexity of information processing demanded of all, he creates space for the cyborg as a unified metaphor for their interpenetration.

Cyborg anthropology extends anthropological holism by positioning humans as entities in technology actor networks, thereby reconceptualizing them as bio-techno-cultural entities. Dennett's careful model of consciousness as a virtual machine, analogous to a computer, leads us to identify strong individual-level parallels among biological, mechanical, and human forms of information processing, thereby giving considerable concreteness to the human-as-cyborg notion. This is its main contribution to cyborging anthropology.

CRITIQUE OF DENNETT'S CULTURE CONCEPT

I am less satisfied with Dennett's account of supra-individual phenomena, however. There is a rather large gap between the stories of permutation told by actor network theorists, whose stress is on competition, alliance building, negotiation among powers, and more or less constant social construction and reconstruction, and Dennett's static, "gifts of culture" discourse. Before we can assimilate Dennett's account of consciousness into anthropology, it must be separated from this account of culture.

As indicated in the section quoted earlier, a conception of super-individual processes is an important part of his story. However, in not recognizing the need to remove the individual standpoint, a simplifying abstraction in the development of a fuller account, Dennett's argument remains mired in another undertheorized moment of Modernism, the bourgeois individualism fostered by this era's characteristic political economy, capitalism. (Dennett's preference for Richard Dawkins as his anthropological guide with regard to "culture" is deeply regrettable; I kept wishing he had chosen Clifford Geertz.)

In line with much biomedical thinking, Dennett presents culture as rapid, "extrasomatic" adaptation, an important complement to the "hard-wired" and "learning-based" adaptations of other life forms. He articulates the relationships among these processes in this way:

> Plasticity makes learning possible, but it is all the better if somewhere out there in the environment there is something to learn that is already the product of a prior design process, so that each of us does not have to reinvent the wheel. Cultural evolution, and transmission of its products, is the second new medium of evolution, and it depends on phenotypic plasticity in much the same way phenotypic plasticity depends on genetic variation. We human beings have used our plasticity not just to learn, but to learn how to learn better, and then we've learned better how to learn better how to learn better, and so forth. We have also learned how to make the fruits of this learning available to novices. We somehow install an already invented and largely "debugged" system of habits in the partly structured brain" (p. 193; his emphases).

For Dennett, culture is primarily an already debugged, largely stable array of entities which therefore can be easily "installed." He believes that we can legitimately think of culture as being like a range of software products. His preoccupation with an individual perspective means that the creation of this product range is not problematized; it exists somewhere "out there," prior to the individual taking it on. (Educationists would recognize in the passage the so-called "banking" theory of knowledge, in which knowledge exists prior to and independent of learning, and where teaching is a job of transferring the commodity of knowledge into the mind of a learner, like transferring money from one account to another.)

To the complex society anthropologist like myself, as to the TANer in STS, Dennett's passage is jarringly simplistic. In it, Dennett sounds like the early "culture and personality" theorists in anthropology (Mead 1928; Benedict 1934), who assumed a one-to-one correspondence between culture and personality, each a mirror image of the other. A.F.C. Wallace (1970) and others have succeeded in displacing this simplistic view of the relationship of culture (particularly language) and personality by one which stresses the extent to which the elements of culture are mazeways for handling diversity rather than one-way conveyor belts though which uniformity is promulgated.

Indeed, Dennett's account of culture is full of the language of progress and implicit goals or teleology. Contemporary anthropology understands diversity as a chief characteristic of culture, as in Pierre Bourdieu's stress on the importance of class in constructing "habitus" (1978). In my own attempts to come to terms with the reproduction of working class culture in Sheffield, England, and in much of the anthropology of gender, the emphasis is on culture as an arena of contestation rather than one of stability. The appearance of stability is often a consequence of an imposition of power, or it may be a result of negotiation, tacit or explicit, between those with access to different, roughly equal, forms of power. Stability is a social construction of reality; tradition, in the current anthropological parlance, is invented. To the extent, then, that Dennett's account of consciousness depends upon culture being a set of debugged, stable, ever improving products, his story would seem to be deeply flawed.

An Alternative Cyborgic Model of Culture, Based on the Ethnography of Information System Development

Dennett's culture concept evokes the computer technician who denies responsibility for system failure by mouthing the nostrum, "garbage in, garbage out." This technician is a character typically encountered by anthropologists executing field studies of information system development (ISD) in real organizations. This work has demonstrated, among other things, the strong preference of systems developers for stability, a preference required by formal, mechanistic, models. Automated information systems work best when they are applied to domains where data change is highly predictable.

Indeed, the fundamental problem in developing effective ISD collaboration between informaticians and anthropologists is figuring out appropriate compromises regarding how stable to treat real world situations as being. The anthropologist is inclined to glory in (and glorify) the complexities which follow from the shifting constructions characteristic of really existing domains of activity. In contrast, the informatician, whose craft pride is located in the construction of effective systems capable of producing predictable results, can ultimately only represent relationships which can be treated as stable. Collaboration can only be built on explicit agreements regarding when to try to reflect complexity, albeit stably, and when to exorcise it.

Dennett reduces the complexity of culture like the technician—by definition, not by explicating a mechanism for handling complexity. The degree of stability at the cultural level posited by Dennett is a poor model of existing culture. It is also unnecessary.

As suggested by the ethnography of ISD, an information simplification similar to Dennett's at the level of individual consciousness can operate on the supra-individual level as well. Culture, whatever it is, reaches deep into the dynamic of Dennett's virtual machine, providing images which constitute a large component of the informational "raw material," many of the patterns which are "recognized." We can better begin to conceptualize what happens at this level by extending his computer metaphor, conceptualizing culture as a virtual network operating on an inter-individual entity level. Similarly run on a parallel architecture, culture flows (Hannerz 1993)—sometimes "automatically," sometimes reflexively ("consciously"), sometimes collectively (textually)—by generating narratives which vary drastically in their plausibility and are subject to the dynamics of power. To understand culture, we must learn how to apply Minsky's metaphor of "a society of minds" to the group/network as well as the individual level. Technological artifacts, and the broader technology actor networks associated with them, have a central place in creating and reproducing the cultural virtual network.

THE CYBORGIC MODEL OF CULTURE ILLUSTRATED:
THE ARCHAEOLOGY OF LANGUAGE

Recent work in archaeology, physical anthropology, and linguistics provides good reasons for seeing cyborgification as occurring quite early in human evolution. This work makes it possible to be much more concrete about how such cultural parallel processing might have come into being. David Armstrong, William Stokoe, and Sherman Wilcox summarize much relevant linguistic data in *Gesture and the Nature of Language* (1995). The problem they set out to address is that of how distinctively human languages came into existence. Much contemporary cultural anthropological theory, both semiotic and that inspired by "the literary turn," takes language as the quintessential cultural activity. To be able to account for how and why we use language, then, is a major step toward being able to account for culture, the capacity which makes us a truly distinctive species.

At least since Chomsky (1965), however, accounts for the development of human language have lacked Darwinian credibility. This is because Chomskian accounts presume a genetically based universal capacity for spoken language, and human language is understood to be quite discontinuous with other forms of communication. In Lyons' widely accepted conception (1981), for example, language is composed of two domains, a set of symbols for things (lexical items) and a set of rules for relating these symbols (syntax) which are related to each other arbitrarily.

It is this capacity to handle the arbitrary, taken as the key to human cultural capacity, which is the most difficult aspect of language to explain. In formalist, Sausseurian linguistics, language is conceived as an abstract system of arbitrarily related units. Consequently, accounts of the evolution of language capacity have had to postulate an extremely abrupt transition from quantitative to qualitative change, or punctuated equilibrium (Gould 1981). Further, the archaeological date for the emergence of a human voice box capable of generating the range of contemporary sounds is quite recent, usually associated with the emergence of Cro-Magnon creatures roughly fifty thousand years ago.

This approach to human language capacity strikes me as being similar to, and as implausible as, the "Cartesian theater" approach to consciousness. Like Dennett, Armstrong et al. set out to provide an account of language capacity evolution which is more plausible. They do this in two ways. First, they expand upon much recent substantivist criticism of the Sausserian approach, by stressing how models of language which emphasize the arbitrary relationship of lexicon and syntax err by taking spoken language as the pattern for all human language. Gestural languages like American Sign Language, they point out, often combine lexicon and syntax in the same linguistic element, the moving sign.

Second, they provide considerable evidence for the notion that gestural languages preceded spoken languages in human evolution. For example, they identify considerable communication through gesture among chimpanzees, our nearest evolutionary neighbors. They suggest the use of especially hand but also other body movements to communicate as a powerful reinforcer of bipedalism. In contrast to gestural language, spoken language is likely a late-emerging, specialized form of speech, particularly valuable in situations where eye contact is problematic, but highly unlikely to have been the first form of true language.

Armstrong et al.'s view of language development requires no single leap to arbitrariness and thus fits better with the gradual fossil record. It is also pleasant that, on their account, sign languages move from the periphery of linguistic theory to the center, a particularly fitting reposte to Graham Bell's vocalism (Lane 1989). Like Dennett on consciousness, they account for information/ communication processes in a way which locates the human more comfortably within the broad developmental sweep of life forms.

Most interestingly for our cyborgifying purposes, however, is the direct connection they make between language and technology. The human hand reached its approximate current form early, more than a million years ago, at roughly the same time as the brain reached its current size and we became fully bipedal. The current bone structure of the upper torso, the structure that makes it possible for us, unlike other primates, to control our vocalizations so precisely, is at most sixty thousand years old. Similar gradual developments like hairlessness were probably, according to Armstrong et al., "[e]nabled by the ability of humans to use fire, to construct shelter, and to manufacture clothing and bedding as protection against death by hypothermia. This again reinforces the notion that the "hard" evidence for human evolution, some time after the adoption of upright posture and the freeing of the hands for manufacturing, followed a path that became increasingly technological" (p. 203).

It seems quite in keeping with their approach to describe the developing gestural language as a communication technology; indeed the body itself, especially the hands, becomes a communication technology. (It is most precisely in this sense that we have always been cyborgs.) It seems reasonable to suggest, moreover, that as the human hand became better able to mimic forms and movements, the form of the hand would with increasing frequency reference other objects. The hand, in other words, becomes a metaphor for the tool, and visa versa.

Unlike Dennett, however, Armstrong et al. recognize that a social moment is as key in this progression as the individual one: "We stated above that the homonid adaptive complex became increasingly technological, and we would amend that to say, 'technological within a social context' (p. 218). . . . It is the ability of the individual to conceptualize and the group to conventionalize that is fundamental (p. 235). . . . A socially cooperating species, becoming more skillful, not only at coping with the environment but also at devising new techniques for doing so, would certainly find communicating with more or less transparent, easily interpretable gestures a great advantage" (p. 229).

In sum, they make a powerful case for seeing the earliest human languages, gestural rather than vocal, as having a very deep history. Deliberate, controlled motion of the body means not only using the body to refer to something else, but also using the body itself as a tool (an additional meaning for the notion that humans "domesticated" themselves!). Along the same lines, Ingold (1995) has demonstrated how our genetic characteristics have been deeply and more or less continuously affected by the capabilities of our technology.

Entities in Cyberspace: Actors, Creoles, Objects?

To what extent is culture carried differently in the presence of Advanced Information Technology? Of the several developments in proto-cyberspace which are suggestive of difference, three are discussed here.

CYBORGS@CYBERSPACE AS ACTANTS IN TECHNOLOGY ACTOR NETWORKS

Are cyberspace technology actor networks different? TAN theory was developed within STS to provide a more satisfactory answer to the question, what is a technology? Rather than answer this question in the terms of the popular culture, which tends to restrict technologies to machines, TAN theory conceptualizes them holistically, as complexes of relationships among human and nonhuman entities which can be treated as unitary things (see Callon 1986).

TANs are unitary in the sense that they have discernible trajectories, but these are influenceable; some entities become actors rather than mere actants, the construction of a particular technological "system" being an active social process. Empirically speaking, "competing" actants become actors by "recruiting" potential network participants into "coalitions" of coordinated action. Successful recruitment has to do with contextually relevant rhetorics and power and cannot be reduced to either external technical "reality" or transcendent "agency."

Analytically, TAN theory developed out of the attempt of STS scholars to free themselves of Whiggish readings of the history of technology, to be more "Kuhnian." Social studies of science are generally relativist in a limited sense, at least to the extent that they reject a "presentist" orientation; that is, it is held to be poor practice to explain the past in terms of the present. The notion that some actants may be nonhuman is an important, and controversial, analytic inference: It would be improperly Whiggish to privilege one type of actant—the human—over others in terms of their potential to be "actors." Through shifting the boundary of potential agency to include the nonhuman, ANT provides yet another justification for conceiving of entities in cyborgic terms.

The enlarged cyborgic capabilities of cyberspace entities suggest the likelihood that typical actants will be "enhanced human" hybrids rather than either human or nonhuman. One implication is a need to rethink fundamental aspects of Modernist ethics, in which agency is strictly human.

CYBERSPACE CYBORGS AS MORE CREOLIZED

Similarly, the capacities of AIT to support group rather than individual initiative will make it more difficult to identify any single point of invention, a common step in arguments over, e.g., authenticity. The term "Creolization" has been adopted by cultural anthropologists like Hannerz (1992) to refer to the process by which new cultural structures/processes or "structurations"

(Giddens 1987) develop into complex dialectic unities out of the interaction of diverse cultural traditions. The term was first used by linguists to characterize the complex speech which often results from interaction between previously separate languages. As applied in, for example, the Caribbean, Creolization perspectives stress the roles of both superordinate and subordinate social groups in the development of something which, though drawing on preceding practices, is itself distinct.

The TANs of cyberspace are "Creoles" in this sense. Instead of having social and technical "sides" which must be "linked together," or talking about organizations as a context for technology, or technology as a context for humans, TANS are unities with complex internal histories. "Creolization" as a linguistic process usually involves systematic asymmetries between unequal groups, such as colonizers and the colonized. Since there are no similarly regular "party" relations in TANs, however, there are some limits to the applicability of the Creolization analogy. Nonetheless, "Creolizing" captures both the relative autonomy of the analytically distinguishable internal dynamics of a TAN (for example the differentiable moments of technological and biological trajectories, or the power inequalities which sometimes mark their interrelationships) while maintaining the ultimately existentially inseparable unity and creativity of the active "Creole" TAN as subject.

Creolization seems to me to be a useful way to think about successful "technology transfer." Each time technological artifacts are introduced effectively into a new cultural setting, the resulting TAN is best understood as a syncretic response to the attributes of both the "spawning" techno-science and the "receiving" social formation. Their extended capacity for syncretism, increasingly symbolic content, and grounding in more diverse practice make cyberspace TANs even more Creolized.

CYBERSPACE ENTITIES AS OBJECTS

Interestingly parallel discussions exist over basic units in anthropology and informatics. Much ethnography of specific cultures involves description of what things there are and how they relate to each other, the cultural categories or constructs, symbols, or semiotics. Any attempt to specify such units, however, risks communicating exaggerated senses of rationality or stability, and thereby oversimplifying the relationship of construct to action.

As ISD becomes more use-oriented, the units out of which an IT system is constructed are increasingly representative of units that already exist in the "real" world. A group of ISD professionals (Madsen et al. 1993) who describe themselves as "object oriented" have developed techniques to automate representation of and reference to these units, as in the icons familiar to Mac and Windows users. Icon use appears to be transparent and icons come to be treated as singular things.

As noted above, real culture units often have internal complexity and ambiguity. There is often controversy over their boundaries, and even the same person sometimes applies cultural categories differently in different situations. The consequent problems of interpretation are exacerbated in systems of formal representation like AITs.

Object-oriented designers have developed techniques to address these dangers. They can construct programs that retain objects' internal complexity; for example, by establishing uniform procedures for processing each object irrespective of its properties; these latter can be defined, manipulated, or changed separately. Thus differentiating the internal from the external, Object Orientation (O-O) allows the programmer to construct a temporary, artificial boundary around the instability so much a characteristic of "real life" TANs /cultures.

O-O is especially helpful in distributed processing, which operates over several artifacts. For example, objects can be constructed to have "inheritance," which means that a change in one instantiation of an object (or an item in a database) is automatically replicated in every other instantiation, irrespective of its physical or electronic location, even in a "separate" information system. Simultaneously "black boxable" and transformable objects more closely approximate real cultural constructs. They should become increasingly key components of the developing worlds of shared information (as in relational databases), although—like ethnographies (the books)—actual O-O systems often fall far short of their representational potential.

Ethnographers and systems developers would seem to have much to learn from each others' approaches to constructs/objects. Such approaches to basic units also suggest powerful metaphors for more general cyborgic properties of cyberspace. Something like "inheritance" must be characteristic of brains for humans to function effectively—if they are to operate, as Dennett, DaMasio, and Rose all agree they do, as sets of "parallel processors" of cultural constructs. Techniques for black boxing internal complexity have similar at least metaphorical relevance to collective, cultural processes: Real human cultures employ constructs more or less simultaneously at many different levels, their symbolic icons embedding numerous complex behavioral proclivities whose diversity, as in "ritual," is ignorable in various contexts.

Additionally, the capacity of AIT TANs to handle objects more complexly is likely to accelerate further the decoupling of space from place; AITed objects "really" can be in more than one place at the same time. Their multi-sitedness and complexity also make such objects less transparent and thus a danger to human freedom and democracy: The person who controls object production is in a profoundly powerful position to influence social reproduction and thus create the future. It would appear that the constructors of AITs will increasingly decide which kinds of diversity (instability) are accommodated and which are marginalized. As life becomes increasingly computer mediated, "object-oriented" becomes more than a metaphor for the human condition: Developing proper objects properly—in a participatory, democratic manner—should become ethically imperative in cyberspace.

Self-Identity in Cyberspace

To what extent are cyberspace entities more modified-human, more Creolized, and more multilocal? What does cyberspace ethnography conclude about the extent to which entity dynamics are actually different in cyberspace?

Although not my personal interest, others have examined closely one empirical issue closely connected to the behavior of cyberspace entities: the way identities are formed in cyberspace and their content. Cyberspace is in an important sense being created first in the imagination of systems developers, designers, hackers, and Internet surfers. The flowering of interface utilities characteristic of the Internet has often been remarked upon, just one of many evidences of rich self-invention. Thus an emphasis on identity is quite appropriate in cyberspace studies.

Sherry Turkle has suggested thinking of the computer as a plastic technology particularly amenable as a vehicle for inventive identity formation. An influential early article (1980) described the "computer as Rorschach" phenomenon of how computered people project onto the computer all sorts of dreams, desires, and visions. In 1984, for her high school student informants, the computer constituted *The Second Self*.

Turkle titles her latest book (1995) *Life on the Screen, Identity in the Age of the Internet*. The evocation of "age" language is one form of her claim that differences between life before and life on the screen are epochal, and that identity formation is the key locus of the change. (Similarly, the dust jacket describes the book as "The first ethnography in cyberspace.") Perhaps the most significant change is the decline she perceives in the necessity for entities to maintain coherence across diverse performances.

To make her case, Turkle focuses on the multiplicity of identities revealed in multiuser domains (MUDs). She first draws attention to the apparent ability of an operating system like Microsoft's WINDOWS (or that of the Apple Macintosh) to run several programs simultaneously. Then she argues that this ability provides a good metaphor for Internet identity, which involves management of multiple "selves": "[Y]our identity on the computer is the sum of your virtual presences" (p. 13). Such MUD existences are not only evocative of Postmodernism; they are an example of how technology can actually bring a set of ideas into everyday life, especially the notion of life as a simulation, referring to "constructing identity in the culture of simulation" (p. 10). A key proof of the spread of this sensitivity is the existence of "net sex." Drawing on her argument in *The Second Self*, she again characterizes computers as intimate machines and as the new location for dreaming, a central identity forming process (1984:26).

Mark Dery is one of several other authors who like Turkle posits qualitatively different identity dynamics as characteristic of the use of new means of computer-mediated communication (1994). He describes the posting of electronic notes in discussion groups like "listservs" as similar in some ways to "public bathroom graffiti, in that their authors are sometimes anonymous, often pseudonymous, and almost always strangers. Which is the upside of incorporeal interaction: a technology enabled, 'postmulticultural' vision of identity disengaged from gender, ethnicity, and other problematic constructions. On line, users can float free of biological and sociocultural determinants." Dery accepts the judgment of a consultant who runs the Science Fiction group (SFNet): 'People are judged on the content of what they say' rather than judged in terms of who they are perceived to be" (pp. 2–3).

In his early examination of the changes in work related to microelectronic technology, Adam Schaff (1982) identifies a potential for substantial self-identity problems for working class people. Because computerization increasingly shrinks the range and the number of jobs to which they will have access, and because such people tend to conceptualize their selves in terms of an occupational role, it will be more difficult to establish positive self-concepts.

Gideon Kunda's analysis of work in *Engineering Culture* (1992) is also framed in terms of identity. His focus is "Tech," a late 1980s "high tech" firm in Boston's Route 128 corridor, where highly sought after engineers earn high salaries within a "no layoff" environment. This is a matrix organization; with no formal lines of responsibility or hierarchy, engineers need only take part in those projects that they themselves choose.

With mounting dispair, Kunda recounts the individual-level consequences of working in this environment made rich by information. These privileged engineers have increasing difficulty locating a boundary between themselves and the organization: they work long hours and have less and less of a "life" away from work; even predictable performances of "burn out" become woven into the work narrative. Kunda's tale is a useful antidote to Tracy Kidder's more computopian *The Soul of a New Machine* (1981; a book which is more about the souls of those who design computers than those of the machines designed). Because these engineers lose the capacity to think for themselves, Kunda sees this new form of work as a profound threat to any political system, like democracy, which depends on independent agency.

CYBERSPACE IDENTITY AND THE COMPUTER REVOLUTION

Chapter 2 argued for making more explicit evaluation of CR Thought a prime focus of cyberspace ethnography. While some are computopian and others compputropian, the self-identity authors are, like Davis-Floyd, "pro" CR. This is the case whether, like Turkle, they focus on differences in the *process* of identity formation, or, like Schaff and Kunda, stress difference in identity *content.*

Should we then conclude that the identities described are "more deeply" cyborgic? Extensive historical work in Cultural Studies (see Stuart Hall 1980) has stressed how apparently new forms of identity formation and content are often strongly dependent upon preexisting social arrangements. Thus, ethnographer Sandy Stone stresses how it is the telephone that first teaches humans to attribute agency to the electronic representation of the not physically present (1995). In their work on a Norwegian home shopping/information service, especially the radically different uses made of the system by men and women, Anne-Jurunn Berg and Marete Lie (1993) stress the importance of prior social experience-based interpretation to what happens when the computers come.

Stefan Helmreich (1995) has carried out extensive fieldwork on forms of "artificial life," described by their creators as harmless, self-replicating computer programs. These forms are alleged to possess an internal developmental dynamic sufficient to justify their agency to be treated with the dignity usually reserved for biological forms. For example, as "actors" with a "right to life," these forms should be allocated memory in every computer systems for self-replication.

Should we think of artificial life forms as significantly new distributed objects? In a series of brilliant explications of their actual practice, Helmreich (1996) demonstrates the extent to which the social relations constructed in the operation of these programs replicate social relations manifest "IRL." Familiar hierarchies of white, male, professional dominance are manifest not because they are "independently invented" but because they are, often unconsciously, "programmed in." Insufficient awareness of how this happens produces a false sense that such "old" hierarchical constructions develop "naturally," an example of the dangers inherent in opaque object construction.

Similarly, is the colonization of worker consciousness that concerns Kunda a consequence of a new, cyberspace form of Creolization? The absence of authority structure at Tech is compensated for by development and promulgation of a distinct organizational culture. As the pun contained in the book's title indicates, this culture really is "engineered," but through quite familiar mechanisms, especially numerous, largely technology-free, ritualistic performances. Indeed, Kunda's critique echoes generations of Marxist critiques of Social Democracy or of British social science interest in those working class Tory voters labeled "Angels in Marble."

In sum, it is difficult to reach a conclusion regarding just how different identity is in cyberspace. Partly this is a consequence of rhetorical style; at several points, for example, Stone warns against taking anything she writes as a definitive statement of a position, preferring instead to strike internally a postmodern "polyvocal" stance. This ethnological equivocality on identity and cyberspace entities also follows from analysts' failure to develop ideas more systematically. Turkle's claim about cyberspace as a "nacent culture of simulation" is provocative, but the argument could benefit from more explicit cross-social formation type comparison. To the extent that they involve imposition of constructs developed in a semiotic rather than empirical manner, all cultures are "cultures of simulation."

We need to know more about workspace culture: If, for example, the absence of an oppositional culture at work is long term, did it revive during the 1990s downsizing at "Tech?" What about the informal work culture bridges between the tier of "permanent" engineering workers and the "temps" who make up the secretarial and other support staff at Tech? We also want to follow these engineers in their lives outside of work: Do they engage in local politics and neighborhood associations? In short, self-identity is related to social relations, like the class imaginings of the Sheffield informants considered in the following chapter. Moreover, as Helmreich's data on so-called artificial life remind us, imaginings of identity in cyberspace may actually be strongly grounded in the imaginings characteristic of previous social forms. As Craig Calhoun argues, processes of identity are always political (1995:233), in the sense that we derive our sense of who we are through comparison with others.

Thus, there is little doubt that, in cyberspace, too, identity formation and content is as cultural as in previous social formation types. At least in part prompted by cyberspace ethnographies, there has been a general complexification of ethnological models of culture, with a resultant complexification of our sense of the relationship of culture and identity and therefore of identity itself. Individuality is not invented out of nothing; it means distinctive selection from among the conflicting, increasingly incoherent, identity options made available through the often ambiguous options offered by culture. It may well be that in the work of Stone, Turkle, and others, a shift in our apprehension of identity processes and contents *in general* is being inappropriately associated with the emergence of a new type of social formation. Indeed, there is a parallel between Turkle's accounts of change in identity process and that of Anthony Giddens (1991). Like Turkle, he identifies an increasing tendency to lodge responsibility for identity in narratives constructed by the individual, but he associates this change with "high" rather than "post" modernity. For Stone, use of a very modern technology, the telephone, is an essential practice in the transition to dialogic narratives, as opposed to personal experience, for the redemption of claims to social authority.

The decoupling of space from place accomplished through use of the telephone implies that "virtual" life has been coming for a long time. Where analysts draw lines between social formation types is especially important in cyberspace ethnography as long as CR rhetorics remain an implicit standard or are much performed inconsistently. As in the early nineteenth century (Anderson 1983), such lines are drawn around various national imaginings. Cyberspace is often described as a self-consciously transnational social formation, but it is also the locus of nationalistic cultural imaginings like the national information infrastructure initiatives examined in chapter 6.

Concern like Schaff's for the social psychological consequences of technology induced unemployment is justified. Indeed, in 1980s Sheffield, Barbara Andrews and I found both more computerization and a more extensive questioning of conventional social labels—for example, what does it mean to "be in the working class?"—than was present in the 1970s. However, because computerization is only one of many political economic changes taking place in contemporary society, such data do not in and of themselves justify Schaff's conclusion that computerization is the cause of these changes in identity content. The fuller political economic argument is also taken up in chapter 6.

I am ultimately skeptical of CR claims like Turkle's. Computer "Rorschachs" may involve new, more complex identity forming processes. Yet the relationship between culture and identity is complex because culture is complex. Evidence of complexity of individual level identity processes is not necessarily evidence of change in social formation type. Moreover, the content of these new identities is largely predictable, like that of Helmreich's artificial lifers, drawing heavily on sources in the existing, pre-cyberspace culture.

Conclusion: Embodied Imaginings

Drawing on various research activities, this chapter has aimed to resituate understandings of the entities likely to carry culture in cyberspace. Events in proto-cyberspace like the cyborgic delivery of Davis-Floyd's baby draw our attention, but analysis of them also illustrates the knotty problems of descriptions mediated through CR Thought.

The entity problem challenges traditional anthropology, but the challenge can be met by an appropriate cyborgification of general anthropology. Dennett's "parallel processing" model of consciousness allows conception of individual-level "units" which "run" adequately. Shortcomings in his model of multi-unit culture carrying can be addressed by appropriate elaboration of the parallel processing metaphor. Three additional amplifications—Complexified Actor Networks, Creolization, and Object-Orientation—build on his metaphors to provide concrete images of how cyberspace cyborgs might be different.

These points were illustrated further through a brief discussion of ethnographic work on self-identity in cyberspace. Some ethnographers make a strong case for difference in self-identity. It is not always clear, however, whether the case for difference is based on processes specific to cyberspace or on cyborgic features characeristic of culture carriers in many types of social formations.

Substantial conceptual work has been necessary to constuct this provisional characterization of culture-bearing entities in cyberspace. Hopefully, a side benefit of the venture is that along the way it has modeled important elements of the unified, nondualistic theory necessary for adequate description of technology. It also suggests something about how participants in the construction cyberspace should approach their practice. For example, the dangers inherent in the "inheritance" of O-O objects implies a responsibility to search out additional democratic space.

In the process of finding language with which to describe experience in a way that provides a modicum of fair representation, cyberspace ethnography requires us to think more carefully about what our descriptive terms mean. By resituating an important object of anthrological interest, the typical carrier of culture, the cyborgic discourse offered here changes the focus of ethnography and makes it more difficult. Driven by the attempt to approach cyberspace ethnographically, this rethinking is an early fruit of *Cyborgs@cyberspace?*

This encounter with the entity problem has highlighted difference, but the chief change identified is between the way we *used to* think of culture-bearing entities—as being bound by the skin—and the way cyberspace encourages us to think of them now. Once we cyborgify our understanding of entities, the more obviously cyborgic characteristics of cyberspace entities appear less different from older life space entities, as does cyberspace as a whole.

Social Relations in Cyberspace
This chapter shifts ethnographic attention from the individual level to the sociocultural, from the entities which carry cyberspace culture and their acts of individual identity construction to the social relations they can actively construct and do effectively reconstruct with others. In line with the effort to problematize CR Thought, the chapter's ultimate aim is to use what we know now to assess just how different social relations in cyberspace will turn out to be.

[5]

The Ethnography of Mid-Range Social Relations in Cyberspace: Community, Region, Organization, and Civil Society

Social relations are the actually experienced, especially the more or less stable, patterns of interactions among culture-carrying entities. They vary in character, from the micro (the tiny group of intimates) to the macro (the global). While all types of social relations may be different in cyberspace, particular attention is directed here to "meso-" social relations—those manifest typically in communities, regions, and/or large organizations, because these have been the primary locus of my ethnographic field work in cyberspace.

Social relations are at the heart of sociology. For classical sociology, the character of such relations formed the fundamental dynamic of social life, changes in social relations reflecting but also driving changes in broader social formation reproduction. This was true whether social relations were conceptualized in terms of roles, as in structural/functional theory about occupations (Parsons and Shils 1951), or in terms of interests and collectivities, as in conflict theories about classes-for-themselves (Marx 1871).

Since macro-relations were the locus of explanatory dynamics, classical theory tended to downplay intimate and intermediate-scale social settings. These latter were associated with socialization and repetition. Anthropologists like Robert Redfield (1930) tended to accept the classical sociological model of community-level dynamics as simple reproduction. As the critiques of ethnography has pointed out (see van Maanen 1983), genre conventions, such as writing in the "ethnographic present" and the tendency to treat any field site as more or less autonomous and isolated, derived from and reinforced the locating of dynamics at the "macro" level.

However, fieldwork in more complex social formations led later social anthropologists (Mitchell 1969) to frame analyses in terms of fluid "social networks" rather than membership roles or interest groups. Networks rather than stable groups were increasingly seen as the basic structure of social relationships in more complex social formations. With degrees of overlap among individuals that are variable, social networks cover a broad continuum of kinds of social relations, allowing for greater diversity in values and behaviors. Still, retaining some discernable degree of durability, they remain measurable.[1]

The shift of attention to networks undermined the classical priority of the macro. Much twentieth century sociological theorizing (Mead 1962; Garfinkel 1984) reinforced this shift; indeed, one could argue that the chief characteristic of the Postmodern analytic moment is to dissolve the macro in the micro.[2] Late twentieth century, more antistructural and deconstructionist theories (Calhoun 1995; Giddens 1991) conceptualize the various levels and forms of social relations as relatively autonomous. The possibility of discontinuities between self-identity and social relations, and among intimate, family, friendship, occupational or ethnic group, class, societal, national, and global levels of social relations, means any multilevel correspondences, especially those presumed by causal notions like CR Thought, must be demonstrated, not assumed.

Contemporary Issues in Meso-Social Relations

This "looseness" in connections between various levels and moments means the problem of social relations in cyberspace is really several different, differentially examinable, problems. Thus, to understand, for example, the dynamics of communities in cyberspace, we need to recognize their differences from social relations with intimates, on the one hand, and macro-social relations, like economic dependence, on the other. Further, because they are normally networks, meso-social relations are somewhat elusive, only occasionally perceived as relevant or strongly "embodied." They perhaps "come to life" (are experienced as relation*ships*) most noticeably in the midst of crises, of a "natural disaster" or economic sort.

For example, I share a sense of workspace culture or community with only some of the people in my employment organization, a large state university, even with only some of those with whom I share a physical worksite, the specific branch where I teach. Yet all of us in the organization share at least one important relation*ship*—the one experienced as relevant, for example, when jobs are differentially dispensable in a time of systemwide downsizing. I share a similarly midrange relationship with all those in Utica, New York—a city of about 67,000 people. The fact that Utica is now half its previous size emerges as significant as we deal with the consequences of cuts in our fire service. Those of us in the Upper Mohawk Valley, the region of upstate New York which includes Utica, felt our relationship of economic interdependence as the consequences of the recent decision to shut down a big local U.S. Air Force base worked themselves out. While I interact directly with only a small set of them, I share a meso-social relationship with other professional anthropologists, which I feel more strongly when competing with them for jobs or when the U.S. government decided to drop "anthropologist" as a distinct occupational category.

PLACE IN MESO-SOCIAL RELATIONS

Several aspects of such intermediate social relations have garnered recent attention. First, they have been presumed in the past to be about proximity or "place," to have a substantial geographic element. The continued relevance of place has been called into question by the notion that cyberspace "accelerates the decoupling of space from place."

Jane Jacobs' classic *The Life and Death of Great American Cities* (1961) aimed to specify the role of place in meso-social relations. As the title suggested, she told a vitalist story about expansive modern urbanism, which she accounted for in largely economic geography terms. Cities achieved greatness by attaining a kind of econo-cultural virtuous spiral. In economic terms, one or more industries developed which found markets outside the city and its region. Inside the city, these industries fostered large and diverse "feeder industries," whose expansion both aided the exporters' competitive position and, as they grew more independent, provided their own economic momentum. All of these together performed social reproduction on an expanding rather than simple scale (Hakken 1987), attracting people and wealth from the outside and achieving "greatness." The geographically embodied character of socioeconomic vitality has been reemphasized in the "economic geography" of scholars like Doreen Massey (1984) or Manuel Castells (1989). Thus, the potential implications of a shift from place to space are profound.

THE FINAL DESTRUCTION, OR THE RESURRECTION, OF CIVIL SOCIETY?

Jacobs' work can also introduce a second contemporary issue, the character of civil relations. In cultural terms, her approach stressed how both export and feeder industries stimulated and in turn were stimulated by various "non-economic" institutions—community organizations, schools, museums, and art institutes. These are frequently glossed as "civil society" in contemporary sociology. The declining quality of general meso-social relations, and the consequent vulnerability of social reproduction, are frequently traced to a decline in such institutions, as in Robert Putnam's "Bowling Alone" (1993). While the notion of "social capital" which he employs is in important ways a misnomer,[3] it does direct attention to qualities, such as a general concept of "sociality," which are necessary to effective meso-social relations. Alan Wolfe's *Whose Keeper* (1989) similarly argues that no society can survive for long unless the people in it share some general sense of responsibility for others, especially those with whom they are not close.[4]

POLITICS AND MESO-SOCIAL RELATIONS

Being mostly posited and not actually experienced, meso-social relations have a "virtual" quality (and did so long before AIT). Rather than having the voluntary "feel" of close social relations, meso-social relationships seem, to Americans in particular, to be "thrust upon us." At the same time, it is precisely these relations, whether in their neighborhood or at work, which are most likely to be activated when people choose to act in concert with others. They may then become a social movement or some other political force able to impact social formation reproduction. The potential for new forms of such mobilization in cyberspace is the basis of the liberatory potential that many feel in the virtual community. Awareness of crisis and this potential for liberation may indeed have something to do with the disproportionate presence of sixties devotees among the more vocal cyberspace pioneers (Rheingold).[5] At the same time, social movements imply collectivity, much of which in the past has been built on shared senses of identity. Theoretically, the time it takes to cultivate the multiple identities described by Turkle might lessen entities' capacities to participate in social movements.

ISSUES IN THE ETHNOGRAPHY OF CYBERSPACE MESO-SOCIAL RELATIONS

In sum, there is a range of intermediate, meso-social relations not overtly apparent but still of significance to social formation reproduction, to which both economic and fellow-feeling dimensions are important, and that have had important connections with place, civility, and politics. In considering ethnographic data on communities/regions and formal organizations in cyberspace, among the important ethnographic questions are:

1. How are communities different in cyberspace? Are they substantially more network-oriented, and even less group-oriented? In the long run, will communities no longer involve proximity—or how much does cyberspace accelerate the decoupling of space from place?

2. How does cyberspace affect the social reproduction of regions, the physically bound spaces within which "modern" humans/cyborgs spent most of their time and which provided them with economically remunerative activity (jobs or social wages)? How tightly, for example, are regions' declining abilities to influence their own

reproduction connected to the de-placing tendencies of AIT, or do less place-tied political "spaces" emerge to "respace" them? If the region becomes less important as a mediator of social formation reproduction, what replaces it?

3. Are organizations in cyberspace moving generally toward a new "cyberfacture" stage of the labor process? Will such changes in work further inhibit "third sector" institutions, or will interventions, perhaps by civil bodies, influence these changes to promote civil society?

4. What are the political/power implications of cyberspacing meso-social relations?

In the following effort to assess the landscape of intermediate social relations in cyberspace, we first take up deliberate attempts to enlist AIT in regional social formation reproduction, in 1980s England, especially in the region around Sheffield, and then compare it with data from the 1990s United States. Data regarding the correlates of computerization in relation to work culture and then in employment organizations as a whole, both profit and not-for-profit, are then addressed.

The Ethnography of Cyberspace Communities and Regions

THE REPRODUCTION OF THE SHEFFIELD/SOUTH YORKSHIRE REGION:
ANALYSIS

As indicated in chapter 3, the cultural correlates of computerization in Sheffield were manifold and complex. Along with the progressive computerization manifest in a worker co-op and other imaginative, local state-supported projects, considerable de-skilling, disemploying, and workspace marginalization of women and minorities also took place. In line with other empirical studies of computerization (e.g., Attewell and Rule 1985), these negatives were not as pronounced as many Sheffielders feared they would be.

> There were numerous examples of the connection between AIT and substantial change in the culture of working class people. Many were attempting to create a new self-identity centering on computers, an alternative to the factory-based worker identity predominant in the 1970s. More or less everyone we met was concerned about what the new technology meant for the future. For many working class people, computers tended to be a locus of both fear and derision. An alternative comic quipped, "I knew a bloke who wanted to do computers at school but he wasn't able to—he didn't have enough money for the lobotomy!"

The connection between computers and class culture turned out to be more complexly mediated than this joke implies, however. Besides macro, nationally-linked political dynamics like the rundown of the British Steel Corporation's Sheffield sites, there were important regional mediators: In the Yorkshire coal field around Sheffield, pits were being rapidly closed and pit villages transformed. The forced introduction of computerized mining technology once rejected as impractical was an essential component of the national government's plan to break the political power of the National Union of Mineworkers (NUM), a goal largely accomplished by the breaking of the strike in 1984–85. Indeed, NUM staffers argued that it might have been possible to maintain more unity during the strike had its focus been on the technology as opposed strictly to pit closures. Along these lines, Geraldine Casey (1992) describes a case where the incorporation of health and safety demands specifically relevant to computing, along with other "new social movement" identity perspectives, were important ingredients of relative trade union success in Puerto Rico.

Indeed, many Sheffielders were convinced that computers could be important, positive tools in the creation of a progressive and less class-bound society. These views were prominent in the political circles where local government programs to promote progressive computing were developed. Both optimism and concern about the impact that new information technologies were encountered, as with regard to changes in gender roles. As one of the women who had been a leader of the Women's Support groups in the 1984–85 Miner's Strike noted: "The new technology makes it more and more possible for women to be doing much of the work that a miner does. But we have not seen women flooding into the coal field."

While there were significant cultural correlates of computing, the Sheffield data do not fit well with the CR notion of an AIT-induced transformation to a substantially different social formation. Even though many opposed it, Sheffielders perceived themselves, their lives, and AIT as clearly still bent to the imperatives of the reproduction of capital. Indeed, the project identified the symbolic or ideological roles of computers as being as important as their material or physical role. To understand the connection between computerization and culture change, we need to recognize how various social groups battled over how computerization was to be understood as much as how it was to be used. The results of the computer initiatives of local government were more limited than the social ones of national government. This was partly a consequence of technical differences, like difference in the computer power available. However, social factors, like the breaking up of establish patterns in working class neighborhoods and villages attendant to nontechnological forces, such as the privatizing of mines, mills, and housing estates, loomed larger. So did semiotic/ideological factors, such as humans' reluctance to confront social forces when will is drained by images of domineering machines.

In short, these data were explicable in terms of modifications in the reproduction of the current, existing Sheffield social formation. The connections
between computerization and social change observed were subtle, more a consequence of the characteristics of the social situation into which the technology
was introduced than the nature of the equipment. In the 1970s, the primary
groups in the region mobilizing to pursue collective interests were owners/con-
trollers of means of production and workers, those whose survival depended on
being able to sell their labor power. In the 1980s, the basic groups were the
same, but the networks of social relations within the groups themselves had
changed substantially. At least some of this change was related to policy intervention at the regional level.

U.S. COMMUNITY COMPUTING

The United States has recently been the scene of several attempts to use computing as a tool to aid communities and regions. Often referred to as "community computing," such attempts have generally focused on computer-mediated
communication (CMC) rather than computer-mediated activity (CMA), as
earlier in Sheffield or in the Nordic countries. Nonetheless, the CMA and
CMC patterns associated with community computing have striking ethnographic similarity.

The Restructuring Social Service through Advanced Information Technology Project

This project, described in chapter 3, is an example of largely fruitless efforts to use AIT to transform meso-social relationships. Of course disap-
pointed, I was not surprised. The RSSAIT project is a good illustration of the
fundamental reason for skepticism regarding the CR. Powerful actors, both human and organizational, wanted to *appear* committed to using AIT to make
decisions, but their actions were most consistent with different actualities:

- Because their course of action had already been determined in relation to political priorities, they had no real interest in getting good
  information, or to using AIT to produce and disseminate it,
- For similar reasons, there was no real enthusiasm for open, shared
  decision-making, and
- The politically available software was inappropriate for the task.

Despite some positive conditions, the actual role of AIT in transforming
social service in Oneida County has been quite marginal. AIT has not been irrelevant but has become:

1. A system for collecting data sent to state government and unused
   locally;

2. A hushed up, embarrassing failure (PROSLCE), and
3. A symbolically evoked but largely unused (that is, quite uncon-
    nected to the actual decision-making and system transforming
    taking shape) justification for networking.

Jay County, Indiana

Prompted by rhetoric about (and funding associated with) a national "data superhighway," residents of Jay County, Indiana, a comparatively isolated, rural area, initiated a community computing effort in 1994: "[T]he taskforce has carried out a county-wide infrastructure needs assessment [and] has addressed issues of network implementation, planning, content and fiscal self sufficiency. It has also taken up matters of equity (a lottery was proposed; public access entry points were identified) and balance (between the diverse user needs and communities). The taskforce also surveyed community-based network models that would bring Internet access and resources to Jay County."

Anthropologist James Nyce and Computer Scientist Peter Stahlke were recruited to help. They concluded ethnographically that the cultural rather than the technical preoccupations of the project warranted most attention: "[T]he Jay County effort raises question about what developers and end users, alike, in community network initiatives have taken for granted. This initiative also reassesses questions about what, in the relatively new arena of community-based network efforts, gets marked or misconstrued as 'obstacles' or 'success.'"

Indeed, they suggest that what happens in community computing projects, as in other forms of computing encountered already in *Cyborgs@cyberspace?*, follows more of a social than technological trajectory: "In the face of repeated technical failure, up and down the scale from glitches to freezes, Jay County residents have carried on more than a year-long network planning process. What is striking is that they have done so when they have had little or no evidence that I-highway technology 'works' or is of use to them. Further, despite these technical failures, they and the taskforce have remained committed to this planning process. As one taskforce member put it, 'We missed the boat on the other [interstate] highway. Let's not let that sucker get by again'" (1996: 33).

Experience here illustrates how community computing's aim is not so much to help individuals establish new personal relations, although this often happens and is generally seen as a good thing. Rather, the point is to help the region's communities, to reestablish some stability in the reproduction of civil society, and to rebuild an effective set of both social and economic relations. It is the existence of this broader agenda which explains why Nyce and Stahlke's Midwesterners remain committed to the community computing project despite massive difficulties in getting the system to actually "work" in a technical sense:

One would think that network advocates and designers would see technical failure, particularly of this order, as a strong obstacle to success: that it would be enough to derail, if not halt, any community-based network effort. In short, for those of us who equate technical competence with success, these technical failures and the community's response to them raise a number of questions (p. 33).

Like the CMA interventions in Sheffield, community computing is caught up in powerful symbolic processes: "This suggests that in Jay County network technology is important but not as a thing in itself. Not tied to any immediate context, imaginatively detached, this technology becomes infinitely manipulatable. . . . In fact, what this technology provides is a field of space and time, and opportunity, to redefine fundamental concepts. As we create networks, we create and give meaning to these concepts."

Paralleling Turkle on self-identity, Nyce and Stahlke suggest here that community computing can involve the reconstruction of meso-social relations. Their project requires reexamination of some basic issues in the way Americans think about their regions:

> Working through these categories has brought to the surface issues of essence—who are we—and trajectory—where are we going—issues that lie at the heart of American community. To put it another way, in American terms community is something that has to be negotiated and built. . . . For Americans, it cannot be equated with a set of sociological 'facts' like town, city, or school district. In classical sociology, categories like these are the basis of social life and are things that no one can escape. . . . In America, at first glance, these categories do appear, are important and do seem to be closed and fixed. However, they are in America anything but. . . . In America, community, authentic community at least, can only emerge from individual choice and action (p. 34).

It is indeed the openness of this community computing initiative—its unformed, inchoate quality, perhaps even its inability to "work" in a technical sense—that has enabled it to become a cultural mazeway for handling diversity, a channel for hopes, dreams, and imaginings, even the "reinvention" of the regional social formation: "Network and Internet 'talk' became a resource for these choices and actions, in a number of ways the network planning process played a critical role. It provided an agreed-upon vocabulary, and from the process emerged a common, shared set of understandings about what is needed to reinvent Jay County. . . . [T]he taskforce participants also had to actively work, through choice and action, to carry this out. For more than a year they have done so: This is what has given this network planning process, in the face of failure, its legitimacy and worth (p. 35)."

One could hardly imagine a clearer example of how it is the symbolic role of AIT, rather than its technical one, which is important in cyberspace meso-social relations. As in Sheffield, community computing endeavors are more about discourse than instrumentality, more about finding a new way to talk about and therefore to approach problems of regional social formation reproduction than about mechanisms to accomplish specific tasks. This is why CMC captures a powerful part of the American social imaginary.

Eastern Washington

Anthropologist Karen Michaelson has also been an active imaginer of cyberspace through a similar community computing initiative, TINCAN, in a largely rural, economically depressed section of western Washington state. The project provides a free on-line information system, with local information on the region as a whole. There are public access sites in community centers, schools, and businesses. Riding the telecommunications lines of various community partners, the network allows anyone in the region to make a local phone call to get on line, eliminating long distance charges, the bane of rural communities' attempts to access information. TINCAN also provides limited Internet access: e-mail and connection to a variety of sites such as federal and state information resources. Users can use TINCAN's lines to access full Internet services if no provider is available in their local area:

> Indeed, the mission of TINCAN is to aid in enhancing education and community development in the rural areas . . . both to enhance the local community, as well as provide access to communities of interest outside of the locality. It at once links a region which is defined by existing social, economic, and political relationships, one which is becoming an electronically defined space whose concept of community may transcend the geographic whole (1995:1).

Like Nyce, Michaelson supports TINCAN technically. Her ethnographic interest is the way such projects intersect with searches for a sense of geographic identity; for example, how rural communities defined a separate existence for themselves, and support local business, while also connecting to urban centers. There were basic disagreement about what the systems was for:

> [S]ome members . . . want TINCAN to be primarily focused on external access, rather than community information. Business and government . . . see the so-called information highway as the savior of

their small communities. Somehow, if they can only get connected, new businesses will spring up and the economy will revive. . . . Schools focus on external services to access new information for teaching. . . . Some towns seem to develop local information systems more rapidly, usually with the prodding of a local activist, and see the connection to the Internet as a plus (p. 2).

Rather than having a single server or each town having its own, a compromise was reached, so that those who chose to could have their dial-in open to their home community menu, and transfer to the main TINCAN menu if they wanted wider information or access. How people develop their own uses is the key to understanding this technology actor network:

In the media, there has been a great deal of hype about the information highway, and about how one or another service is an "on-ramp" to that highway. Certainly, TINCAN provides access and a place to get "on." But once people are on the highway, where do they go?

Tom Grundner, the founder of the community networking movement, points out that the real role of community networks is to be an "off ramp"—a place to get off, explore, and understand. And, as at every off-ramp, new organizations arise to serve the needs of travelers and local residents alike. So community networks have tourist guides (one of TINCAN's rural affiliates has listed every hotel and restaurant in their small town), as well as new ways for local residents to explore their own community (p. 4).

Michaelson sees this development as "turning of the tables" on consideration of "place" in the debate over civil society. She sees networks like TINCAN as a new kind of Oldenburgian "third place," to engender a sense of commitment and community. Unlike Rheingold, Michaelson does not reduce civil society to intimate social relations. By "heightening" difference, such networks create a more geographically dispersed "meso" community:

In some sense, Americans have always dealt with the alienation of the greater society by creating smaller communities based upon difference. [Shared ethnic identity,] the Crips and the Bloods, the mega-churches, are ways of defining a like-minded community and a sense of group identity lacking in the sheer physical proximity of neighborhood and town. . . . [Networks like TINCAN similarly let] small groups within the community keep in touch, excluding others from their parochial discussion. With few restrictions on participation, marginal political groups and others gain access to a broader audience, as well as use the medium to organize for action. As long as they obey the "rules of the road"—no hate speech, no flooding the e-mail—they are welcome to put fourth their ideas in their own forums, and let the public make a choice (p. 6).

ETHNOLOGICAL ISSUES IN COMMUNITY COMPUTING

Re-coupling Space and Place?

Like Douglas Schuler (1996), perhaps the primary scholar of community computing, Michaelson underlines community computing's capacity to re-create the local, "place"-centered nature of past forms of social capital.

> But, community networks also pose an interesting and perhaps power-
> ful means of engendering broader commitment and fostering action
> within a locality. . . . While it is certainly possible to join an interest
> group on-line composed of people all over the world, it is also possible
> to locate individuals with similar interests in your own geographic lo-
> cale, whose existence may have been obscured by differences of class,
> color or other categorization. Such interaction has the potential to cre-
> ate the political engagement and commitment that is associated with
> the term "community" (p .5).

All her examples of TINCAN cyber-politics have a local focus. Michaelson presumes that new forms of meso-relations shall have a local, geographic focus, a place, in order to accomplish political reinvigoration; she doesn't demonstrate it. Summing her analysis in terms of the civil society discourse, she gives central emphasis to locale, but in a moderately de-geographied form:

> Community networks provide a sense of place in an essentially alien-
> ated society, using the freedom of cyberspace to create new kinds of
> participation in community life. Individuals from outside the geo-
> graphic area rarely become registered users, entitled to participate in
> public debates. Thus, while the communication takes place in cyber-
> space, it is at the same time highly localized. To describe such partici-
> pation in terms of virtual space versus physical place is to create an
> artificial construct. Geographic communities in American life rarely
> exist in the sense of a "community" where proximity is the primary ra-
> tionale for interaction. To the degree that participation in community
> networks enhances the commitment to a locality, then these networks
> enhance community in the traditional sense of locality. The fact that
> they serve as "on-ramps" to allow residents to participate in broader
> groups has the potential to detract from that local commitment, and it
> is unrealistic to contend that this does not frequently happen. But

such broader participation can also create an awareness of [how] global issues . . . are manifested in one's own geographic locale, and serve as the focus for organizing community action at a local level, reinvigorating the public debate (pp. 7–8).

Cyberspace ethnology also points out how the notion of locale, at least as normally understood, can also be reconstructed. As humans/cyborgs spend even an inordinate amount of time connected by modem via telephone lines to virtual spaces, they often report a peculiar sensation of "'thereness'; an uncanny resemblance to wandering the hallways of some labyrinthine mansions. . . . One of the most striking features of the WELL, observed a user named Ioca, is that it actually creates a feeling of 'place.' I'm staring at a computer screen. But the feeling really is that I'm 'in' something; I'm some 'where'" (Rheingold 1993). Further, virtual reality interfaces, facilitated by high-bandwidth "information highways" of the sort proposed by the Clinton administration, will concretize Ioca's "feeling of 'place'; at last there *will* be a 'there' there" (Dery 1994:7; emphasis in original).

The slippage in Dery's language, from a "*feeling* of 'place'" to the confident statement of the actual presence of a "there" in the future, should be noted. Still, the comments help us recognize that even so-called local relationships are socially constructed. To be able to evaluate the extent to which a politics of cyberspace can replace a politics of local place, let alone a Rheingold-type argument that such a replacement is likely, we need clearer ideas about the construction of and the importance of such "there's."

Civil Society as a Policy Issue

In discussing scholarship on contemporary meso-social relations, the question of the declining presence of a "third sector," neither market nor state, is a key issue. Whether arising through earlier support for specific computer-mediated activities, as in Sheffield, or through newer interventions into computer-mediated communication, as in community networks, "third sector/social capital" discourses seems to arise quite regularly. Discussion of the wider implications of these meso-social relation efforts is hampered by implicit presumptions that "third sectors" must be based in local geography.

Perhaps no one has done more to highlight the potential of AIT for progressive meso-social relations that cyberspace colonizer Howard Rheingold. Referring to virtual communities as "a full-scale sub-culture," Rheingold describes himself as participating in "the self-design of a new kind of culture . . . [where n]orms were established, challenged, changed, reestablished, rechallenged, in a kind of speeded-up social evolution" (1993: 2). Nonetheless, he clearly has in mind broad, civil society as well as close personal relations; indeed, he feels that formation of new civil communities is more or less inevitable in cyberspace:

My direct observation of on-line behavior around the world over the past ten years have led me to conclude that whenever CMC technology becomes available to people anywhere, they inevitably build virtual communities with it, just as microorganisms inevitably create colonies. . . . I suspect that one of the explanations for this phenomenon is the hunger for community that grows in the breasts of people around the world as more and more informal pubic spaces disappear from our real lives. I also suspect that these new media attract colonies of enthusiasts because CMC enables people to do this with each other in new ways, and to do altogether new kinds of things—just as telegraphs telephones, and televisions did (p. 6).

In pursuing the theme of communo-genesis in cyberspace, Rheingold is occasionally willing to employ technicist rhetoric—"We now know something about the ways previous generations of communications technologies changed the way people live" (p. 6), or changed "our experience of the real world" (p. 4). Generally, however, he chooses more optative, contingent language: "Most people who have not used these new media remain unaware of how profoundly the social political and scientific *experiments* under way today via computer networks *could* change all our lives in the near future" (p. 4).

It is important to recognize that, by and large, Rheingold pays no attention to the kinds of public policy initiatives examined by Barbara Andrews and myself, Nyce, and Michaelson. Indeed, his only attention to sustained public initiatives—ARPANET in the United States, and Minitel in France—is to stress how hacker-like cybernauts seize the artifacts and use them for purposes different from those intended. The presumption of his argument is that, if cybernauts are to succeed in broadening civil society, it will be through defeating the anti-communitarian tendencies inherent in states.

Politics and Democracy

Rheingold has an abiding concern with the issue of democracy. His approach is framed in terms of the extent to which timely intervention by net pioneers like himself, in the face of macro-social pressures, can make a difference: "What we know and do now is important because it is still possible for people around the world to make sure this new sphere of vital human discourse remains open to the citizens of the planet before the political and economic big boys seize it censor it, meter it, and sell it back to us" (p. 5).

In Rheingold's story, CMC technology offers a new hope for democracy because of its capability for "many to many" communication, rather than the only "one-to-many" capability of current broadcasting. Whether cyberspace is good or bad for democracy, however, is contingent upon the actions of pioneers: "But the way such a [many-to-many] capability will or will not be used in the future might depend on the way we, the first people using it, succeed or fail in applying it to our lives . . . whether it is possible for us to build some kind of community together" (p. 12). Finally, he posits the mechanisms which created close or normative community in the WELL, the computer conferencing system which is the aspect of cyberspace in which he has had the most experience, as the ones which will convince the pioneers to take the necessary steps.

As here in Rheingold, too much discussion of "virtual" community reduces the differences among levels, presuming that what is demonstrated on one level is true for others as well. His book is mostly about intimate social relations, the shared identity which tends to grow up around extensive use of MUDs, MOOs, and BBSs, rather than the meso-social relations most typically seen as connected to democracy. Rheingold has provided perhaps the most well known argument that CMC means new social relations: "People in virtual communities use words on screens to exchange pleasantries and argue, engage in intellectual discourse, conduct commerce, exchange knowledge, share emotional support, make plans, brainstorm, gossip, feud, fall in love, find friends and lose them, play games, flirt, create a little high art and a lot if [sic] idle talk. People in virtual communities do just about everything people do in real life, but we leave our bodies behind" (1993:3). In this comment, like other cybernauts, Rheingold mixes discussion of micro- and meso-social relations. While these data are intended to make the case that CMC is inherently communo-generative, the broader networks of meso-social relations are seldom in focus.

Such analytic shortcomings are often connected to inadequate theories of culture. As in Dennett, "shared values" are presumed to be the basis of both specific communities and culture in general. *Accounting for* the emergence of sharing (in a town, region, even a nation), the really difficult problem facing social science, is not addressed but presumed.

Rather than restricting discussion of cyber-community to the micro level, participant observers like Nyce, his collaborator Stahlke, Michaelson, and activists like Schuler (1996) open cyberspace meso-social relations to analysis. Like my work with Andrews in Sheffield, their ethnography also alerts us to the connection between such relations, policy initiatives like community computing, and ethnogenesis, the generation and extended reproduction of cultural constructs. In addition, they help us see how ethnogenesis can be closely connected to what in other discourses is called politics.

These ethnographies of community computing open an additional possibility, that cyberspace can support the production and extended reproduction of meso-social relations both more and less tied to place than previous meso-relations. Just as public cyberspaces need not, *pace* Michaelson, undermine locales, their existence also demonstrates that public spaces may not necessarily need locale. Unfortunately, these latter possibilities are seldom developed analytically. "Really existing" communities, whether in cyberspace or not, manifest as much dis-census as consensus, and managing to stay together in the presence of the former can be exceedingly difficult. Micro-, meso-, and macro-social relations all play parts in this process, but not in lock step.

Computing and Workspace Cultures

From the first uses of computers to process large data sets like payroll records, through the 1980s enthusiasm for robots, to, most recently, eloquent statements regarding CMC's capacity to support "virtual work," AIT's implications for work institutions have prompted the largest volume of speculation. The considerable part of this speculation that addresses national and cultural difference and the broadest structural implications of labor process transformation are addressed in the following chapter. Here we focus first on the work cultures that underlie the dynamics of organizations and then on the labor market institutions through which organizations connect to each other.

As pointed out in chapter 2, the reemerging sociology of work of the mid-1970s included a large ethnographic component. One of the important contributions of ethnography (see Lamphere 1979 and Shapiro-Perl 1979) was documentation of the importance of workplace cultures, the worker-generated patterns of and for behavior manifest in each particular workplace, to labor process dynamics. Work culture, often misread by more formal research methods, is an important mediator of the quality of working life and a determinant of practicalities like productivity. The new fieldwork on work also stimulated and was informed by a reinterpretation of labor history which stressed the role of close relations at work, especially in their gender and race dimensions, as relevant to, for example, workers' willingness to strike.

Initially, computerization affected work culture through mediation of various activities (CMAs) in the labor process itself, the formal and informal activities which result in particular commodities. Computers' automating uses eliminated some activities (hand cutting), added others (programming and reprogramming), and/or rearranged the mapping of jobs on remaining activities. While changing such things obviously affects work culture details, does it also change basic dynamics?

Currently, CMC is perceived to be the primary channel of workspace change. In general, work culture is closely tied to speech and other forms of communication, and changes in patterns of communication are related to changes in other patterns of work culture. As elsewhere, CMC and CMA together are perceived as even more likely to result in fundamental change—such as when new communications media promote the sharing of different messages with people doing different things, especially those in different physical locations and times. One specific adjustment in terminology—substitution of "workspaces" for "workplaces"—flags this increased potential for broader change in computered work cultures.

NETIQUETTE: EMAIL AND PROFESSIONALISM AT NR

During our fieldwork in 1993 and 1994, workers at Norsk Regnesentralen on numerous occasions took pains to explain to Barbara and I how their various social institutions, especially organizations, support basic commitments to egalitarianism. In work groups, for example, those who wanted to suggest a new initiative introduced it only briefly—preferably indirectly—and then waited for further discussion until another mentioned the idea again at a subsequent meeting. Among more formal institutions supporting egalitarianism is the *all-moete*, a yearly meeting of everyone in the organization in which, we were told, each person irrespective of status had the right to speak out on matters of common concern. Work groups and organizations also have an annual *julibord*, literally a "Christmas table," which in addition to feasting often includes a range of status leveling activities, possibly including raucous parodies of organizational leaders.

This was why everyone interpreted the failure of the NR Managing Director (MD) to show up at the julibord as "not Norwegian" and therefore a sign of an impending organizational crisis. Indeed, within a week, the MD had written two scathing messages, one about a researcher, the other about a group leader, and circulated them on the internal organizational communications system, PORTACOM. The first message resulted in a formal appeal to the trade union, the second the decision of an entire research group to leave.

Barbara's and my initial inclination was to view these developments as resulting from an attempt to apply authoritarian, top down, "American-style" management in an egalitarian Norwegian organization. A steady stream of NR researchers, making it their business to apologize for the un-Norwegian situation, offered a different, technological explanation: The crisis was a predictable consequence of inappropriate use of PORTACOM. The MD insisted on using CMC to communicate the wrong kind of information—things that should only be said in person, for example. It was just too easy, in the heat of the moment to fire something intemperate off on the computer, and then compound the problem by hitting one additional key and sending *everybody* a copy. People respond to email as formal communication, like a letter or memo, not as informal "chit chat." Email messages, they said, should be short and limited to communication of facts, not interpretation or commentary; to use them for other, more complex organizational purposes was likely to lead to confusion:

When something is not clear, my experience is that a person-to-person talk clarifies things better than flows of [email] memos. Heated discussions escalate over PORTACOM, between people who are sitting literally 20 meters from each other. They become a caricature; they show how new technology may actually cause the quality of human communication to deteriorate.

It is predictable that the NR technologists would locate the problem in a lack of fit between technical system and behavior. What made this situation ethnographically striking was the fact that NR got much of its income by promoting CMC, helping firms become "learning organizations" by implement sophisticated internal electronic environments, including PORTACOM itself. Indeed, the same people attributing the problem to inappropriate use of CMC were putting considerable energy into developing tools to help users crawl out from under email mountains—tools, in other words, to restrict the very communication they were paid to encourage! That skilled technologists could hold such contrasting views simultaneously is evidence of the power of the technicist mind set. It is also suggestive of the difficulties of seeing the influence of social relations in a technological arena.

THE SCANDINAVIAN APPROACH TO INFORMATION SYSTEMS DEVELOPMENT

"Intranets" and similar electronic internal communications systems like PORTACOM are key components of contemporary strategies to "reengineer" organizations. "Information system development" (ISD) is a blanket term for referring to the entire process through which any computer-based system, whether CMA, CMC, or both, is conceived, implemented, and serviced. The most sustained appreciations of the complexity of ISD, as well as the most sophisticated efforts to intervene deliberately in it to achieve social objectives, are Nordic, a primary reason for studying the cultural construction of computing there. Work there during the 1980s, including a range of unique ISD initiatives, provide the chief empirical data to support the idea that workspaces can be computerized in ways which empowered workers both individually and collectively. Concentrating especially on the involvement of users in Nordic ISD, anthropologists like Hendrik Sinding-Larsen (1991), Lucy Suchman (1987), and Eleanor Wynn (1991), as well as informaticians like Joan Greenbaum and Morten Kyng (1991), Pelle Ehn (1988), and Gro Bjerknes and Tone Bratteteig (1995), documented a unique imagining of cyberspace.

Similarly, "system developer" has emerged as a distinct occupational specialty in computer science more in Scandinavia than elsewhere. Scandinavians need a developer rather than merely a "systems analyst" because more attention is given to incorporating the needs, situation, and views of users in ISD (Allwood and Hakken n.d.; Bjerknes et al. 1987). Scandinavian systems development is contrasted with the machine-centered, "turn key" approach, the dominant comparable professional conception in the United States. Turn key approaches are artifact- or machine-centered. The system analyst is to be skilled at quickly extracting from a customer a statement of system specifications—functions that the system is supposed to perform. She then uses resources—her professional knowledge, existing hardware, and the skills of programmers whose labor she manages—to develop a system to be delivered complete to the customer. He need only "turn the key" to make the system fully operational.

Rather than merely seeking out a set of specifications, the good Nordic systems developer (not a "systems analyst") embraces users' knowledge dialogically. Often (Greenbaum and Kyng 1991) the dialogue takes place best in groups. It should also include attempts to incorporate users into activities like brainstorming before collectively making decisions regarding the nature of the system to be developed. Users' knowledge of information technology is often to be enhanced as part of the process; users should be incorporated into developing and testing prototypes of the system, providing feedback for redesign, and so forth.

User involvement throughout ISD (including the more or less continuous postimplementation redevelopment which is characteristic of contemporary computerized workspaces) affects workspace culture, often resulting in a high degree of worker participation and influence, even control. High levels of user participation were an important feature of a series of important and well-known research projects that aimed to institutionalize it in Nordic ISD. These began in Norway in the 1960s and spread to the rest of the Nordic countries, through the Sydpol project. These efforts, which have continued into the 1990s, demonstrate the viability of user-centered ISD and its potential to create more proactive work cultures.

Assessing the Work Culture Correlates of the Scandinavian Approach

An interest in assessing the correlates of this Scandinavian initiative work culture was a prime motivation of the Nordic National Computing Project described in chapter 3. How widespread were the new work culture dynamics described?

In the Nordic countries, many academically trained systems developers are taught this theorists' discourse on use. They know, for example, the linguistic forms through which "users" are to be evoked—for example, through interviews and other techniques. However, we met many practicing systems developers who were skeptical of this theoretical discourse. They pointed out how, when "user" was conceptualized at the beginning of a project, it would be done primarily through an "interest" perspective. This means that the situation of use was politicized, even a bit dogmatically. Further, while definitely anxious to keep users a presence in ISD discourse—we might say, to attribute an ontological status to users—they also frequently characterized the Nordic ISD user discourse as somewhat "burnt out."

The most sustained skeptics regarding just how different the results of Scandinavian ISD actually are include some academics themselves involved in the projects (Bjerknes and Bratteteig 1995; Dahlbom 1990). After listing "some examples of what theoreticians say system developers in the field are doing or should be doing" (p. 127), including democratic design in real cooperation with users, Dahlbom asserts: "As we all know, system developers do very little of this sort in their practical work—at least knowingly." He goes on to ask rhetorically, "And the theories of system development that take up so much of our discussions, are they only so much 'syntactic sugar?'" (p. 128). Dahlbom rejects the idea that the Scandinavian approach has resulted in substantively different because more participatory workspaces.

Controversy among ISD observers over the actual consequences of user involvement has been heated. Joergen Bansler is a Danish social theorist who has published several influential articles and books on systems development, while Philip Kraft is a similarly influential American work sociologist. In a paper to the 1992 Participatory Design Conference in Cambridge, Massachusetts (1994a) they argued that national-level corporate institutions of industrial relations in Scandinavia effectively preempt the substantive effectiveness of user involvement in system development. In their view, the perception of substantial user impact, which is presumed to follow from mandated user involvement in Scandinavia, is inaccurate. Their view is supported by researchers at the Institute for Work Research in Oslo. They described the socially constructed partners—the national organizations of employers and of employees—as using their formal participatory powers to impede the generalization of transformative practices fostered in local sites. Successful local projects were perceived as threats to the reproduction of the power of both large firms and the trade unions built around existing craft and skill demarcations. Psychologists Allwood and Kalen (1993), like Bjerknes and Bratteteig (1995), are pessimistic about participation channeled through unions alone.

Others argue for a more mixed evaluation of the extent and character of user involvement. Joern Flohr Nielsen and Niels Joergen Relsted from the Institute of management at the University of Aarhus in Denmark call for "A New Agenda for User Participation" (1994). They begin by asserting that there is a considerable degree of user participation in current Scandinavian system development and implementation—indeed, that participation is institutionalized and constructed socially as necessary. Yet their experience has convinced them that practitioners "face severe problems in defining the right way of involvement." Their survey research led them to conclude that the usefulness of participation is highly dependent on user type and organizational function; specifically, that participation is of little use if organizational development issues, as opposed to strictly technical ones, are not on the participation agenda. They argue, moreover, that the recent penchant for decentralization in organizations has actually broadened opportunities for user participation. Similarly, sociologist Trond Knudsen (1993a,b) finds evidence of substantial user involvement, but primarily in worksites where users already have substantial influence, often due to their professional status and prestige being at least comparable to that of systems developers. The quality of participation, in other words, follows from factors more internal to the preexisting specific work process than national tradition, legislation, or professional action.

In contrast, other Scandinavian ISD scholars remain positive about the importance of "use" measures. Developers like Kristin Nygaard and sociologists and colleagues at the Center for Working Life (Sandberg et al. 1992) argue that, despite problems, user influence in Scandinavia has been and continues to be uniquely substantial. The national policies which support user involvement are claimed by many (Andersen and Kramer 1994) to have had important workspace culture consequences.

Summative Assessment:
While the Critiques May Be Overdrawn, Less Was Accomplished Than Hoped For

While obviously some of the differences here follow from different conceptions of "user" (see Allwood and Hakken n.d.), there remain different assessments of what was accomplished. Morton Kyng, an important Danish theorist in Scandinavian ISD, argues (1994) that the critics of the actual importance of users in Nordic ISD like Bansler and Kraft both exaggerate the claims of proponents and oversimplify the discourse on users. Yet even in critiquing Bansler and Kraft, Kyng acknowledges that what was accomplished through user participation in decisions regarding technology was limited. In their rejoinder to Kyng, Bansler and Kraft (1994b) concentrate primarily on why little can be expected from participatory design in the United States, again because of the particular relations of social forces and the cultural construction of the 1990s economic crisis. In his most recent work, Sandberg (1994) has drawn attention to the willingness of "Swedish" capital to abandon participation in pursuit of globalization—the rundown of Volvo's "participatory" workplaces. These comments must be taken as moderating to some extent the claims he has previously made about the importance of user involvement.

In sum, as Barbara and I participated in projects and talked to professional developers, ISD academics, and social scientists studying Nordic ISD, we came to share this mixed assessment of the cultural correlates of Scandinavian systems development. Use perspectives are incorporated into ISD and user involvement is associated with changes in some work process, but less of the former, and much less of the latter, takes place than was suggested by earlier observers (Hakken 1997a). Such a conclusion does not preclude users playing roles in ISD, or mean that, for example, participation cannot be important in obtaining system acceptance. It does suggest that no "natural" role for users in ISD may exist. By extension, one cannot conclude much about the long-term correlates of user involvement in ISD on Scandinavian workspace culture, and even less about computerized workspace culture outside of Scandinavia.

Nonetheless, growing out of the Scandinavian experience is both some acknowledgment of the importance of users to system success, as well as specific initiatives to incorporate such understandings into ISD. One such initiative, referred to variously as Computer Supported Cooperative Work (CSCW), or Group Support Systems (GSS), starts from a recognition that much professional work is carried out in groups and teams; therefore, computer interfaces should be designed to support groups, not just individual "man–machine" interfaces. CSCW, in particular, has been a major cause of the incorporation of an ethnographic sensibility into ISD: If one wishes to design a system to support group work, one first needs to understand the work of the group. Among the important findings of CSCW research is the importance of informal relations to effective group work, that the "socializing" uses of CMC should be encouraged.

COMPUTERIZATION AND COMMUNICATION IN PROFESSIONALIZED WORKSPACES

As described earlier, Trond Knudsen found the greatest influence among users with high professional standing. Some observers have argued that computerization, especially in the form of computer-mediated communication, changes the dynamics of professionalism. Anthropologists like Yvonna Lincoln (1992) and Barbara Joans (1992) emphasize and endorse informants' willingness to frame their activities in computerization's terms, for example, professional "virtual communities" supported by new technology. Lincoln argues that computer-mediated communication produces professional dynamics superior to those of previous modes. Cyber-social relationships are said to be less formally organized into a structure of roles and more flexibly mediated as networks of connections; the Internet, as it were, replaces the prestige hierarchy of the typical university as the fundamental pattern of and for professional social relations. For ethnographers like these, the personal connections of discursive interaction replace the structured anonymity of bureaucracies, with important implications for professional life.

Ethnographer Lee Komito, in contrast, finds little to differentiate pre-CMC from CMC communication patterns in professional work groups (1995). The primary difference he observed in the patterns of a civil service office space after implementation of an email system was the use of the system by younger staffers for socializing relatively unrelated to work. Once this pattern had been established, senior staffers discouraged more developed use of the system. Indeed, if the experience at NR were indicative, one could project the following as course of the typical organizational CMC experience:

- Some resistance;
- More or less enthusiastic adoption by at least some segments of the work force;
- CMC-connected exacerbation of the preexisting difficulties of communication in the workspace, perhaps with especially dire implications for those who adopt "telecommuting"; and finally
- Substantial restricting and "domestication" of CMC.

Lincoln fails to consider how the current relatively accessible communicative experience of U.S. emailers is highly contingent, a consequence of factors like the "accidental" history of email's development within an academic rather than commercial milieu. This ease is reinforced by the fact that, since the right to operate an Internet node is for academic institutions a single item cost, there is no easy way to calculate the marginal cost of each additional use and therefore to charge "real" costs per user or use. This may change as Internet access becomes more mediated by private organizations. In general, however, it is difficult to reach a strong conclusion regarding the long-term implications of the computerization of professional work cultures.

The Ethnography of Organizational Culture in Cyberspace

While ethnographers use "work culture" to refer to the patterns of and for behavior created among those in direct contact in a workspace, they use "organizational culture" to refer to the more anonymous level of meso-social relations manifest within large organizations. Because most people's access to the means of subsistence is mediated through employment, organizations are the predominant institutions in employment social formations. Moreover, as pointed out by innumerable social psychologists, those of us who live in such social formations locate much of our identity in our occupation or profession, the things we do for which we get paid. Thus much of the popular sense of how different cyberspace will be from its predecessors turns out to involve judgments regarding the nature and extent of changes in organizations. Anthropologists like Marietta Baba (1992), Patricia Sachs (1995), and Sharon Traweek (1988) are only a few of the large number who have examined the relationship of computerization to workspace dynamics at more general levels (see also Suchman 1987; Hakken 1993; Anderson 1995; Dubinskas 1988).

CR Thought presumes that computers change organizations directly, not merely by mediating preexisting activity or communication. In such discourses, organizations devoted to the development of AIT—Microsoft, Xerox, IBM—

receive considerable attention. While this attention may really have more to do with their importance to the current moment of the reproduction of capital, work in such organizations is typically treated as prototypic of cyberwork and is thus of special concern to at least the rhetorics of cyberspace meso-social relations.

Tracy Kidder's *Soul of a New Machine* (1981) is a vivid ethnography of a workspace where a new computer was developed. The book is taken as an accurate depiction of cyberwork despite the fact that neither CMA nor CMC play much of a role in the labor process on which Kidder focuses. It sets the pattern for the breathless tropes evoked in subsequent descriptions of "high tech" organizations, including celebrations of:

- Work groups under siege that nonetheless overcome monumental obstacles emanating from the rest of the organization;
- A collective consciousness of unique professional standing that allows patterns of interaction opposed, sometimes overtly, to formal organization culture;
- Authoritarian if charismatic leadership;
- Long hours and harsh conditions; and yet
- An ultimately close worker identification with the organization in spite of the above.

Such descriptions are repeated so often in the hagiographic "high tech" management literature as to suggest generic convention. Indeed, Kidder's strong but unacknowledged identification with the way in which managers construct the ISD process, as well as his general lack of comparison with other workspaces, leaves him open to the charge of mythinformating.

While Kidder tends to give the work culture a heroic spin, Gideon Kunda's *Engineering Culture* (1992) inverts the trope. Kunda's professionals, although highly paid and with job security, find decreasing space for authentic self-development, the highly manipulated organizational culture driving out work culture. Characteristic of CR Thought and like Kidder, Kunda remarks little on how the computers themselves, either directly or through their mediation of other activity, whether direct labor or communication, change the workspace. Yet ethnographies like these are often evoked to justify the CR view of ISD. An extreme example is Stacey's (1987) CR account of work in Silicon Valley. "High tech" rhetorics fit poorly with descriptions of Philippino women working at home dipping galenium oxide chips into pots of chemicals heating on stoves also being used to heat baby formula. They are more clearly an evocation of eighteenth century "putting out" than a futuristic cyberspace!

Frank Dubinskas' work describing the run up of a new factory for making Apple Macintosh computers (1992) is perhaps the most instructive regarding how cyberspace work processes can force change in organizational culture. The factory was designed around a production "transfer line," a TAN that integrates human and robot workers into a single assembly process. The line was first constructed by a Japanese robotics firm in Japan and then disassembled and re-assembled in Cupertino, California. The run up was filled with problems that Dubinskas traces to national differences in engineering occupational cultures. Japanese industrial engineers design for work groups for which harmony is an important actual and explicit goal. In contrast, American engineers—especially the "cream of the crop" then at Apple—are rewarded for being "cowboy" individualists, which leads to macho, competitive, "all singing all dancing" engineering. When the Americans tried to implement the Japanese design, problems were predictable. The problems had little to do with the use of computerized robots per se but everything to do with the characteristic approach to solving the inevitable problems which crop up in implementing any new technology actor network, especially when there is an important cultural/national difference dimension.

CONTINUITY IN CYBERSPACED ORGANIZATIONS

In a review of ethnographic studies of workplace computing published prior to the most recent flowering of interest in CMC (Hakken 1993), I reached two general conclusions. Especially when initially framing their work, cyberspace organizational ethnographers tend to employ CR rhetorics as uncritically as other writers. However, the *analyses* of these researchers tends to *undercut* CR Thought, stressing instead the continuities between pre- and proto-cyberspace organizations. Among the continuities demonstrated by these analyses, important justifications for CR skepticism are discussed below.

Occupational Cultures

Kathleen Gregory's early exploration of Silicon Valley (1983) explains dynamics in terms of conflicting occupational cultures rather than in strictly "machine" terms. So does Frank Dubinskas' early study of the consequences of differences between managers and scientists in genetic engineering firms (1988). Marietta Baba (1991) argues that finding means to overcome these semiotic discrepancies between workers and managers becomes a major preoccupation of new work process development, a problem which she elsewhere (1991) traces to previous occupational socialization.

Gary Downey (1991?) has given attention to the various ways in which computing approaches (computer-aided design/computer-aided manufacturing) have become integrated into the occupational culture of engineers. His current work focuses on the role of engineering education in the creation of an occupational culture coming to terms with new technology. Bryan Pfaffenberger identifies several points at which the fate of on-line information systems intersects with the occupational culture of librarians (1990).

Organizational Dynamics

Nontechnological outside factors and previously established patterns internal to an organization can also substantially influence the correlates of AIT. Baba (1988) presents the changed relationship between universities and industries as linked as much to the decline in federal spending for universities as to recent technological change. In examining how time is culturally constructed in various high technology organizations, the authors in Dubinskas' collection *Making Time: Ethnographies of High-Technology Corporations* (1988) analytically stress prior organizational experience. Sharon Traweek's *Beamtimes and Lifetimes* (1988), a comparative ethnography of particle accelerators in the United States and Japan, is also about time. She focuses on the mutual co-construction of organizational forms, the machines designed in them, and the occupational culture of elite physicists, especially experimentalists. Computing and its artifacts are not so much a cause as a leitmotif in her discussion of the Stanford accelerator. For example, computers are ever present in the offices of experimentalists but not in those of the theoreticians. Distinctly symboled in its architecture, the concrete fortress computer building has its own separate IBM developmental staff. The switching of electronic beams, the core activity at the accelerator, is controlled by computers. Switching is one of the few occupations held by both women and men in significant numbers, for some women have been promoted from clerical to accelerator operator.

Management Strategies

Kunda (1992) effectively assigns causative agency to "organizational culture," illuminating how "the culture" is used instrumentally by "Tech" to constitute the organizational structure (actually a "quasi-"structure or matrix). Certainly the structure requires AIT artifacts like those that are the firm's primary products, but it is not determined by them. Kunda appropriately places this organizational strategy within the context of previous approaches to controlling workers. June Nash's ethnography of Pittsfield, Massachusetts (1987), a regional study like ours of Sheffield, acknowledges that technological innovation may lead to enterprises that employ different segments of the population. However, she argues that such shifts must be seen against the backcloth of "old" management control strategies. What is new is not the strategy but that it is being implemented on a world, rather than national, scale.

Gendering

Louise Lamphere's (1979) studies of the clothing industry indicated what could be accomplished through participant observation of the labor process and thus were important contributors to an early stage in the anthropology of work. They modestly reference computing, such as the manifestly machinofactured fact that it was the cutters, the only male workers, who wielded the

AIT machines introduced into the industry. Her more recent studies of new technology in the Southwest (1992) develop the gender and technology theme further. For example, in discussing women's employment in electronics, she draws attention to both the relatively higher wages and the lower security, health, and worker power through trade unions that women experience in new technology industries.

Robotics and other forms of computer-based automation in production have potential for eliminating the salience of physical capacity at work and therefore for lessening gender differences. In her studies of New York City newspaper computerization, however, Eve Hochwald (1982, 1991) found little evidence that computerization had changed the pattern of workplace gendering. Similarly, Traweek's (1988) is perhaps the most nuanced work on how gendering constitutes new technology while also being constituted by it.

Race/Ethnicity

Although she makes a formulaic reference to the disemploying impacts of AIT on Black men, Annie Barnes (1986) gives little further attention to technology in her discussion of Black women and discrimination in the workplace. Karen Sacks (1982) addresses how largely unrelated dynamics of race came to the fore on the occasion of an attempt to introduce a new computer system into a hospital. The impact of their research is to represent AIT as terrain on which racial relationships are reworked rather than as a cause of new racial dynamics. The authors in Lamphere's collection on immigration (1992) stress the importance of differences both within and between ethnic groups who enter the U.S. economy. Like several other ethnographers of markets, both in labor and other commodities (petty traders), collaborators Grenier et al. (1992) analyze economic fate in terms of relative experiences in the informal (non-waged) and formal economies.

Virtual Work

"Telecommuting" is a term used to refer to work arrangements in which workers spend less time in a central workplace but relate to it via CMC. Telecommuting is frequently used as an example of a very different work process. Yet in her ethnography of early telecomputing initiatives, Constance Perrin (1990) found that only a small number of the workers who could telecommute actually chose to do so. For most workers and managers, the notion of working at home violated deeply held notions regarding what behavior qualifies as work and what doesn't. Perrin connects many of these cultural constructions to the "panopticon" or surveillance conception of work. Perrin concludes that telecommuting will not be statistically significant until there is a fundamental change in the cultural construction of work. Even increased globalization is in her view likely to reinforce rather than replace panopticon presumptions: "Yet as national and international computer networks proliferate and substitute for in-person coordination and communication, managerial suspicions of the . . . familial and invisible processes [which they associate with telecommuting] are likely to deepen" (p. 36). On Perrin's reading, telecommuting, like the bulk of the AIT-mediated employment relationships examined here, is indicative more of continuity than fundamental change. Carla Freeman's review of new forms of "home" work (1990) also stresses AIT as more facilitator than cause. That is, the sweatshop conditions (long hours, stressful conditions, low benefits) of much clerical teleworking are more like a pre-Fordist "putting out" system than some postmodern cyber-transcendence of the commodity form.

Computing and Preliminary Studies of Organizational Culture: A Summary

In sum, computered organizations tend to replicate earlier dynamics. There is a similar pattern in electronic scholarly publishing, where the accoutrements of paper journals seem to migrate more or less intact into cyberspace. Irrespective of authors' rhetorics, descriptive anthropological studies of the early forms of cyberwork document how the relationship between computing and change is highly mediated. Since the specific mediators stressed are the same as those of previous cultural studies of work and despite the occasional CR rhetorics, early AIT/work anthropology is not indicative of a new social formation.

The Recent Emergence of a Cyber–Culture–Facture Stage in the Labor Process

One can argue that as long as work is mediated substantially by the commodity form—that is, as long as most people access material subsistence through labor, or selling their capacity to do work—work institutions will remain essentially the same. More recent cyber-work ethnography suggests something different, not so much a new social formation type as a further, fourth stage in the development of the labor process *within* the employment social formation. The following examples give dimensionality to the dynamics of this possibly emerging cyber-cultural workspace.

MEAT CUTTING

The highly ideological function of computing in the cyber-cultural labor process is suggested by Ken Erickson's recent studies of meat cutting in the U.S. Midwest (1995). Pointing out the extensive interest in and talk about computer-based machines for "high tech" animal disassembly, Erickson finds virtually none of the rhetorically featured artifacts actually in use "on the shop floor." The primary recent technological innovation has been to increase to three the number of protective layers (of leather) worn by workers. This "armor" separates meat cutters' activities from their bodies, which continue to disassemble carcasses hung from automated moving overhead chains in more or less the same way they have since the 1880s.

While the artifacts may have changed little, the TAN has. Trade unions have virtually disappeared from the industry, as has most of the experienced workforce. There have been drastic cuts in average wages, substantive worker skills, and length of employment (which in the plant Erikson studied now averages about six months). Workspace accidents have increased, as have the number of Third World workers.

Accompanying these changes, which are similar industry-wide, is a noticeable growth in time spent on safety training, Quality of Work Life Circles, and other "culture" committees, all so frequent as to constitute a new meat cutting regime. In new age meat cutting, actual computing is "virtual" but not irrelevant. Frequently invoked but rarely used, its primary role must be ideological, technological incantations wrapping unrelated labor process interventions with an aura of general inevitability. A discourse "bridge to the future" decouples the labor process from a material place and recenters it in a cultural space.

TRANSFORMATIONS TO QUALITY ORGANIZATIONS

In organizations with high turnover rates like Sun Microsystems, an expanded army of "culture workers"—trainers, information sharers, communication specialists—support the large proportion of time allocated to "team building" and similar activities. Sun, which has staked its business strategy on developing long-term relations with a small number of big clients, and which is therefore quite vulnerable to the resignation or pirating of key employees, has chosen to make work as public as possible.

As organizations like Sun reengineer themselves into various "virtual" forms, the "terms and conditions" of the job become more difficult to define, precisely because the creation of actual social interactions has become as important as "product." In this Ivan Boesky/hostile takeover era, my colleagues and I in state universities spend our time responding to ever more bizarre initiatives to form badly conceived "partnerships" and "strategic alliances." These are coupled with thinly veiled attacks on the very notion of accessible public higher education. Whether through Business Process Reengineering, Total Quality Management, Joint Application Design, or Quality of Working Life Committees, the business of the contemporary organization is the production and manipulation of culture, the marketing of the organization itself, even to itself.

CYBER-LABOR AS A SOCIAL ACTIVITY: UBIQUITOUS COMPUTING

In an earlier era, the problem of how to design a usable computer was conceived in individualistic, psychologistic (as well as sexist) terms, such as "the man/machine interface." As evidenced by the popularity of approaches like

Computer-Supported Cooperative Work, Groups Support Systems, and Participatory Design, computer professionals have finally discovered what work ethnography knew all along: Work is a profoundly social activity. The background design problem of cyberspace, how to develop information systems that effectively support work's social aspects, has moved to the foreground.

At Xerox Palo Alto Research Center, this imperative is addressed through "ubiquitous computing." This is partly a question of designing office environments with the equivalent of "a monitor in every sandbox"—for example, "live" white boards which, like an Apple Newton, automatically convert written script into digitized information. This is only one of a wide range of input/output devices that everywhere allow rapid access to "the system." More important than the hardware, however, is the conceptual shift involved in allowing everyone equal access to, while convincing them also to be responsible for, shared databases.

ORGANIZATIONAL "CHAIN OF COMMAND" AS OXYMORON: TEAMS, MATRICES, AND INTERNAL NETWORKS

For such labor processes to work, information must be a truly shared resource, not something held closely by those with power. Organizational theorists are no longer the only ones to have less and less tolerance for the traditional hierarchical organization, in which information flowed up from the bottom, and control flowed down from the top. Instead, organizations are encouraged to adopt

- "Team" forms of organization, and more cooperative, role-permeable, basketball or soccer-like, rather than American football-like, teams;
- Matrix organizations, where people take up multiple roles in different projects, based on their personal preferences, and where there is no permanent responsibility structure;
- Internal networks, perhaps congeries of mini-hierarchies, teams, and matrixed projects, within the "same" organization; and/or
- External networks, similar to internal ones except that they cross organizational as well as geographic boundaries.

In such situations, it becomes increasingly difficult to talk about "the organization" and "the work" as we have in the past; both organizations and work practices become "virtual."

REINVENTING GOVERNMENT OUTSIDE OF GOVERNMENT:
EXTERNAL NETWORKS

It is but a short step from making computing possible everywhere in an organization to seeing an organization as possible wherever there is computing. Contemporary organizations are increasingly decoupled from place. For at least some organizations, this also means their boundaries become socially permeable as well as geographically diffuse.

For example, Phil Endress, the Mental Health Commissioner with whom I work in Oneida County, New York, likes to describe his job as "reinventing government outside of government." The labor is similar, but privatized public workers are employed by twenty or so not-for-profit agencies on thirty-odd different contracts.

However, the "end of Welfare as we know it," managed care, and block granting together mean further changes. Health Maintenance/Behavioral Health Care organizations will not enter local markets if they must contract with each agency or individual service provider. "Networking" is the future for those organizations that are to survive when programs are no longer mandated but outcomes are. Similarly, without services to provide, or regulations to enforce, what happens to the public organization, such as the County Mental Health Department? It either disappears or finds new roles, perhaps as:

- Mediator between HMOs/BHCOs, on the one hand, and networks of providers on the other;
- Facilitator of networking, through identifying and removing blocks to establishing relationships;
- Collector of data and promoter of information sharing, both about existing organizations and of data about populations served and unmet needs; and
- Monitor of the public good, especially identifying "holes in the safety net."

In sum, organizations seem destined to become increasingly virtual. This is not because of the character of AIT artifacts but the Technology Actor Networks of which they are a part. The new TANs result from a coming together of new social policies and other social developments with the capabilities of new artifacts. Yet despite considerable effort to find them, I know of no NFPs making sophisticated use of AIT to model, let alone create, these new virtual organizations. Instead, like most private and public organizations, they use AIT, if at all, for management information systems. The AIT, in other words, follows and supports the organizational innovation; it does not generally lead, let alone compel, change.

A FOURTH, CYBER-CULTURAL LABOR PROCESS?

The contemporary organization took shape in the late nineteenth century, when a paper labor process was carried out by engineers, managers, and clerks in parallel to the physical labor process executed on the "shop floor." The workspaces described above are different in that they increasingly manifest a second parallel labor process, a cultural one. In this perhaps-to-become-dominant fourth, increasingly virtual, cyberfacture stage of the labor process, the well-spring of value added appears to be not knowledge but the collective performance of the workforce. The successful organization is able to realize capital by getting its workers to participate fully in the act(s) of labor, while at the same time convincing customers of the performance's authenticity. It is the job of this second parallel labor process to "improve performance" in a highly anthropological sense. At Kunda's "Tech," new workers take classes in "the culture" and "Tech talk." Core staff participate in and give public testimonials at the frequent, periodic speeches by top managers, speeches which are more like a high school pep rally than a New England town meeting.

Whereas machino-facture meant replacing skilled labor with machines wherever possible, the new stage involves something of a retreat from manic mechanization and a reemphasis on eliciting persons' readinesses to perform the approved culture. In cyberfacture, it is the effectiveness of the ensemble that counts. However, the thrust of previous labor process evolution has been to individuate the labor process, to "break it down" and inhibit social relations. While CSCW is important as a source of ideas for alternative approaches to the building of systems, it can also facilitate the individuation aimed at in Taylorism (Hakken 1997b). How momentous the reversal may be is acknowledged by the management literature on "quality." The key to improving "quality" is located in the ability of the organization to attain a high level of commitment to shared corporate objectives from each individual, "spontaneously" rather than coercively. As indicated by Susan Irwin Anderson (1993), efforts to achieve a "spontaneous" organizational culture are highly structured and take a great deal of time. Nonetheless, they frequently manifest contradictions: As I was told during training for a job with a Washington, D.C. "beltway bandit," I had to learn to "lie honestly"! Organizations must expend considerable effort to achieve the performances increasingly at the center of the reproduction of capital.

When first applied, computers were used largely like other machines in machinofacture, to enable the elimination of skilled labor. At the moment, the role of computers seems to be shifting. Indeed, many of the conflicting outcomes characteristic of work practices mediated by AIT arise from the contradictions between the older, replacement role of cyber-technological artifacts as part of machinofacture and the newer role, where they are subordinate to cyberfacture. The prevalence of these contradictions is itself one indication that this "cultural" phase is no passing fad.

To an anthropologist, this process of making the culture in the workplace explicit and representing it as the key to value, a glorious new form of commodity fetishism, is the contemporary workplace development worth watching. The development has significant practical implications as well. There is a large business literature indicating that the profitability correlates of AIT are highly variable. It may be that variation in the degree of support for the production and marketing of workplace culture is the best explanation for variation in the profitability correlates of AIT, that it is their contribution to the reproduction of workplace culture which is most predictive of AIT's contribution to profitability.

What do these developments suggest about the characteristics of meso-social relations in a fully developed cyberspace? The mark of the stabilization of each of the previous stages of the labor process was the development of a distinct social geography: the city with manufacture, and the working class suburb with machinofacture. What social geographies may correspond to cyberfacture?

Three possibilities seem likely. Option one is that suggested by early ethnography of computer-mediated organizations, that CMA was "just another technology," another face of machino-facture. A second option is a social geography characterized by an "information rich, information poor" fault line. The specter raised in popular accounts (see Jeremy Rifkin 1995) is that of a small group of highly qualified, AIT "with it" individuals who derive substantial social privilege from their control of the technical infrastructure of cyber-facture labor processes. A mass of "non-techies," in contrast, find themselves without social support because of their marginal role in the dominant labor process, with an unstable or no job, living in deteriorating cities or suburbs, in "Max Headroom-," "New Jack City-", *Neuromancer, He, She, and It*-like states of social collapse, their geographic "communities" increasingly existing in only the merest empirical sense. Public sector programs have largely disappeared, and states have shrunken to more or less ineffective apparatuses of repression.

This option, in social formation reproduction terms, is more accurately seen as a devolution back to a social geography quite like that associated with the bulging cities of early manufacture. A break in the Fordist social contract has apparently already taken place, with masses no longer able to purchase the goods they produce. Indeed, the revival of virtual home work, misidentified by some as evidence of a neo-craft stage, just as easily fits with a "putting out," "neo-feudal," labor process.

The third plausible option is harder to define. Since the middle of the nineteenth century, much of the discussion of social evolution has drawn attention to development in worksites. A stream of progressive social evolutionism stemming from the German Edward Bernstein, for example, has stressed how the educative consequences of the workplace experience, both of struggle and socialization, eventually create a working class both capable and powerful enough to introduce real social democracy.

Some have seen the "teamwork" and relaxed hierarchy emerging in some cyberspace worksites as the inevitable result of "informating" (Zuboff 1988) or even the long awaited arrival, finally, of social democracy. Cyberfacture, by institutionalizing decommoditized social interaction at work, would also provoke a relative demediation from the wage form. Increasingly, such individuals would construct relationships of solidarity in cyberspace as well as "in real life" (IRL). An increasing range of other social relations would become, relatively speaking, de-commoditized. At least in identity terms, relatively more "labor free" individuals (the term suggested by ex-coal miners in the English North) would construct an even more flexible identity out of multiple, both physical and virtual, often non-labor-based activities. Those most able to contribute to the social construction of such relationships would be valued out of the recognition that they provide the social qualities essential for value realization in any form, including as capital.

Early in the computer era, the typical use of computers to replace workers pointed toward devolution to neo-manufacture as a more likely option than cyberspace. Recent waves of downsizing and contractions in effective local, regional, and national state powers can also been seen as more compatible with option two.

However, the fact that downsizing has generally not occurred in phase with the most extensive computerization, and that the phasing of computerization and declining state power are similarly weakly related, leaves space for option three. Moreover, the virtual labor process can be framed in more collective terms (as in, for example, CSCW or GSS) and allows more semiotic, less simplistically materialist, readings of the various cultural performances encompassed by it. A labor theory of value, reenergized in this way, would explain the retreat from Taylorism in cyberfacture as strategic, not just tactical.

Conclusion: Virtual, or Virtually No Work/Community?

It is not at all clear that this fourth stage in the labor process will achieve stability. As with other social innovation, however, it is important to realize that a major source of this indeterminacy is itself social. The outcome depends upon how people act: Will we choose to act collectively in ways more likely to result in option three, or won't we?

How we act is to some extent dependent upon our institutions. The weak state of the labor movement in the United States is something on which I can comment given my career as both a labor activist and work scholar. The business unionism model in the United States (and, to an only somewhat lesser degree, the social democratic unionism of Britain and Sweden) appears to be less and less relevant to general social formation reproduction. In a labor process organized around cultural performance, trade unions whose chief tool is protective job demarcation via collective bargaining become marginal, both interfering with individual performance and stifling collective innovation.

At times in their history, however, trade unions have been less tied to collective bargaining. As social unions, conceiving of themselves in broader social terms, they have unleashed collective social and well as individual creativity. Nordic experiments involving and legislation mandating worker participation in the design of work, like the later forms of work computing described earlier, provide new terrain on which such a social unionism might be built. Current U.S. trade unions have "the local" as the fundamental unit of organization. If able to transcend its current dependence upon localism, a trade union movement could be built around extending more substantive forms of workspace participation. To be successful, such trade unions would have to establish strong links with other progressive social movements, perhaps in coalitions with community computing projects or in regard to other consumer issues.

A broader understanding of the characteristics of computered employment organizations is needed before any specific conclusions regarding the adequacy of CR Thought in the realm of organizations can be reached. The glaring contradiction between the vision of individual empowerment and the elimination of collective empowerment in many current labor processes remains itself a potential source of inspiration for new democratic social movements. It is also within this context that a long-term view of community computing should be developed. Such projects are rich in possibilities for identification of either place- or space-grounded forms of solidarity. The Internet has already demonstrated its value as a tool for communicating outside of broadcast and official channels, as well as a way to alert public opinion and organize at least some forms of support—for example, of the Zapatistas of Chiapas, Mexico. Both depend upon discovering creative ways to transcend the local, a topic that seems a rich area for the kind of collaboration between community computers and researchers for which Doug Schuler has called (1996).

Advocates of virtual community like Rheingold, Stone, or Turkle sometimes treat close relations as the only problem of interest. They fail to give separate attention to the mid-range or meso-dimensions of community in their arguments for virtual communities as an acceptable alternative to local, geographic communities. (This tendency parallels the "ethnomethodological" fallacy of some cyberspace anthropological ethnographers or the "social psychologistic" fallacy of Kunda.)

Indeed, community computing projects seem a rich ground for exploring the various decommodifications that might be a prominent form of cyberspace social geography. Community computing projects could engender better ways to balance the reproductive needs of multiple parties, including:

- Individuals, for both meaningful activity and income;
- Humans for rewarding relationships (many of which can be built on barter rather than wages);

- Neighborhoods and cities for life enhancing spaces and built environments, as well as
- Investors for profits.

Advocates of the "civil society" or "third sector" perspective, like Michaelson, tend to make a different although in some ways complementary error: they tend to presume that effective meso-relations are necessarily place-bound. Two problems with this presumption were pointed out. Meso-social relations themselves, like close social relations, were already less likely to be developed with those in close geographic proximity (Stein 1960). Computing seems to accelerate this process; for example, electronic mail can be a powerful impetus to support and build personal relationships with others in one's profession who live in a different place. In short, the effectiveness of a strategy to rebuild via computers the capacity for effective social formation reproduction by encouraging place-based meso-social relations may be sharply limited by the decreasing density of such relations.

Another problem is the failure to explore what to this cyberspace ethnographer seems to be an obvious alternative perspective, the possibility of the creation of spaces for effective meso-social relations which are not as tied to geographic place. (Perhaps the most important historical example of such spaces are the "imagined communities" called nations explored by Benedict Anderson [1983]). An activist "cybernaut" can conceive of an array of meso-social relation types, some with a strong geographic focus and others with different spatial focuses. Some would have more and some less of an economic or material needs (work) focus, but each would be capable of providing effective mechanisms for the pursuit of social objectives. If the pressures for a fourth stage of the labor process are strong, they will create additional opportunities for the creation of such virtual meso-social relations, as well as chances for strategic community computing. From such perspectives, one can begin to talk seriously about a meaningful politics for cyberspace.

What are the prospects that cyberspace will re-create a viable civil society, one with renewed "public spheres" or "third sectors?" In order for substantially new communities to coalesce around CMA and CMC, these communities must, as Rheingold argues, be actively imagined; they will not just happen. At crucial points in the past, the emergence of social space for such entities has been dependent upon state action. Like Wolfe, Rheingold tends to ignore the question of the extent to which the state is likely to have to continue to play an important role in the construction of "third sectors" or "virtual communities." How likely is this? It is to the correlates of currently existing proto-cyberspace for the largest forms of social relations, like those connected to states, and the structures which underlie them, to which we turn in the next chapter.

Introduction

While some talk about cyberspace stresses its voluntary character, much of it has a more compulsive quality, such as evoking "systems." Cyberspace is treated as a framework for social life, something with wide ambit, as a set of macro-social relations.

Larger than community, region, or organization, macro-social relations have features whose connections to people's immediate actions or experiences are highly mediated. Discourses about the macro-social

[6]

Macro-Social Relations and Structure in Cyberspace

often employ the rhetorics of structure[1] and thus open themselves to the Postmodern charge of essentialism, treating as permanant characteristics of objects properties that are more likely a consequence of interpretive frame.

Essentialism has caused significant problems in social science, but instead of abandoning structure, talk about it can be better grounded in practice, the dynamics of actual macro-social relations. What do these dynamics suggest about the reproduction of future social formations?

THE NATION: A DECLINING FORM OF MACRO-SOCIAL RELATIONS?

Since much cybertalk involves the state (government) and formal public policy, we begin with the nation. In employment social formations, strong nations have long been projected, at least by those who would lead them, as necessary for general well-being. Successful social policy, the connecting of governmental actions to popular discourses, and general mobilizations of collective will all presuppose substantive national independence.

In the era of Modernism, we have come to think of policy as "social" when national forms are harnessed to collective ends; a preoccupation with "the national" corresponds to the hegemony of "the societal" in social thought. Especially when under the influence of Parsonian social theory, Americanist anthropology accepted the nation as the prototype for "normal" macro-social relations, for "society." It used national difference to illustrate the relevance of "culture." A "normal" society or culture, for example, was complete, with its own economy, social structure, politics, and culture—in other words, an independent nation/state.

To lack any of these meant relegation to a lesser level, to be a "subculture."

The presumption that identity was normally unitary followed from the equation of the national with the societal. The ethnocentrism implicit in this practice—it implies, for example, that "national" difference is more fundamental than subcultural difference—is one source of critical anthropologists' discomfort with Americanist theory. This discomfort underlies the preference for talking about social formations rather than societies (Hakken 1987).

Recently, hostility to the theoretical hegemony of the nation has gone mainstream in social science. Immanuel Wallerstein (1976) projected a notion of a "world system" into which nations were highly integrated. It was this totality, rather than individual nations/societies, which were the proper units of sociological analysis.

Extending Anderson's point (1983) about nations as "imagined communities," Calhoun (1995) locates the shortcomings of nation discourse in the modernist, closely connected constructions of "people" and of "the public." In these imaginings, nations have typically demanded a plausible, even if quite fictional, public, one moreover rooted in a preexistent, relatively homogeneous people. Such a nation could project itself as a "natural" form, the expression of an already shared identity. Moreover, "the people" are presumed to have a "will," articulated in forums that bear some resemblance to a Habermasian "public sphere" and performed through public acts like voting.

As the nation has lost its analytic appeal, talk about national forms of macro-social relations has been displaced by a discourse of globalism. It is now common to refer to "globalization" as the dominant contemporary macro-social moment, as a "New World Order" sweeping aside the capacity of nations to control their reproduction. "Globalization" is evoked (like AIT) as an autonomous source of the perceived disruption of existing macro-social patterns; it has marginalized the nation as structure. Along these lines, Jürgen Habermas has suggested that "supra-regions" like the European Community may take on the "steering" functions previously performed by nations (1997).

"Poststructural" theorists particularly concerned to avoid essentialism now react against macro-social relation language. Ulf Hannerz, for example, argues (1992) for coming to terms with contemporary cultural complexity, especially macro-phenomena no longer channeled nationally, through conceiving of culture as "flow." (In this metaphor, he draws explicitly on AIT theory.) Reference has already been made to George Marcus' (1993) rejection of "closed . . . systems narratives of macro-social processes." Some poststructuralist ethnographers, rejecting any attempt to develop an alternative to national macro-social relations discourse as yet more "master narrative," would restrict anthropology to the "local."

All too often, this restriction becomes its own master-narrative. Because of the historically important rhetorical connections between "the nation" and "the culture," a substantial component of anthropology's current problem with "culture" can be traced to our conflicts over macro-social relations. The continued, largely unquestioned use of "subculture" is one indication of how deeply embedded in our analysis the national model of macro-relations remains. There are parallel political developments—a worldwide withdrawal from nation state policy punctuated by periodic eruptions of ineffectual "New World Order" rhetorics. The hegemony of the nation is being deconstructed in current social practice as well as theory, but as yet neither "reconstructed" terminology for describing macro-social relations nor viable structures for democratic control have emerged.

My ethnographic experience, especially in the Nordic countries, convinces me that the nation remains important to the imagining of cyberspace. In this chapter, I attempt to establish why this is so without deploying discredited national rhetorics. My alternative rhetorics present nations as only one of several largish macro-social formations imagined in diverse geographic conditions, often containing within them a wide range of human groups with different characteristics. We must continue talking about nations while avoiding their misleading self-representations. Calhoun suggests the following guidelines:

> First, the idea of a single, uniquely authoritative public sphere needs to be questioned and the manner of relations among multiple, intersecting, and heterogeneous publics needs to be considered. Second, identity formation needs to be approached as part of the process of public life, not some thing that can be fully settled prior to it in a private space (1995:245).

My approach to nation builds on the argument of the previous chapter, which highlighted the multiple, partly distinct but also intersecting, levels on which the social relations of cyberspace are being constructed. Nations include the identity forming, "public" discourses essential to effective understanding, let alone the democratic construction, of cyberspace.

STRUCTURE AND MACRO-SOCIAL RELATIONS

Cyberspace talk often involves typification of social totalities beyond the nation, of general "systems," even if of an open, quasi-"organic," evolving sort. Totalizing slogans for the social formation in waiting—"Information Society"—adopt the abstract, allegedly more general, rhetorical level typical of economics. Similarly, despite occasional comments like how it is "villages" which manifest a "global" quality, most talk of "globalization" is essentialist and thus appears incompatible with interactive discourses like those callled for by Calhoun. In a word, such talk is structural.

Postmodernism's discomfort with "structure" is its association with discourses of mastery. It has developed out of the substantial critique of the structuralistics of classical social theory in Symbolic Interactionism and Ethnomethodology. Calhoun is among those who describe themselves as a "post-structuralist." Anthropological colleagues echo this position when they claim that there are only actors and their projects, no discernable interests and certainly no structures. Having impact "behind peoples' backs," is not the structural dimension irrelevant to an experiential approach, one which tries to keep in the same frame that which is and that which is perceived to be?

I believe effective analysis of cyberspace cannot avoid talk of structure. First, some sense of structure is necessary to ethnography. To communicate at all, especially across languages, ethnography must use categories with substantially shared meanings, sharing achievable only through talk about what is generally the case. Explaining things holistically—that is, developing accounts for specific practices in terms of type—also requires generalizing discourse. A common trope of such general discourses is to speak of "eras" and to conceptualize eras in terms of the type of social formations characteristic of them. To construct policy, one must similarly speak in generalities.

A second, similarly "weak" justification of structural talk is that, in practice, to provide an alternative episteme, ethnography requires a substantial alternative structuralistics. A large proportion of humans/cyborgs currently relate to their world through concepts which presume structure and thereby experientially "create" it. In this way, dominant forms of talk about cyberspace "cause" actual connections. Since the late nineteenth century, most public intellectuals in the West have approached questions regarding social formation reproduction through formal, neoclassical economic models. Talk of "Information Society" similarly fosters quasi-formal, related-to-as-structural properties. As these practices actually marginalize the experiential dimension, ethnographers must provide alternatives; they cannot merely reject structuralistics altogether.

The third strong case for thinking structurally is that collective human action (or inaction) can itself become structure; it can have something like momentum, a cumulative, material impact on social formation reproduction. As particular technology actor networks become central to social reproduction, they make some forms of reproduction easier, others more difficult—in Langdon Winner's phrase, "Technologies have politics" (1977). It is appropriate to describe such momentum in structural terms, as long as one recognizes that structural language typically involves abstraction—and, as such, simplification—from the actual complexity of social formation reproduction. In sum, ethnography needs a way to talk about nations without presuming their hegemony, and it demands a "structuralistics" capable of accounting for the notions about the structural with which people operate and their consequences, as well as the momentums that accumulate in and are characteristic of "systems as wholes."

ISSUES IN THE IMAGINATION/REPRODUCTION OF MACRO-SOCIAL RELATIONS IN CYBERSPACE

National-level facets of cyberspace are developing at the same time as the crises in "nation talk" described earlier. Thus, both conceptual and empirical issues in the cultural construction of computing are relevant to macro-social relation forms:

1. How empirically extensive and important are national differences in the construction of cyberspace? For example, how important is their differential availability (such as the Internet in the U.S. vs. cellular phones in Sweden) to the way peoples use AITs?

2. How does the locus of cultural reproduction change in cyberspace? (Even figuring out how to ask this question is difficult, given its long and so often inappropriately presumed connection to the nation.) How connected to the rise of cyberspace are the declining capabilities of national social formations to influence their own reproduction? For example, given its marginalization, does it still make sense to strive to create a *national* information infrastructure? Are there prospects for reconstructing the nation as a meaningful social formation—for salvaging national/social policy—through cyber-technologies?

3. What are turning out to be the most general "structure-like" features of cyberspace? What differences emerge in the way social formations reproduce? For example, does the importance of scarcity decrease or increase? What is the connection between cyberspace activity and change in social structure? Are there changes in what is socially valued and by whom? How do these changes interact with the kinds of developments referred to popularly as "globalization" and with other decouplings of space and place?

4. What about social power? How are its sources shifted? Do new mechanisms for influencing social reproduction acquire increased potential? For example, how suggestive are proto-cyberspace governance structures like that of the Internet for refounding democratic political practice within, alternative to, or supplementary to the nation state?

This chapter first provides ethnographic data that establish the continuing importance of national and cultural differences to the construction of cyberspace. It then outlines and critiques both standard, neo-classical economics cyberspace structuralistics and a more "critical" but ultimately no more satisfying "political economistic" alternative. These are contrasted to a more effective structuralistics based in ethnography and on institutionalist economics.

National/Cultural Aspects of Computing

This section surveys some of the more obvious ways in which macro-social relations are relevant to the dynamics of cyberspace. As a social world that exists in an important sense only in and through electronic representations, cyberspace is a notional projection. In this sense, it is even more about *Imagined Communities* than the nineteenth century nation-making described by Anderson (1983). Yet while much of our 1980s project in Sheffield concerned *computing myths,* we also addressed *class realities,* the importance of computing to changes in the way that the broader social formation was actually reproduced. For example, computing was central to the program of the national government during the 1984–85 Miners' Strike, the definitive moment in the Thatcherite remaking of Britain:

> During the coal strikes of the 1970s, flying pickets from coal districts [already] strongly supportive of militant action had been used to bring out pits in other regions. Early in the 1984 strike, police prevented the use of flying pickets. This was done, on the one hand, by physically surrounding and effectively cutting off coalfield regions from interaction with each other and the rest of society. On the other hand, roadblocks at motorway [interstate highway] interchanges and on major trunk roads were used to interdict miners' cars and those of their supporters and turn them back from non-strike areas. Remote access to the national computer database of motorcar registrations enabled the police to identify these vehicles. Indeed, the miners' strike marked the coming of age of a wide variety of new computer-based electronic repressive equipment and technologies, many of which had been previously tested in Northern Ireland (Hakken with Andrews 1993:123).

Being a direct means of its reproduction is only one of the important roles computing has taken on for "states" in the general, European sense. Computing can also be an object of state action, as in the passage by the U.S. government in 1996 of a "Communications Decency Act" or efforts to construct national information infrastructures (NII), "data superhighways."

UNITED STATES AND NORDIC COMPUTING COMPARED

At the same time, cyberspace is constructed differently in different national/cultural spaces in ways that have little to do directly with the state. Swedes are generally proud of their advanced CMC actor network, claiming in 1994 that the (until recently) state-owned telecommunications monopoly had already installed the technological artifacts (wires, switches, and so on) necessary for a "state of the art" "infobahn" or NII. This infrastructure had the highest rate of institutional interconnectivity in the world. Then why, even though affiliated with the Department of Social Anthropology at Stockholm University, did it take me more than four months to get a simple, workable email connection?

When computing resources became widely present on U.S. campuses, as they did at my branch of a state university in the early 1980s, these resources tended to be made available in large "labs" which any member of the college community could use. (While possibly a consequence of the largesse of computer scientists, this relatively open access probably had more to do with how placing them in labs meant they didn't have to be paid for out of departmental budgets!) A pattern of broad access (albeit largely restricted to the academic community) was established. The subsequent public funding of the Internet reinforced the extent to which email was built on open access.

In Sweden, however, labs were set up *within* departments. Outside of Informatics, most 1994 Swedish graduate students (as well as visiting scholars) didn't have automatic Internet access and were at a comparative career disadvantage.

Differences in AIT conditions in the U.S. and Norway were discussed by faculty at the University of Oslo Department of Informatics. Their Norwegian students tend to begin their education with a strong ideological commitment to user involvement, as well as a naive enthusiasm for it. As their education progresses, however, awareness of the difficulties of achieving effective user involvement tends to displace and temper some of their enthusiasm.

In the U.S., students presume the form and substance of a technological system are "given"; they have to be convinced, and it takes time, that it is even possible for any non-technologist, let alone an ordinary person, to influence technological development. Awareness of this U.S.–Norway difference helped us understand the unease that several of our informants, especially "theorists," expressed about American enthusiasm for "Participatory Design." In explaining her hesitation at using this term, for example, one informant said that PD sounded too much like "yet another American 'product' to be marketed." Instead, she preferred to speak of "user involvement in system development."

While they appreciated the privileged attention to Scandinavian practice in the "PD" (Markussen 1994) and Computer Supported Cooperative Work (CSCW) discourses, these Nordic informants insisted on maintaining a separate Scandinavian discourse over system development, as through the annual IRIS (Information system Research In Scandinavia) Conferences. As researchers, they are fearful of being overwhelmed by American tendencies to exclude social impact. Their caution may well be justified; there is, for example, an important sense in which American culture emphasizes the "performance" of participation over its substance, confusing enthusiastic language for substantive commitment. One Swedish informant who had worked for several years for an American computer company, including time as a U.S.-side manager, eventually gave up on pursuit of a management career in it. He was particularly irked by regular organizational failure to "follow through" on campaigns for which loud public endorsement was demanded of managers; he never quite knew what to take seriously. He contrasted the apparent American preference for showy public display and easily shifted enthusiasm with the Swedish preference for understatement coupled with long-term connections and commitments. If successful user involvement depends upon cultural predilection, there is reason to be dubious about the long-term impact of PD in the United States.

In general, differences between Scandinavian and American AIT discourses and experiences can be traced to multiple sources. They have to do with different endowments, histories, institutional structures, and habits—different patterns of social formation reproduction—as well as specific national policies. It is only recently that calls for user involvement have moved from the margins toward the center of American discourse, and their place is still ambiguous. (In Scandinavia, movement is in the opposite direction). Michael Hammer' and James Champy's (1994) Americanist calls for worker empowerment through business process reengineering coexist with calls for letting information technology, and not workers, determine the proper shape of all business processes. As in the older discourse over Total Quality Management, the empowerment of individual workers is presumed to be compatible with the elimination of any vestige of collective influence based on preexisting work practices.

Moreover, no social policies on AIT similar to the Nordic ones developed in the United States, although there were important public economic policies (such as support for techno-science through the National Science Foundation and the military) with major consequences for AIT. At least some of the trans-Atlantic miscommunication over user participation is traceable to different national discourses/experiences, including specific differences in what gets recognized as an appropriate object for policy. Given the general American insensitivity to national difference, miscommunication has as much to do with national narrative styles as with substantive differences of value or of technical capabilities. National/cultural miscommunication can result from either a failure to acknowledge difference (for example, presuming that the state takes similar roles in both Scandinavia and the United States) or from exaggeration of it (such as presuming that corporations in the United States, because of their great power, would have no interest in worker participation).

SECOND WORLD IMAGININGS

In 1988 ethnographer Eleanor Smollet helped me complete a preliminary survey of conditions in Bulgaria for a study of the cultural construction of computing. Bulgaria had been suggested to me by a Dutch researcher as an appropriate site because of its unique place in COMECON, the effort to construct a single transnational socialist economy. Shortly after World War II, Bulgaria was selected to concentrate on production of electrical products, which over the years developed into a specialization in AIT. Bulgarian hardware and software were central to the Soviet space program, and in the mid-1980s, a Bulgarian PC was briefly marketed internationally. Internally, computing implementation was centralized. (At one time, I intended a study tracing whether such centralization was correlated with social policy in a class manner, different from what we had experienced in Britain and more like that attempted in Sheffield. The chaos of late 1980s social transformation made this impossible.)

What I might have found is suggested in Joern Braa's account of hospital computing in Mongolia, which highlights the negative side of centralized computing, especially when combined with a technicist approach to medicine. As official organizations of a Soviet constituency republic, Mongolian hospitals participated in a centralized information system. Since the breakup of the Soviet Union, AIT actor networks have faced considerable challenges. Braa described how in 1993 that information system was no longer adequate:

> In Hatgal, there is a [regional] Hospital. . . . I asked how the socio-economic situation affected the health-situation. In 1992, the IMR [infant mortality rate] was as high as 11.6 percent, and the question was if the mortality was affected by the present crisis. I was told that the high IMR was due to some statistical problems. Many of the deaths were infants from other municipalities dying in the Hatgal hospital. But the calculation of IMR is based on the number of infants in Hatgal. This is a well known problem but difficult to correct, they explained [and] there was no data or analysis about how the situation really was.
>
> [T]he IMR increased in 1991, after having decreased during several years. In the same period the number of births have [sic] decreased. This situation normally cause [sic] a decrease in IMR, but not in Hatgal. It is reason to believe that the increase in the IMR is related to the similarly increasing economic hardship in Hatgal [but] apparently nobody paid attention to the increase. I also asked [a] question about birth weight and measurements of the growth of infants, but this information was not known or not available as such from the hospital. This information was collected by the pediatric office and apparently kept there without distribution of any analysis.
>
> Information about the real catchment population, its socioeconomic and geographic distribution, is not available. . . . Such an analysis is not possible to perform based on the available . . . aggregated data (Braa 1993: 23–24).

What Braa developed subsequently in his Mongolian work is an approach to computing that, like the RSSAIT project in Oneida County, aimed to put information at the disposal of local communities so that they could make their own priority decisions.

THIRD WORLD COMPUTING

In my work promoting attention to the anthropology of computing, my greatest disappointment has been that few cultural anthropologists who specialize in the study of "third" let alone "second" world societies have chosen to take up computing among "their people." Most of those who participate in the Committee on the Anthropology of Science, Technology, and Computing of the American Anthropological Association do their work in standard American institutions. Few of those doing community computing in minority communities have chosen to focus on cultural difference as a matter of interest rather than a problem to be overcome. While some in STS now take techno-science in non-Western nations as a serious topic, their research normally focuses on "traditional" rather than "cyberspace" topics.

Benetta Jules-Rosette's *Terminal Signs: Computers and Social Change in Africa* (1990) is one of the few exceptions, but her insistence on restricting ethnography to the study of narratives alone results in an incomplete analysis. Bryan Pfaffenberger's account of Tamil computing careers in London is a better indication of what a broadly cross cultural anthropology of AIT might offer. In a paper entitled, "The Second Self in the Third World" (n.d.), Pfaffenberger modifies Sherry Turkle's ideas to develop a "cultural theory of user appropriation": "Although there are ample signs of an identity response [like that of Turkle's U.S. informants] among London Tamil computer users, they are informed by a totally different cultural discourse" (n.d.:10). He illustrates this different mediation with the following story:

> Virtually all informants insisted that of all peoples, Tamils would be the least likely to fall prey to the [computer] addiction trap, a fact that, for Tamils, helped to distinguish them from the English. . . . Computer addiction . . . is from the Tamil perspective both foolish and morally wrong, because it restricts the range of activities and destroys the precious equilibrium towards which Tamils strive.
>
> In our search for Tamil computer addicts . . . we found several individuals who seemed, at least on the grounds of outward appearances, to match the stereotype. But on closer inspection we found something very different. For example, we found a Tamil personal computer user [who] related the following extraordinary narrative about the origins of his quest for computer mastery:
>
> "I was two weeks late for [the beginning of his academic program]

because of immigration problems, and I went straight away down to the college from the airport. I noted down the item and room of my course in maths, and I walk into this maths class, and this lecturer came around and put an equation on the board, and said, 'solve this.' And I said, is that all this is about? This is easy. So in three minutes I am finished, and I took it up. He was, 'Oh, you're finished?' Then he showed my paper to the whole class and said, 'look, he's finished.' The whole class laughed. Then he said, 'my last two lectures were wasted.' Then I said, 'I have come only this morning.' Then he realized he had made a mistake, he can't remember all the faces. When I said that, he said 'Oh I am so sorry, I didn't realize.' What actually he meant was to write a *program* to solve this . . . a FORTRAN program. . . . So the whole class laughed at me, and I say, 'OK let's see about this programming.' And I said, 'I will be the first.' With that incident, I forgot about electrical engineering, and said, 'Right, I'll teach all of you about programming. So forget everything, all the time programming.' The whole class came to me for help with the final exam. That is how I got involved in computing."

This is the Jaffna Tamil way: to fight against fate. For London Tamils, this narrative is hilarious because it shows them their character, which they themselves willingly concede to be eccentric, even fanatic; it attests to their extraordinary competitiveness, uncompromising ambition, and unwillingness to accept the hand that fate has dealt them. . . . If Tamils seek to master the computer, it is a broader set of adversaries that they engage than the challenges of programming languages and operating systems (n.d.:15–18).

John Sherry's work on Navajo computing (1995) is similarly suggestive of what a developed cross-cultural gaze has to offer AIT. He is particularly insightful about the ways in which the Navajo are marginalized in ostensibly open competitions for public resources, as by the modernist predilection for discursive redemption through precise, written logic, in contrast to a Navaho preference for face-to-face talk.

In "CAD/CAM Saves the Nation?" (n.d.), Gary Downey accounts for the developmental trajectories of both Computer-Aided Design and Computer-Aided Manufacturing in terms of an unfolding narrative of nationalism: "Over the past decade, an elite, official community has applied a rhetoric of nationalism to elevate CAD/CAM technology and give it distinctive significance as crucial to the resolution of a national identity crisis" (p. 2). Given the inability of the American economy to function in the integrated fashion required for successful competition in the age of high tech, the historical mission of CAD/CAM was literally to construct a single, integrated nation in the form of integrated design and manufacturing (pp. 8–9). As is so often the case with the actual construction of a technology actor network, things don't work out as planned:

> However, rather than fulfilling the nationalistic dream of an integrated technological savior by producing an integrated CAD/CAM community, the development of CAD/CAM has brought into existence three distinct technological communities, each consisting of a network of researchers, vendors, users, and computers. . . . [T]he creation of distinct categories of CAD/CAM technologies intersected with existing distinctions among categories of technical groups in design and manufacturing to produce the three community networks. . . . [T]he historical development of these distinct communities has made fulfilling the nationalist agenda a tall order, for it means integrating these three communities, as well as other communities, into a single coordinated network" (pp. 2–3).

One cannot understand CAD/CAM in isolation from this nationalist narrative, just as understanding this nation is impossible in isolation from its technologies. While relative, substantial claims can be made about the importance of national/cultural styles to computing, although specific cases often have much complexity with which to deal.

Transnational CMC

Sri Lankan Tamil or Navajo computing can be described in terms of ethnic or cultural as easily as national difference. An example of cyberspace macro-social relations more difficult to fit into such rhetorical frames is the international currency markets. Accounting AIT made this international market possible, and its current form—trading is more or less "real time" throughout the world—would be difficult if not impossible without CMC. Nonetheless, the dynamics of this market continue to be influenced by the conditions of its development out of the Euro-dollar market after World War II, the rise of transnational corporations, and the spread of the global factory. The dynamics of innovative artifacts are generally tied to series of other social innovations operating at multiple levels of social relations.

INTERNET

The popularity of the Internet is very dependent upon its formal commitments to connectivity and open architecture. Like the commensurate, strong ethical commitments of its users to netiquette, access, and "shareware," these proclivities have structural foundations. Fundamental tasks—ensuring that network connections are adequately maintained and connectivity appropriately promoted—are handled by decentralized technical committees, overall policy being in the hands of an ad hoc group, the Internet Society. In an important sense, the Internet is merely such commitments engineered; that is, as opposed to seeing the developing computerized communications system as a seedbed for the development of various proprietary technologies (the fate, essentially, of U.S. cellular telephony), the Internet was constructed around a shared protocol or standard. Anyone wishing to compute with others had to use equipment compatible with this protocol. The result has been a rapidly expanding system which takes connectivity as a given. (In Scandinavia, the creation of a cell-phone system took place under conditions of a much stronger public stake in telephony, resulting in a much higher degree of connectivity and more rapid uptake; Germans refer to the cell phone at the ear as "the Scandinavian disease.")

Current discussions of "information infrastructures" are more or less modeled on the global Internet, which is also evoked by diverse groups as a model for future politics. Market enthusiasts (of the "Chicago School") see a commercially oriented Internet, marginalizing the nation/state more or less permanently, as the "infrastructure of choice" for worldwide steering. Those who see the state as necessarily involved in promoting general welfare also evoke the Internet's history. The huge boosts to its development from the U.S. military, the U.S. National Science Foundation, and the public telecommunications monopolies in countries like Sweden, Norway, and Great Britain are presented as prime examples of necessary state involvement in cyberspace.

Populist critics of transnational corporate power also read important political lessons in Internet texts. They stress, for example, the way in which Internet governance could be a model for systems of social control which are neither based on the nation as the key unit (like the United Nations) nor bureaucratic and hierarchical.

THE WORLD WIDE WEB

Essentially the same antiproprietary dynamics contributed to the explosive growth of the World Wide Web. At the time of this writing, many for-profit companies have invested huge amounts in the development of Web sites. This has given them a further problem: How to get potential customers to visit a site so advertising can influence their buying. This in turn means diversion of advertising effort (and money) into promotion of attention to the Web in general. Paradoxically, this huge investment in on-line advertising is one reason for moderate optimism about the ultimately general accessibility of computing and against an "information rich, information poor" scenario for cyberspace: The more corporations depend upon Web-based advertising, the less likely that potential consumers will be left out. Something like telephone access seems probable.

There is another reason for optimism that access to transnational on-line media will grow. The continuing difficulties in developing technologies to prevent customers accessing electronic goods via the Net for free, a legacy of the hacker culture, reinforces the "open access" trajectory strong because of its use for advertising. Imposition of draconian punishments to enforce rigid proprietary claims, justified as defending "intellectual property rights," seems unlikely.

NATIONAL INFORMATION INFRASTRUCTURES

What does the Internet experience suggest about the fate of the various "national information infrastructure" initiatives? In the United States, NII initiatives have had contradictory national dimensions, a contraction of state regulation of the communications industry but an expansion of support for NII funding perceived as contributing to "national well-being."

The general decrease in nation state influence on social reproduction leaves me pessimistic about what states will be able to accomplish as we enter cyberspace. Since information infrastructures like the Internet are already global rather than national, efforts to position one nation in a better competitive position vis-à-vis others may be a waste of time, may be corrosive of cyberspace, and may only further marginalize the initiator (Hakken 1994). Hanseth, Thoresen, and Winner (1993) are critical of NIIs as national politicians' cyberfetishisms with the wrong focus, as "technology-" rather than "user-driven."

If the experience of Internet suggests that public support of cyberspace remains essential, of what kind? Instead of "building the highway and hoping that people choose to drive on it," public support should help specific organizations identify information which it makes sense to share, then aid development of systems to link them. That such meso-social relation-based approaches are viable is suggested by the literature on evolutionary ISD (Kautz 1993).

Scandinavia and National/Cultural Differences in Constructing Cyberspace

NORWAY, SWEDEN, AND NATIONAL AIT

This section places the NNCP, a detailed examination of cyberspace macro-level dynamics and a project executed in a strategically important place, in the context of other macro-cyberspace ethnography. The intent is to convey a detailed sense of both the scope and the limits of macro-relations in cyberspace.

The Nordic experience of AIT is special for several reasons. These nations have long pursued policies of openness to and participation in world scientific and technological discourses, policies that recognize the centrality of appropriation of these innovations into national culture. This openness includes a trans-Nordic network of scientific, technological, and policy workers who interact frequently among themselves and with colleagues from around the world. As economic disorganization and reorganization take place on an increasingly international scale, these nations' capacity to thrive depends even more upon getting right their relationship to much bigger political economic units.

Fenno-Scandians have made disproportionately large contributions to many AIT-related branches of knowledge. A strong case can be made for their preeminence in Computing Studies, where they were early and continuing contributors to the integration of social considerations into the construction of computing and especially the desirability of user participation in development. Nordic scholars and organizations have been important in drawing attention to the range of interventions, by both state and non-state organizations, such as trade unions, in the construction of computing. They have also been leaders in drawing attention to the gender dimension of computing and in developing mechanisms to influence computing and the reproduction of gender. It is not an exaggeration to describe the main lines of development of fields like Computer Supported Cooperative Work or Participatory Design as involving a transnational response of North American and European to Fenno-Scandian scholars.

While the differences between American and Nordic computing are those most talked about, are there also important differences, either in discourse or practice, within Scandinavia? The degree of the national frame's relevance to the cultural construction of AIT in two quite similar nations would be indicative of its potential for continuation of its broader relevance.

Recent Nordic scholarship in Science and Technology Studies (Fugelsang 1995) has given analytic weight to intra-Nordic national difference, stressing, e.g., the correlates in technology policy of specific "national technology styles." It is predictable that a focus on the malleability of national technological practices would emerge strongly in Fenno-Scandian scholarship. National social formations come to integrate into a common "package" many of the social factors in the AIT dialectic at least in part because they often aim explicitly to do so though policy. In much of Norden, policy was an early motif of CR discourse, essentially about extending the already large role of the state further into the reproduction of social life. Nordic technology policy is related to these countries' long tradition of national/cultural self-consciousness, fostered by an ongoing dialogue regarding both the differences between Nordic and other regional cultures and states (for example, Continental European) as well as differences within the region. While the various Nordic national dialogues on technology have deep roots in the complex history of the political, social, and economic relationships in the region, they continue to be distinct. While in theory part of an all-Nordic Council, each nation has pursued a distinct national policy with regard to military alliances, politico-economic communities, social welfare, internal political structure, and extended trade relationships, all of which affect AIT.

Thus there were several good ethnographic reasons for focusing ethno-graphically on the national dimensions of how cyberspace has been and is be-ing imagined in this part of the world. The NNCP presumed that, because they aimed to do so, it was plausible to concentrate on how Nordic national social formations strove to integrate into nationally explicit "packages" policy relevant to the social dimensions of AIT. Further, it was presumed to make sense to try to differentiate those characteristics of AIT in use which followed from preexisting national "endowments" from those coming from the policies themselves. This differentiation required separating patterns which tend to be characteristic of all computing from those characteristic of Scandinavian com-puting alone, separating general Scandinavian patterns from those characteris-tic of single countries, and these last patterns from those which vary at some subnational (such as lan/laen [county], worksite, or idiosyncratic) level. What does the Nordic experience suggest about how much room there will be in cy-berspace for national influence over technological processes?

National Technology Discourses

Like all well socialized natural scientists, Nordic AIT professionals initially state propositions in abstract, non-nationally-tied, language: "A Mac is a Mac wherever it's plugged in." However, descriptions of specific use situations, espe-cially those in which participation was significant, were often quite specifically nationally connected, either policy specific—such as referring to a particular nation's co-determination or work environment legislation—or more cul-tural—for example, invoking things like "a Norwegian national habit of partic-ipation."

Some differences between the way Swedes and Norwegians compute can be associated with different national discourses in general. While most Scandi-navians live a material life crafted about similar entities, including the welfare state, produced largely in the last fifty years, the particular ways these entities have clustered diverge noticeably. For example, an early Norwegian computing company, NorskData, was internationally significant until the late 1980s, when it collapsed. Many Norwegian organizations, especially in the public sec-tor, were in 1993 still coping with up to forty years of IT developed to be run on NorskData hardware and software.

Part of NorskData's ability to survive was the fact that it provided a concrete answer to the question, what is the Norwegian way to compute? The extended history of NorskData thus intersected with the continuing, very public dis-course in relatively young Norway (winning independence from Sweden only in 1905) for a distinct national identity. Its prominent role in this discourse ac-counted for some portion of NorskData's success at winning public contracts.

The distinct Norwegian discourse on technology was neatly captured in two texts encountered in the field. One was a poster used in the domestic shop-based advertising campaign to market official 1994 Winter Olympic sweaters. Its text read: "Tradition and Unbeatable High Tech." The fact that the caption was in English reflects contradictions in Norwegian popular culture. The recently expanded popularity of such sweaters, especially among the young, was a key symbol of resurgent "national pride," but the interest was kindled, paradoxically, by successful participation of Norwegian performers and organizations in international pop culture. This music, like the poster, contained numerous inside/outside semiotic references.

A second poster, part of another marketing campaign built around the celebration of 350 years of book publishing in Norway, was a clever depiction of an apparently very old wood painting of Petter Dass, an eighteenth century Norwegian hymn writer/poet. This Dass, however, was holding a floppy disc. Perhaps to encourage a second reverberation of the joke, the tail of a white mouse (bio-form variety) trailed off a table, and a green apple rested on the table next to Dass' arm.

Norwegians appear to want both tradition and high tech, to incorporate the new technology, the computer, into the old, the book. In the process they consciously embrace contradiction (Bjerknes 1993). As performed fantastically during the Lillehammer Olympics of 1994, a narrative of national distinctiveness, based more and more on something like a distinct Norwegian "national character," is very present in Norway. This story stresses values like "dugnad" (voluntary cooperative work, like a U.S. "barn raising") and "deltagelse" (a notion often raised in discussion of cooperation and participation which places primary emphasis on assuming shared responsibility for outcomes). Such values, rooted in rural rather than corporate workplace experience, may be displacing social democratic values. The newly emphasized "old" values were an element of the successful 1994 "Nei til EU" (No to the European Union) campaign, for example.

One can identify several presumptions in this Norwegian discourse:

- As long as adequate deference is given to nature, technology is not necessarily to be feared.
- As long as they remain free of constrictive relationships (with Brussels "Eurocrats?"), the basic good sense of ordinary Nordmenn, along with the egalitarian tradition built into institutions like trade unions, ecologically sensitive technologists can be trusted to get on with the business of integrating forefront technologies into the social fabric.
- While solutions which optimize Norwegianness, nature, and high technology may not be ideal, they will suffice.

This confidence in selective adoption of technology resonates strongly with the deliberate naiveté characteristic of Norwegian interventions in the international arena.[2]

While contemporary Norwegian and Swedish national discourses are both no longer dominated by images of Social Democracy, they are moving in different directions. How their approach contrasts with Swedish centralism is obvious to Norwegians. The Swedish version of the technology story places emphasis on the necessity of more formal promotion of technology initiatives through state intervention at strategic points. Svante Lindqvist (1984) documents the long history of state involvement in the promotion of technology, continuing to the present day. Small Sweden, with large public subsidies, accounts for a full percent of the world's spending on research and development. Recognition of the uniquely strong state commitment to research is one of the few residues of a distinct Swedish national discourse, especially over the "Swedish model" of issues like social development and industrial relations; the only other may be over nuclear power. Generally, however, the discourse on technology is less nationalist and guarded, more positively technicist than the Norwegian one.

Ex-Prime Minister Carl Bildt's public enthusiasm for the "Infobahn" fit with a "technology-driven" discourse. The way the national and technology discourses intersect in Sweden is illustrated in a comment made by a government minister to the BBC. He argued that Swedes used to think of their society as being like a Volvo driven by Bjorn Borg—a bit lacking in style but ultimately successful. Now they think of Sweden as like a rusty Volvo badly in need of repair driven by a drunken Bjorn Borg.

The universal *in*attention to June 6th, the Swedish national day, contrasts strongly with effusive Norwegian talk about May 17th. In 1994 Sweden, the absence of public emphasis on social democratic values was predictable under a conservative national government. In contrast to Norway, there was less nationalistic discourse, let alone an attempt to reroot it in a deeper past. In the face of state budget crises and high levels of unemployment, strategies for social recovery tended to emphasize increasing resources to techno-science, as well as a turn to Europe. Bildt's much publicized commitment to Sweden entrepreneuring the "infobahn" or "information superhighway," or the later campaign to make Stockholm the "IT capitol of Europe" were indicative of this practice/discourse.

In multiple ways, informants tended to divert discussion of national culture, describing Swedes as "the first citizens of the global culture," and Sweden as "boring"—that is, lacking in cultural patterns distinguishing it from the rest of Europe or the United States. Swedes are very widely traveled. Bildt's infobahn campaign, which located its value in support for commerce, employed distinctively non-Swedish rhetoric borrowed across "normal" political lines from Bill Clinton. In appointing a government rather than parliamentary commission to investigate the information highway, Bildt and his colleagues pointedly rejected the allegedly deep Swedish commitment to corporatist consultation and compromise (including user involvement). The successful campaign to promote Swedish membership in the European Union similarly employed a technocratic discourse stressing how entry would support Sweden's ability to compete in the high tech market place. Unlike Norway, opposition stressed material factors, such as rising taxes and costs, rather than defending the "Swedish model."

Early Characteristics of Norwegian and Swedish Computing Infrastructures

These discourse differences regarding technology relate to a complex history of actual computing TANs. As in the United States, many early efforts to develop computing took place within Norway's and Sweden's defense establishments, and these efforts are credited with early (1950s) successes. A distinct Scandinavian theoretical interest in computing was also institutionalized early in both countries: Noteworthy is the relative importance given in theory to the role of users, especially in the development of systems, as in the work of Boerje Langefors, the recognized father of Informatics in Sweden. A commitment to use perspectives is also perceivable in the preferred early computing languages—the Norwegian Kristen Nygaard's development of SIMULA as an object-oriented alternative to COBAL. Equally noteworthy was the identification of computing as an important site for action research. This applied social science perspective, developing out of the British Tavistock Institute, emerged first in projects at NR and AFI (the Norwegian Work Research Institute) and was quickly copied by the Swedish Arbetslivcentrum or Center for Working Life.

Theoretical informatics interest in Norway was institutionalized outside the academy in the 1953 establishment of NorskRegnesentralen as the center for research. The early and continuing emergence in Sweden of two types of academic loci for research is noteworthy: an interest in information systems, housed in schools and departments of economics and business, and a more narrowly technical interest in computing machinery, more often connected to engineering/natural science schools.

National Policy

Sweden was a relatively early advocate of national policy and programs to support the development of computing technology. This interest in policy can be connected both to the general history of using the state to pursue detailed social objectives and to the fact that, while several firms developed unique applications of computing, no Swedish firm comparable to NorskData emerged.

Several proposals for national-level action have been developed and implemented. *IT 2000: SiREN, Ett initiativ till nationell samverkand inom IT-området* (IT 2000: SiREN, an Initiative for National Cooperation in the IT Domain) was proposed to run projects from 1993 to 1999 in support of computerized telecommunications. More or less related to planning have been several highly publicized computing initiatives, more recently a national "infobahn" or information highway.

Hans Glimell (1989) argues that one can identify five distinct periods on Swedish IT policy. In the 1950s and early 1960s, public support was given to researchers to develop artifacts, many of which were quite innovative. Public support was not given to develop markets for these artifacts, however. In the next period, support was given to applications of computing within the state sector itself. By the mid-1970s, computing policy had become primarily social, addressed to issues like personal privacy, de-skilling, and unemployment. Through co-determination laws, AIT policy became the single most important arena for a much broader attempt to extend social democracy.

By the early 1980s, however, influential Swedes had become convinced that the social emphasis was too extensive, and policy was reversed very quickly to be once again "technology/artifact driven." Glimmel finds the current situation difficult to characterize. The national state has recently greatly expanded money for technology research and development. This is a consequence of a conservative government's decision to divert massive funds intended to extend public/worker ownership into support for research. Like many informants, Glimmel argues that too much attention has been given to artifact development and not enough to technology transfer/social implementation.

In contrast to the developed Swedish policy, Norway was one of the last European nations to develop a national IT plan. The accomplishments of the plan finally developed in the late 1980s and its successors, as well as whether there should be plans in the future, are matters of heated debate. In a survey of information technology initiatives in Norway, Ivar Solheim (1992) is critical of FUNN-nettet, an early attempt to create a national data network that was eventually abandoned. He is similarly critical of the attempt to implement a more general national information technology policy, because effort so far merely reinforced existing practices rather than changed them. Interpreting these events as examples of inappropriate technology policy, Solheim stresses their failure to connect desired alternatives to the particular features of the Norwegian social formation, among which he includes localism, participation, and cooperativeness.

In Norway, the number of relevant technology institutions is small; indeed, the general Norwegian approach to any policy area thought to require detailed development is to create central institutions. As elsewhere in Scandinavia, networks formulate policy. Vague and diverse responses to our questions about the central individuals in national computing policy convinced us to abandon plans to use formal techniques of analysis; the Norwegian computing policy actor network is difficult to specify. This may be because competing conceptions of the appropriate aims and role of policy remain unresolved, as indicated in Solheim's evaluation quoted earlier. Among the important points of difference are whether policy should concentrate on support for artifacts or whether it should focus on sharing information: the slogan of the IT "plan" being considered when we were in the field was "IT: From nice to have to nice to use." Recent government preferences for market models, which have lead to competition between supposedly central institutions, have increased the disparate impact of framing activities, as has decentralization of funding. Perceived-to-be toothless "competence centers" replace more powerful bureaucracies. Several informants argued that, appearances to the contrary, there was effectively no Norwegian computing policy, and thus no easily recognizable actor network (contra Ferne 1989).

The situation in Sweden was historically and remains much more formal. Indeed, the most frequently reported characteristic of the "Swedish model" (a term used by Swedes almost interchangeably with "Scandinavian model") was the stress on institutionalizing consensus, usually bureaucratically. Our field experience in 1994, however, revealed a radical contraction of the influence of the two central consensus-building activities in Sweden. One is national level collective bargaining, more or less abandoned unilaterally by the Swedish Employers Federation in the late 1980s, concomitantly weakening, if not completely marginalizing, the economic power of Swedish trade unions. A second is the relative abandonment of the use of Royal Commissions to bring together all interested parties and to take enough time to hammer out a consensus on policy issues. The proposal to develop a Swedish infobahn was not developed by a royal commission but by an ad hoc group convened by a private group, the Academy of Engineering Sciences. Informants repeatedly stressed the extent to which institutions perceived to be established had been eviscerated rapidly, and that it was very difficult to describe the basic structure of current Swedish society. This is also true of technology actor networks.

SECTORAL CASE STUDIES OF NORDIC NATIONAL DIFFERENCES IN AIT

Disability

The history of new technology for people with disabilities illustrates well the accomplishments and limitations of the Swedish approach to computing. To a knowledgeable outsider, the extent to which people with disabilities are actors in the social democratic "folkhemmet" (the people's home) is impressive. Rejecting charity as a means to improve their lives, the organizations of people with disabilities have succeeded in institutionalizing an ecological rather than individual/essentialist conception of disability. That is, disability is conceived in law and to a great extent in practice as inhering in the environment and the individual's relationship to it rather than in the individual herself.

The capacities of AITs to extend the capabilities of adaptive technology, and therefore independent living, were quickly grasped by these organizations. They convinced the state labor market board to set up TUFFA, a participatory program to promote indigenous AIT-disability technology development. A large state contract, one element of a sophisticated set of inducements, prompted excited competition among major organizations like Ericsson and was eventually won by the state telecommunications company, now Telia.

On the one hand, user-involved structures like TUFFA succeeded in successfully institutionalizing delivery of new disability technology. Given their zeal for *arbetslivet* ("the life at work," the essential goodness of which nicely complements the Norwegian commitment to *naturet,* "the nature"), Swedish authorities are willing in practice to spend large sums (up to one million Swedish crowns) on technology to support an individual with disabilities in a job. As a result of TUFFA, a firm called TeleNova has an international reputation for effective development of individualized workplace adaptations.

On the other hand, the Swedish attempt to influence the general character of disability technology, though fostering an indigenous industry, is a failure. While TUFFA created TeleNova, this organization was spun out of the private sector and is now owned by the organization of the blind, SRF. TeleNova in particular and Sweden in general are technology takers, not makers; there is no longer a substantial Swedish element in AIT-disability technology development.

Some understanding of why this is so can be gleaned from SRF technology politics. In the era of social democratic hegemony, a general policy of advocating improvements in the lives of people with disabilities was sufficient to produce ever-rising public sector spending on adaptive technologies. The combination of a more assertive bourgeois government, cost cutting in the state sector, and the high development costs of new AIT-disability technology have made the SRF task with regard to adaptive technology much more difficult. Current discourse over technology policy is reduced to consideration of particular, individual items.

In 1992, for example, the organization debated at length the issue of access to mobile telephones, a widely available AIT in Sweden. Whatever one may think of the particular position arrived at—that every blind and visually impaired person in Sweden should have one, irrespective of need—it is evident that an approach which requires building first an organizational and then a political consensus with regard to every particular computer-based adaptive device is doomed. Any attempt to become more proactive on technology is complicated by the recent decentralizing of decision-making over access to home and school adaptive technology to the "laen" (county) and "kommun" (town or city) level. Because SRF is preoccupied with repeated mobilization of organizational resources to secure access to already existing technology, user involvement in general technology development is marginalized.

Individuals within Swedish disability organizations have reacted to the situation by shifting their focus away from attempts to foster specific artifacts and toward affecting the context within which projects develop. First, they identified as an important issue the extent to which AIT innovation can further marginalize people with disabilities; for example, the way in which icon-based interfaces make computers harder to use for those impaired visually. Second, they identified affecting the minimal standards to be met before access to the broad European market is allowed as the appropriate focus of activity, such as the creation of a standard which supports multiple interfaces, including less visual acuity-dependent ones. Third, they organized Nordic-wide support for such a standard, and they are now pushing the standard in various EU bodies and projects.

The disability-AIT situation in Norway is comparable but less developed. Several programs to promote indigenous disability/health technology have had little to moderate impact. A current ambitious program to promote the building of "smart" houses is an example of an initiative that is primarily technology-driven. A shift toward creation of competence centers rather than strong policies, with simultaneous implementation of decentralization policies, has created a situation where the national competence center to evaluate new disability technology is dependent upon its "fylke" (county) government to fund equipment, which it has only recently begun to get.

In sum, there is much to admire in both Swedish and Norwegian disability AIT experience, including their efforts to be participatory in development. While it would not be unfair to describe the former as somewhat "overdeveloped" while the latter is "underdeveloped," in neither case has policy been particularly effective at shaping the general nature of technology in use.

Gender, AIT, and National Policy

When Barbara Andrews was first in Norway in 1987, she encountered substantial activity around and a developed practice on gender and AIT. This included:

1. Projects both in academic informatics and in social science/humanities with an explicit technology and gender focus;
2. Vigorous discussion/action groups on this issue; and
3. Discourses on gender within more general system development projects and in the organizations doing system development.

In 1993, a technology and gender discourse still existed in Norway, but it was much less public. There were few currently explicit projects, and they tended to be historical, focusing on previous projects rather than on new research. Many women told Barbara that they regularly censor themselves from raising gender issues in AIT discussions.

Consequently, the gender and technology discourse was difficult to participate in. In fact, we would have missed the discourse had we not been driven to search for it by our commitment to exploring issues raised by the debate over standpoint epistemologies. Our reading in the discussion of situated knowledges helped us recognize a suppressed discourse when we encountered it, and we were encouraged as outsiders to raise the gender issue by the self-censors.

How can one account for the fact that consciousness of gender was an important part of the Norwegian AIT discourse in the 1980s but that this discourse had been greatly silenced by the 1990s? Does this change matter?

Of course, the extent to which one sees the decline of gender and technology research and discourse as problematic depends on one's conception of the gender and technology issue (Hakken with Andrews 1993). For some, the problem is primarily one of gender *in* technology, getting enough women into AIT. The proportion of Norwegian women entering AIT has declined recently. Still, some informants argued that the disappearance of a public gender discourse in technology is somewhat positive. It is evidence that the actions taken thus far to recruit females into technology may be sufficient, the remaining differences being a consequence of "personal choice."

The personal choice perspective draws on a tradition of "difference" research and analysis, a tradition which stresses how men and women continue to have different orientations to basic life issues despite positive (affirmative) actions, and that these differences should be respected. (A similar argument is used to minimize concern for the explosion of part time work, almost all of which is done by women.)

Another set of more negative explanations, offered by more informants, drew attention to professional practices that discouraged gender research. In the late 1980s, funding was denied to several proposed gender-related projects—projects that in previous years would likely have been funded—because they were "not commercial." A gender research interest became perceived to be not a good basis for building one's career: Not only was gender research less likely to be supported, but it was also more likely to lead to public controversies, as was the case with a book on professional careers.

Negative attitudes toward "women's research" were exacerbated by an increased Norwegian preoccupation with obtaining externally perceptible "credentials"—for example, the Ph.D. The difficulties involved in pursuing women's research in technology are related to the critique of the methodology, action research, characteristic of the 1980s projects. These difficulties may themselves contribute to a widening gender gap in some fields and less progress toward gender balance in others.

While relevant, such "difference" and "scholarly discrimination" explanations are incomplete. There is additional evidence that, despite the comparatively positive status of women in the Nordic countries (the government of Norway is sometimes ironically referred to as "state feminist"), their choices remain highly structured by existing social features. These include a continuing shortage of enough inexpensive, full-time child care places and gender inequalities in housework. These reproduce the need for women to follow "two careers" while making it more difficult to do so.

The gender and technology research carried out in the 1980s supports the "difference" perspective but extends it with a more negative twist: Not only are attitudes different, but the technology itself is gendered against women. A masculine bias both discourages women's involvement in technology careers and directly reproduces gender inequality. Because this "gendered technology" position implies that the problem is much more rooted in general social reproduction, it makes policy development more complex. One response taken by some radical feminists, to reject the world of technology altogether, further marginalized those who would have done gender and technology research. (It should be kept in mind that gender-conscious research into technology is strongly supported by other feminists, especially those concerned with epistemology and in science.) Another response, an ambitious program of reconstructing technology in a way that rids it of its gender bias, was not welcome in an era dedicated to market-oriented "bottom line" considerations.

In short, one can account for the change between the eighties and the nineties in gender and AIT research and policy in Norway in the following way. It was possible in the 1980s to support both positive action for women in AIT and relatively open research on gender and technology irrespective of whichever of the three views—more or less benign difference, scholarly discrimination, or gendered technology—you held. This is no longer true.

On the surface at any rate, the situation in 1994 Sweden appeared to be different. There had been some research relevant to gender and information technology in the 1980s but less than in Norway. Indeed, some feminists were critical of high profile "user participation" projects like Utopia for their blindness to gender issues. In the 1990s, informants tended to stress how funding has become available for gender and technology research, including a new professorship in gender and technology at the University in Luleå and funds for research and conferences at Tema in Linköping. The issue was of more public concern: The results of several projects supporting "difference" and "gendered technology" perspectives were well publicized.

How might one account for the difference between Norway and Sweden with regard to this issue? Women engaged in this research, as well as feminists looking at gender issues in other areas, were quick to qualify the relatively healthy picture of Swedish gender and technology research presented here. For example, they pointed out that the new funding came within the context of the more general increases in funding for academic and technology research described earlier. They also drew attention to the big disparity between the public ideology, that Sweden is "the world's best place for women," and conditions actually experienced by women. These feminists suspect that the current economic crisis will likely have negative consequences for women, such as cuts in welfare spending and reduced support of child day care, and the possibility of increased unemployment for women in the state sector, where most new jobs for women have been created. Perhaps the major center of 1980s research on technology and gender, a group at the Arbetslivcentrum, had been largely disbanded. The commitment of the chastened, much reduced, renamed Center for Work Environment Research to doing more research on contemporary gender and technology issues was doubted.

The mere possibility that a separate "women's party" might be organized created a great deal of public discussion early in the field period. This might indicate a comparatively greater public sensitivity to the gender issue in Sweden, an impression reinforced by the open grumbling of some Norwegian politicians that it had been "ruined by state feminism." The reality of gender politics was reinforced by evidence that opposition to joining the EU was much stronger among women than men. In other words, the support for technology and gender work was contingent upon economic and political concerns not well integrated into technology policy.

Along these lines, one informant argued that much support for gender research was justified primarily in terms of equality policy. As is typical, this policy is more institutionalized in Sweden than in Norway, leading to, for example, a more institutionalized system of child care centers and more thorough-going integration of positive action with other areas of policy, such as regional policy, than in Norway. When one dug more deeply into the results of positive action, however, one found evidence that these programs ultimately served to reproduce gendering at a different level. In short, the differences in the patterns of gender and technology imagining in Norway and Sweden are not very deep and are epiphenomena of more general national trajectories: The more institutionalized Swedish state, the particular fluke of increased general funding for R&D despite a more severe economic crisis, and other similar differences in the reproduction of the two nations' national projects.

User Participation in ISD and Social Formation Reproduction

Chapter 5 described the famous Nordic systems development research projects. These demonstrated that extensive user involvement is possible, that involved users tend to be more satisfied with the systems developed, and that involvement can lead individuals to a more radically democratic attitude. However, they had little demonstrated impact on work culture or organizations, nor have formal entities (such as mandated trade union negotiations over technology) had much impact beyond the sense that the possible negative impacts of technological change "had been dealt with" and thus promoted quicker acceptance of technological change.

The unexamined coexistence of multiple goals in Nordic discourse on users, a discourse assumed by those outside to be singular, added substantial ambiguity to attempts to evaluate user participation (Allwood and Hakken, n.d.). When asked whether in their experience the special features of Scandinavian IT systems had to do with specific social policies (work environment legislation) or with general features of Nordic culture, informants typically stressed the latter. (Of course the character of specific social policies is indirectly connectable to such cultural factors.) Their comments followed the previously common but now less frequent pattern that the special features were manifestations of a Swedish/Scandinavian/Nordic "model" or alternative approach to social issues. This alternative is described as more participatory, more democratic, and therefore more effective, a kind of positive syndrome.

While discourses critical of dominant American organizations (such as IBM) were present in both Swedish and Norwegian ISD communities, there were differences in the way that similar user involvement institutions developed in the two countries. These differences were sometimes conceptualized as differences in politics that cut across national boundaries. Those more convinced of the need for a revolutionary transformation of society saw user participation as a "non-reformist reform" to achieve social transformation. Others, evolutionists, saw participation as about better systems (both more efficient and more humane) which would lead in the long run to better nations. For conservatives, participation was justified as increasing system acceptance. These goals are not necessarily mutually exclusive, but unexamined coexistence in a single Nordic discourse added ambiguity.

The debate over participation described in chapter 5 is complicated by particular contradictory myths/practices about each of the Nordic countries. In Norway:

- "There has never been an indigenous ruling class," but there is reason to fear foreign domination;
- The contradictions within Norwegian notions of participation referred to above;
- The pride in egalitarian practices vs. the suspicion that these are more often ritual than substantive—the belief that consultation is really only over the trivial, or that "when we do consult, we never get anywhere."

These latter contradictions are connected to the Norwegian celebration of the individual, the active creator, whereas participation implies collective responsibility. Along with awareness of the more "material" factors which underlie them (oil and gas and the small size of most Norwegian enterprises), such cultural constructs must be integrated into use discourses to provide a satisfactory understanding of Norwegian computing. While the recent debate over user involvement has spawned more reflection on Nordic system development, insufficient attention to the specifics of national experiences has limited its applicability to the more complex present.

In sum, while there are many underlying similarities, one can often identify differences in nuance between Norwegian and Swedish computing. The differences are perceived to have more to do with hard-to-specify factors like national history and narrative than particular, specifiable policies, let alone particular technological artifacts. The Nordic case shows how one can only construct effective accounts of the characteristics of computing in particular places by combining sensitivity to national differences, both in discourse and in distinct historical trajectories.[3]

THE FATE OF THE NATION AND NORDIC COMPUTERIZATION

The NNCP did not presume any particular degree of national difference nor anything about the particular forms that such difference might take. The reason for doing a comparative project in two so similar countries was to investigate just how relevant (or irrelevant) national differences are to AIT. The project shows how "material" factors corresponding to particular organizational structures must be integrated with discourse factors like intentions to provide a holistic account of the contemporary reproduction of computing on the national level. This practice is "overdetermined" at the macro-social level, its characteristics an outcome of the interaction of several discourse practices, social structures, developments in international political economy, and more strictly technological trajectories.

Having accounted for national distinctiveness, we now consider the nondistinctive. The distinctiveness of Nordic computing, as well as the distinctiveness of Norden in general, is declining in all three of our specific areas, disability technology, gender and technology, and state mandated/fostered user involvement at work. Why?

The failure to "make a democratically substantial difference" does suggest an overriding pattern rather than disconnected developments. There remain several alternative explanations for this relative success at institutionalizing worker participation and yet failure to reach an explicit democratizing policy objective. Bansler and Kraft explain this relative Nordic failure to the centralized structure of trade unions, an explanation echoed by scholars at the Work

Research Institute in Oslo. The failure of the Danish trade union movement to provide an institutional structure to "exploit" the democratic opening created by mandated participation, or the similar failure of the Swedish movement to build on the transformative possibilities created around the Center for Working Life, could be accounted for in similar ways.

Professional Politics in Scandinavia

While much is appropriately made of Nordic success at institutionalizing a more social approach to system development, some informants described current discourses as prime inhibitors of participation's liberatory potential. The general discourse in computer science is an abstract, internationalist one. This means that Nordic professionals in ISD demonstrate their competence by participation in an overtly abstract international discourse, expressed in English and therefore subtly, but seldom explicitly, inclined toward the United States. The presumption in this international professional discourse of a distinct "Scandinavian approach"—with specific, rather fixed properties—continues to have paradoxical consequences. It serves as an initial resource for Nordic researchers as they start international careers, but it later becomes a limitation. It is a form of distinctiveness in a practice that privileges universality. Further, constructions of the Nordic approach based in previous experience restrict understanding of current practice. Adding to the paradox are the diverse images— place of origin, national identification, and political standpoints—evoked when the label of the "Scandinavian model" is applied.

There are consequences whether Nordic ISD professionals choose to perform the notion of Nordic distinctiveness—as the notion of a special attention to safety helps to sell Volvos—or to critique it, pointing out its shortcomings. What is most difficult is to try to ignore the notion. Indeed, there were several occasions when informants seemed to be of two minds, drawn on the one hand to perform the distinctive "Scandinavian approach" discourse, while on the other wishing to be freed from it. One informant expressed his frustration over "this wretched English language discourse over systems development in Scandinavia." There was a noticeable pattern of performing "Nordic uniqueness" in English, while critiquing actual practice in "Scandinavian." (Even the distaste for the term "PD" shown by some Scandinavians seemed less an objection to actual content than to its American/English heritage.) Following Erving Goffman, we should not expect a perfect correlation between "backstage" and "public" performance (1959). The complex "political" problems of having to develop an AIT professional career simultaneously on national, regional (Nordic), and internationals stages is both a demonstration of modernist identity problems in cyberspace and an additional relevant dimension of macrosocial relations.

Neo-Classical Approaches to Cyberspace in Economics

It is important to understand that significant political events took place along with, even superseded, the discourse over the practical consequences of user participation on work culture per se. For example, at the center of Bansler's and Kraft's argument (1994b) is the strong claim that no Scandinavian participatory practice broadened social democracy. The intended increase depended on increased trade union power and democracy, but this did not happen. Kyng, too (1994), traced the downscaling of the Danish participation/democracy initiative to the failure of the unions to institutionalize a broad program, not a failure of policy vision but of inadequate power to achieve it.

ISD professionals Bjerkness and Brattateig, like Dalhbom pessimistic about the long-term potential of existing Nordic trade union-mediated participation to promote social democracy, also suggest a profession-related explanation. Whether phrased in terms of a willingness to assume a "moral" rather than "political" definition of their role, or a willingness to be seduced by "syntactic sugar," system developers' professional history provides at least a partial explanation for AIT-related participation getting "off the democratic track."

Alternatively, one could account for these patterns in terms of the prodigious expansion of the influence of capital over general social formation reproduction. Both Reaganism and Thatcherism are at base accommodations to the reproduction of transnational capital; they are matched by changes in Wallenberg family–controlled—which is to say effectively all—capital in Sweden. This change is symbolized by the emergence of ABB with its chameleon-like "the best corporate citizen wherever we happen to be" as the most visible example of what used to be referred to as "Swedish" capital.[4] Danish and Finnish social formations have made similar accommodations to the globally exercised ambit of capital. Even Norwegian enterprises and institutions, despite their potential for relative autonomy, have increasingly adapted themselves to the demands of capitalist institutions. As loci of decision-making have shifted to supra-national cyberspace in the absence of substantial restraint, nation state–mandated participatory structures have been marginalized, and their potential for promoting real democracy diminished.

Moreover, it seems to me that something in the technology "black box" still remains ambiguous and paradoxical, not reducible to the functional, cultural, professional, or political economic dynamics described here. What I have in mind is the gradual yet obvious development of a unitary, Microsoft style of computing throughout the world, albeit one with admitted Mac, UNIX, and other variants. This singularity has, for example, transformed the activity of the systems developer from designer/creator of entire systems to the wielder of a "tool belt" and its array of instruments for "*bricoulage*": the knitting together of off-the-shelf hardware and software products already in use into a passable "system." How can one account for the dominance of this style of computing? Has a particular TAN become so stable that it bends social reproduction to itself? This sounds like a technological determinist argument and is acknolwedged as such by Nordic systems developers. In raising such questions, we pass over from discussion of specific macro-social relation dynamics to discourse on general structures or, as I prefer, social formation reproduction.

CHANGING DYNAMICS OF EMPLOYMENT SOCIAL FORMATIONS

In the 1960s and 1970s, the reproduction of those social formations in which employment institutions were most dominant (particularly in northern North America, southern South America, Europe, and Northern Asia) manifest tendencies toward:

- Expansion of employment-based institutions, as more and more spheres of social activity became mediated by the commodity form;
- An expansion of the state;
- Automation, or replacement of labor by machines;
- General acceptance of the right of owners or their agents, whether private individuals, corporations, or states, to make the important economic decisions;
- Stabilization and formalization of relations between labor and management, mediated increasingly by states, trade unions, and/or professional organizations;
- Experiments at work humanization; and
- Increased intervention in certain restricted domains of the employment relationship by the state to promote objectives like occupational health and safety, environmental protection, and equal opportunity.

In addition, there was increased concentration of control of for-profit organizations, where these dominated the economy, and expansion of non-governmental not-for-profit private organizations where these existed.

A comparable list for the 1990s would include some of the same tendencies, equally strong or stronger:

- Comparable expansion of employment-based institutions, as ever more spheres of social activity became mediated by the commodity form;
- Comparable automation;
- Expanded acceptance of the right of owners or their agents to make the important business decisions; and
- Even more concentration of control of and by for-profit organiza-

tions, especially transnational corporations that have a much wider ambit.

However, other tendencies are reversed or greatly transformed:

- A contraction in at least some areas of state and not-for-profit organizations;
- A deinstitutionalization of labor management relations, manifest in downsizing, part time and temporary work, increased supervision, marginalization of union and work group influence over the labor process, and a general contraction of worker power;
- A shift in state intervention from regulation and worker protection to support for the reproduction of capital; and
- Transformation of work humanization into explicit productivity promotion, along with more thorough colonization of work culture.

Some old forms of meso-social relations reemerged and new forms emerged:

- A resurgence of exploitative "putting out" or home working;
- The emergence of telecommuting; and
- The emergence of groups of workers who distinguish less between work and non-work times and spaces.

It is certainly the case that AIT has supported some of the continuing tendencies, such as the ability of capital markets to "go global," new forms of automation, and some of the reversals, as AIT-based technologies of surveillance at work tilted some additional power toward capital. At the same time, AIT is technically just as compatible with expanded work humanization, expanded state intervention (computerized monitoring of the environmental effects of production), and expanded worker control, as demonstrated by, for example, Nordic systems development projects. To what extent are the changes in these patterns a *consequence* of the preexisting distribution of power, or did AITs *cause* these changes?[5]

THE HEGEMONIC CYBER-STRUCTURAL NARRATIVE

Typical accounts of the AIT/macro-social change relationship employ the formal models dominant in academic economics since the late nineteenth century neo-classical "Revolution." N-Cers presume that the structure of all societies is similar, because they all respond to the universal condition of limited resources or scarcity with the same allocation mechanism, the market. Further, since N-Cers also presume psychologistically that individual exchange of commodities is the prototype human action, and individual exchanger's actions are pre-dictable (in terms of preference curves), markets are analyzable in terms of laws and can be treated as "really existing" deep structures.

Actual economies are not the same, however, because of various complicat-ing mediators "external" to the core market relations. Some externalities im-prove the result of market dynamics, while others impede them. Given their stress on the desirability of equilibria in market supply and demand, N-Cers see collective human intervention as an externality likely to distort the market and thus generally discourage state policy.

Cyberspace Neo-Classical Structuralistics

Because conditions of scarcity will still obtain, the arrival of cyberspace will not mean changing the basic N-C approach to models of dynamics. Like state intervention, technological development is an externality, but this one is gener-ally applauded; N-Cers perform CR rhetorics enthusiastically. The Organiza-tion for Economic Cooperation and Development (OECD) is a kind of "think tank" for leading capitalist economies. Its *Jobs Study* (1994) is the strategy doc-ument adopted by the world's twenty-five most powerful economies and the focus of the Spring 1996 meeting of the G7 nations. "Apply new technologies to create new jobs" is how the U.S. Chamber of Commerce summarizes the *Jobs Study*; this is the key among the "strategies recommended to overcome rigidities that cause unemployment" (1995).[6] New technologies create jobs be-cause economic growth is attributable to the development of technology and industrial research and development (RD): "Research and development—and protection of the intellectual property RD produces—raises living standards, thus boosting demand for labor and generating high-wage jobs" (1995).

N-Cers' cheery optimism about cyberspace is possible because they "black box" technology; that is, they treat its dynamics as anterior to the operation of the formal economic laws which they celebrate. AIT, like other technologies, can change the content of actual economies but not their structure. As an ex-ternality, technological change does not demand structural explanation. In this way, N-C both reinforces the technological determinism discussed in chapter 2, while, fit into the Parsonian "Theory of Action," the economy retains a the-oretical independence equivalent, in explanatory power, to technology.[7]

Public discourse on jobs, work, and AIT takes N-C structuralistics as com-mon sense, but their vulnerabilities become clear through closer examination of the public discussion of the *Jobs Study*. The Norwegian government and the permanent secretariat of the OECD have some concerns about the simple "ap-ply AIT" strategy. In a search to find alternative approaches to the persistent rise of unemployment and declining family income associated in the recent past with the spread of AIT, these two parties organized a 1996 Conference in Oslo on the theme "Innovation, Creativity, and Job Creation." (As evidence of their interest in unorthodoxy for delegates from the more than forty countries represented, most of whom were economists, several speakers stressed how "even anthropologists" were included as speakers!)

AIT and Unemployment

Issues contested at the conference included whether AIT destroys or creates jobs, and whether the AIT/jobs relationship is the same in the short, medium, and long terms, and in both process and product innovation. Since the elimination of jobs is often the intent of the designers of AIT and of those who choose to implement it, the premise that AIT creates jobs is questionable on its face. There is some evidence that it destroys jobs (Rifkin 1995; Aronowitz and de Fazio 1994). Similarly, while "protection of intellectual property rights" may create some jobs for lawyers, it does not otherwise systematically create jobs. Since it is mostly about figuring out how to protect corporate profits in the sale of digitized content, such protection may protect monopoly, which, in the standard N-C account, decreases jobs.

While disemployment was a correlate of computerization in some of the worksites we studied in Sheffield, it was not generally so; the association was, contrary to our expectations, more indirect and marginal than massive. Our results were consonant with several contemporary computerization studies discussed by Attewell and Rule (1985) as well as other aggregate level studies.

Further, the massive downsizing in large organizations characteristic of the mid-1990s in the United States, although partly enabled by new technology, is not associated temporally with the period of the technology's most massive introduction into workplaces. At a minimum, one could only retain a CR explanation for these changes by introducing some notion of "time lag" due to "mediating factors." Obvious factors include:

- the decline of trade union power,
- the ineffectiveness of previously relatively effective working people's (for example, Labour, Social Democractic or, in the U.S. Northeast, Democratic Party) politics, or
- the increased power of ideologies which inhibit working class influence more effectively now than they did in the recent past.

To justify viewing such factors as mere "mediators," one would also have to show that they are not themselves better independent explanations for the presence of both disemployment and AIT, that they are more effects than causes. Indeed, in Sheffield we witnessed the results of a number of national government policies, such as denationalization, which led directly to the shedding of regional labor.

In sum, while there are connections between computerization and changes in working class culture like increased unemployment, they are complicated. Because of difficulties in attributing causality, we need to be wary of facile rhetorics of transformation or simplistic presentations of the impacts of computerization. Any link between computerization and employment levels is probably substantially mediated. While AIT, as argued in chapter 2, enhances and in some cases enables "forces" like those conceptualized in the N-C narrative, OECD version, its use is not, in the simple sense implied here, the way to "cause" growth (or contraction) of jobs. By structuring technology as an a priori independent cause, the N-C narrative preempts empirical investigation and obscures actual causation.

These issues have important implications for a wide range of policies, including the creation of national (or international) information infrastructures as well as educational, industrial, and investment policy. At the same time, as I argued in my paper for the Oslo conference, the socially marginalizing consequences of AIT for those with less social power—more marginality—are quite clear. The disemployment consequences are more complex, but these factors combined make the public position of most governments, which call on workers not to resist, highly suspect.

Neo-Classical Economics and Globalism

The typical N-C narrative's approach to another "externality," "globalism," is also adaptationist. An Internet OECD article on implementing the *Jobs Study* (1995) describes the "central finding of the Jobs Study" as "the pressing need to deal with the inability of our economies and the workforce to *adjust sufficiently rapidly* to changing circumstances" (p. 1). Economies need to "*adapt* to new technologies, intense competition, and globalization" (emphases added), these three patronizingly referred to as "all sources of vast opportunity in the future" (pp. 1–2). Such forces are inevitable, irresistible; in this techno-econo-global deterministic trope, adaptation is the only rational policy stance. Technology and globalism are structures which carry on independently of either the intentions or interventions of most actors. Presented as "inputs" with predictable "outputs," neither are subjected to general control.

David Harvey (1995) questions the recency of globalization, pointing out that the operational arena of the wage-labor-based economic system has been near-global for quite some time. What is new is not economic globalism but the misleading narratives which cast it as such. The power of transnational corporations to control the conditions of their own reproduction has vastly expanded, but this is not "inevitable." It is the complement of the rapid marginalization of most of the nationally based, public mechanisms to influence capital reproduction, mechanisms deliberately replaced by programs (NAFTA, WTO) advocated by N-Cers and designed to aid the accumulation of profit.

Like technology change and the global reach of the corporation, the sense of increased competition is real, but it is not a consequence of inexorable "economic laws." All follow from deliberate policy interventions, including the weakening of nation-based trade unions (the only effective trade unions there are, yet) to control access to labor. Such interventions even weaken the capacity of nationally tied capital to enhance the conditions of its reproduction through tariffs. Forceful performance of globalist "mantras" do impact social reproduction, not because they reflect structural "truths" but because of their influence in policy discussions.

Alternative #1: Technicist Political Economies of Cyberspace

In the approach to globalism David Harvey prefers, there is no boundary between the global structure, on the one hand, and the economy, on the other; they are all part of the single macro-structuration (Giddens 1984) of social formation reproduction. At various times, social scientists—including some economists, economic sociologists, and anthropologists—have developed effective substantive, less purely formal, structural models of the general productive and allocative characteristics of social systems. The strain of substantive structuralism choosing to call itself "institutional economics" rather than "economics" alone stresses the power of various social institutions to shape economic behavior in ways not reducible to scarcity discourses alone. Thorsten Veblen's theory of the leisure class is a famous example of institutional economics (1934). The sociological variant identifies with "political economy" (PE), the self-label of economics before the neo-classical revolution. PE stresses the importance to structure of active macro-social processes, such as the protection of social power or extension of privilege. Harry Braverman, for example, explains the choice of workplace technology in terms of a capitalist class's preference for technologies which reproduce its social power over the working class (1974).

As a practice which in general aims to recognize the importance of both emics and etics, anthropology shares more with institutional/political economic perspectives than with neo-classical economics. A group of self-identified anthropological "substantivists" arose in the 1970s (Sahlins 1972) to counter the simplistic adoption of neo-classical terminology by ethnographers. These scholars, for example, critiqued the presumption of a universal "social surplus" whose allocation was the scarcity-driven, necessary preoccupation of economic activity (Hakken 1987). Because a satisfactory ethnology of cyberspace has to both identify and account for substantial change in economic dynamics, it is more properly grounded in PE than N-C economics.

THIRD WAVE WORKERS OF THE WORLD, UNITE!

In 1995, a critical voice reemerged in public discourse over cyberspace. Cliff Stoll's *Silicon Snake Oil* was one of several books blowing the whistle on a recent trope of techno-hype, the one accompanying talk of national information infrastructures/data superhighways. A favorite, rhetorically speaking, is Kroker and Weinstein's *Data Trash: The Theory of the Virtual Class* (1994). Jeremy Rifkin chimed in with *The End of Work* (1995). These works may have been only a temporary eruption occasioned by Newt Gingrich's facile talk of dealing with poverty by giving each poor person a laptop. Still, through attacking the common CR/N-C wisdom, they opened a space for serious consideration of alternative perspectives on cyberspace, like PE.

Unfortunately, two "left" technicisms, replicating the "compputropian/computopian" *contretemp* described in chapter 2, diverted this recent eruption. Some Marxists developed accounts which attributed to AIT responsibility for many of the current negative changes in economic and work institutions (e.g., Aronowitz and DiFazio 1995). These writings echoes David Noble in their advocacy of an analytics which blame technology for much of our current plight.[8]

In 1994, once New Leftists Carl Davidson, Ivan Handler, and Jerry Harris launched *cy.Rev: A Journal of Cybernetic Revolution, Sustainable Socialism & Radical Democracy.* In contrast to Noble et al., *cy.Rev* claims that a celebration of the CR, not a critique of it, is the key to the revival of an American left:

> [A]n important revolution going on in the world today . . . [is] being driven by new developments in information technology. . . . Digitalized knowledge has now become the major component in the production of new wealth. The information society is supplanting industrial society as surely as industrial society replaced agrarian society. The depth of these changes, however, have been largely ignored by much of the left community (p. 1).

Appropriate attention can be facilitated by revising previous Marxist notions in light of the CR:

> The changes here are having a dramatic impact on both the relations of production and the nature of work. There are new social divisions being created along with a realignment of classes and strata around many critical issues. The ground for organizing the class struggle is shifting; there are new dangers of prolonged joblessness, repression, chauvinism and war. But there are also new opportunities creating new possibilities for a democratic and ecologically sustainable socialism (p. 1).

Because of their "new insights into the nature of changes in the economic base where knowledge has become the most important tool of production . . . [in] what we'll call information capitalism" (p. 4), Davidson and Harris add Alvin and Heidi Toffler to the list of important contemporary PE theorists. We should take from the Tofflers the idea that

> [T]he main reason for today's ongoing revolution in the productive forces was the invention of the microchip. This revolution began in the 1950s with the merging of transistors, themselves the first major practical application of quantum mechanics, with the mass replication of miniaturized integrated circuits. . . . The microchip's impact is changing everything about our world and the way we live. Civilization is undergoing a quantum leap on the order of the agricultural revolution launched 6000 years ago and the industrial revolution launched 200 years ago. We have now entered a third period of human history (p. 29). . . . Intellectual capital, developed and held by knowledge workers and encoded in software and smart machines, is the key element of wealth in today's information capitalism. Physical labor and industrial machinery are now secondary to the value added by information (p. 6).

"[N]ew challenges for Marxism and radical theory" follow from changes in basic class structure:

> Knowledge workers today are in the position of the old industrial proletariat. They are key to the enhanced production of surplus value. Just as blue collar workers contained two sides—the conservative labor aristocracy as well as the most progressive sector of labor supportive of democracy and socialism—knowledge workers will divide in two as well. One sector will form the social base for the defense of information capitalism regardless of its excesses. Others will deeply understand the potential the new technology has for creating and sustaining a new social order. This progressive side also is born from the conditions of its own labor, which are enmeshed [sic] in the most advanced forms of capital (pp. 10–11).

As a final jibe at those unable to appreciate the CR, they warn:

> [W]hat is worse than the dangers posed by the third wave is the attempt to ignore or stifle the information technologies fueling it. This was a deep flaw in the structure of the "command economies" of the Soviet block. . . . The growth of the new technology requires open, accessible, and decentralized sources and outlets for the flow of information (p. 31).

POLITICAL ECONOMISTIC TECHNICISM

These PEistic authors fail to treat the problem of computing and social change in a sufficiently empirical manner. Their typical rhetorical move is to posit a relationship between technology and social change, identify a case which could be interpreted in terms of the posited relationship, and treat the relationship as proven. The empirical demonstration of a link is much more complicated in practice, especially when one takes into consideration interpretive flexibility.

Further, they draw upon a set of largely unarticulated values (commitment to "progressivism") which the reader is presumed to share, encouraging an ossified, overly structural, inevitablist analytics. PE cyberspace structuralistics like these are flawed. My discomfort with master narratives extends to anticapitalist forms like these which employ an econo-technic determinist framework, indeed to any account which grants so much autonomy to structure as to presume its impacts to be inevitable.

In the "lite," Davidson version, science-caused AIT is responsible for a revolution in the forces of production, one which moves social dynamics onto new terrain, a naive positivism about AIT. These rhetorics echo Bernal and the other inter-war socialists committed to the scientific-technical revolution as an inevitable way forward (Hakken with Andrews 1993).

While dark siders, Aronowitz and DiFazio are equally presumptive about the determining force of new technology, seeing an "ineluctable" tendency in AIT toward the destruction of jobs, especially good ones. Pessimists, they are nonetheless just as much "forces of production"-ist, like Davidson, as committed to productivism as the typical Stalinist. Both technicisms mirror the N-C discourse. cy.Rev adopts a capital theory of value parallel to that of the OECD: "Digitalized knowledge has now become the major component in the production of new wealth."

Involvement in the neo-Marxist battles over political economy of the 1970s taught me two lessons. One, from the Althusser wars (Althusser and Balibar 1970), can be stated, if overly simplified, as the priority, in the long run, of social relations over technical relations of production. A second was to emphasize the extended rather than simple reproductive, the recurrently transformative, richly dialectical character of social dynamics, and the relative autonomy of multiple moments within them (Hakken 1987).

These lessons are lost on Davidson/Aronowitz-deFazio. While there are occasions when it makes good analytic sense to abstract the mechanical elements out of the congeries, Actor Network Theory recognizes that any permanent such abstraction—as when, for example, one attempts to identify a tendency in the machinery itself, as distinct from the broader TAN, toward either employment or disemployment—amounts to distortion. From the TAN perspective, knowledge is a potential which must be concretely actualized, not a simple "factor." Further, technical capability, like knowledge, is contested, constantly requiring reproduction, and, in the process, frequently reconstructed differently. Since TANs vary greatly in their degree of stability, it makes little sense to speak of anything, whether disemployment or free flow of information, as an "ineluctable" quality of AIT. It is better to concentrate on the various ways in which social groups differentially appropriate artifactual potential and, in the process, actively transform the relevant TANs.

There are strong disemploying potentials in contemporary employment-based social formations. However, accounts of these tendencies which trace them largely or fundamentally to something inherent in technology, in the sense of a collection of machines, are facile. The most important factor in contemporary, edge of cyberspace structural change, the one on which to place the onus for disemployment, may well be capital as a social relation, not technology. Downsizing has been used before to strengthen capital vis-à-vis labor. As Braverman argued, selection of technology is filtered through a class sieve; to distort this process into technological determinism is hypostetization.

Critique of the Historical/Evolutionary Moment

While most obvious in the particular case of employment, interpretive flexibility in cyberspace PE is also needed at a more general, historical level. While Davidson et al. are right to frame their work, as do the Tofflers, in terms of evolution, the specific sequence of technological forms they offer is questionable. Like most sociologists, they foreshorten human history prior to the "industrial revolution" into one long, effectively a-technological, "traditional" period. A metaphysical leap in dialectics brings them into an antithetical, "modern, technological" era, the synthesis being the "third wave."

Chapter 2 outlined a more varied set of evolutionary options for cyberspace: as a new, cyborgified, species; a new mode of production or social formation; a new, "fourth" form within the labor/commodity mode of production; or merely another manifestation of the existing machinofacture stage of the labor process. Equally important was the notion that cyberspace might just as logically "devolve" to a prior form.

This framing provides much more space to capture the many possible nuances of change than the Davidson/Toffler option. More nuanced structuralistics enhance our capacity to identify which account best describes the actual, empirically observable relationship between AIT-based actor networks and broader cyberspace-related social changes. Are these highly correlated? If so, what are the implications of their most likely causal links?

There is an alternative, "social relations of production" rather than "technical relations of production" reading of the current situation. In this view, the contemporary era is one of renewed, very great if not unprecedented, capitalist dominance and hegemony, certainly comparable to the 1920s in the United

States, Britain, and even the Nordic countries. This hegemony follows from several sources, including defeat of the Soviet Union, historic limitations on the role of the state, reassertion of capitalist cultural legitimations in the face of the challenge of the sixties, and the nineties AIT-employing reorganizations of the labor process explored in chapter 5. There can be little doubt that AIT added options for reorganization of many labor processes, nor can there be much question of the legitimation value to capitalism of the notion that such reorganization is necessitated, "ineluctably," by the technology. It is precisely this ideological value, however, which should make Marxists suspicious of the "AIT as technological imperative" line of argument.

When examined empirically, the correlates of AIT turn out to be both interesting and mixed, even ambiguous. De-skilling and disemployment are indeed often correlates of the computerization of specific labor processes. At the same time, advanced technology does lead to new jobs and the utilization of new, if not necessarily more (or less) complex or difficult, skills. Perhaps the most typical correlate of AIT, however, is to shift the terrain of class power. New skills and jobs rarely carry the same gender, trade union, class cultural, and/or workplace-based political power as the ones they replace.

One can find new jobs, both in the original and other sectors, which emerge more or less simultaneously with computerization, and one can also find increased unemployment. The empirically difficult problems include, as Kusterer (1978) discovered, finding some way to compare skill levels while also recognizing the politics of formal skill evaluation or, like Eric Olin Wright (1979), assessing the impact of shifts in labor market composition at the aggregate level.[9]

Alternative #2: Substantive Political Economies of Cyberspace

Probably because its writers were interested in institutional perspectives, the 1996 Oslo OECD Conference "Call" acknowledged some concerns about the N-C master narrative, acknowledging instead that "innovation destroys some jobs." Further attention was drawn to some of the "technology equals jobs" formula's possible down sides, such as the social psychological costs to workers of lost workplace identity. These are identified as reasons for wanting alternative narratives: "There is a need for a debate on alternative ways of organizing labor and the use of technology." (By defining "innovation" in purely N-C terms, as "the creative process through which additional economic value is extracted from the stock of knowledge," the conference organizers did themselves no favor in the search for alternatives, however.)

Nonetheless, at least some participants saw the conference as a breakthrough in the introduction of institutional economic perspectives in the jobs/technology debate. Keith Smith, head of an important policy group funded by the Norwegian Research Council and chief conference rapporteur, summarizing the conference as:

- presenting innovation as a learning process, one cumulative over time, which leads to the idea of differing national technology paradigms;
- viewing technology as flexible; for example, much of it is tacit, not easily constrained, so there are questions to be asked about how or even if it can be codified;
- seeing knowledge as not individual; rather, its creation is collaborative, inhering in organizations as much as people; and therefore
- recognizing how the use of knowledge rests on specific, even cultural, infrastructures, on concretely different systems of innovation.

With its increasingly strong economy and oil wealth, the so-called "Sheikdom of the North" is in a position to think very differently about jobs and technology. In his conference paper (1997), Norwegian economic historian Francis Sjersted argued for a radical experimentation with ways to conceptualize social participation in which the job is much less central, beginning the process of decoupling access to social wealth from the particular job one finds oneself with (or without).

The explanatory strategies of the institutional economists in Oslo were not oriented toward identification of the presumed formal, machine-like processes "built in" to all economies. Rather, the search was for new capacities for and exercise of alternative social power based on different national/cultural dynamics.

SHOE WORKERS IN THE THIRD ITALY

Some cyberspace ethnographers develop similar alternative accounts. In calling the "global factory" the most significant structural feature of the contemporary world, Michael Blim does not mean a specific organization form. Instead, the term is used

> to stand conceptually for [a] complex of empirical activities and their intersection in the globalization of industrial production, . . . the contemporary manifestation of the continuing combined and uneven development of the world capitalist system in which the production of commodities and the creation of value have dispersed capitalist productive activity through the world. [The global factory] occurs in an environment in which the capitalist relations of production and exchange generate new, if uneven, possibilities for economic growth and for increased exploitation of labor by capital (1992:8).

Blim sees AIT as a facilitating factor in this phenomenon—"Important technological advances in telecommunication, aided by air transportation, have facilitated the creation of new networks" (p. 15)—rather than a determining one. He offers the following abbreviated account of labor agitation among shoe workers in a Central Italian region, an unlikely arena, to illustrate "the coincidence of how industry, class, and community can still unleash an increased potential for working-class militancy in the global factory:"

[There] the social relations of production internal to the household were ordered by patriarchal norms; a mix of clientelism and paternalism cloaked the typically exploitative external relations between sharecropping households and landlords. In all, a tremendous export boom in the shoe industry during the 1960s that provided first-time wage labor for many individuals and profitable small businesses for a quarter of the local households would seem to have created an inauspicious base for a progressive labor movement.

Nonetheless, shoe workers in the region nurtured a union movement . . . , culminating in three industry-wide and community-wide strikes . . . [which] resulted in local entrepreneurial acceptance of the national shoe industrial contract. Barricades obstructing traffic in and out of the bevy of central Italian hill towns were erected and controlled by workers and their families. Autonomous groups of women factory workers constructed and superintended their own blockades. The strikers, as in many other labor struggles, won by successfully shutting down the entire shoe industry which, in practice, amounted to the entire economy of the area.

Blim offers four reasons for success: favorable external circumstances, including successful national labor militancy; the expansion of production, which outstripped local productive capacity and the labor force and shifted production from workshop to factory, with a new system of labor control; the new coextensive labor and community forms of social life; and households and kin network support of the strike, which, through interconnected social ties, were sustained by the community itself. Blim recognizes that "this case is only one among many potential accounts of worker resistance in the emerging global factory" but goes on to stress another case of decoupling space from place:

[I]t would be mistaken . . . to confine analysis of sites of resistance to shop floors and factory gates. The global factory, as discussed here, simply represents more concretely the progressive incorporation of peoples throughout the world in capitalist production for the world market. . . . Consequently one of the principal products of the global factory is struggle in a variety of forms and with a plenitude of potential. The highly variable interaction between and among these pervasive classes of agents furnishes anthropology with a formidable research agenda (pp. 23–26).

CYBERSPACE PE IN 1980s SHEFFIELD

Our mid-80s research convinced Barbara Andrews and me that soom of the cyberspace-related patterns of Sheffield culture were similar to pre-Fordist social patterns of unemployment and class degradation, more compatible actually with a devolution to a previous form of the labor social formation than with some new stage or a nonlabor form. At the same time, some interesting interventions and people's general willingness to appropriate AIT discourses in new identity work seemed indicators of potentially new social arrangements.

At that time, we accounted for the negative computer-related transformations of 1970s Sheffield working class culture in terms of what Nash and Fernandez-Kelly (1983) called a new international division of labor. The accelerated internationalization of capital accumulation was an important mediator of computerization. The development of London as the center of the world market in currency and other forms of speculation was draining capital from the domestic economy; computer technology was a necessary precondition to the development of such markets, and computerization has contributed mightily to the volatility of financial markets. Rates of investment in British industry in 1987 were still below those of 1979, and lack of capital was one of a series of economic problems facing Northern English regions like South Yorkshire.

We also adopted "disorganized capitalism" (Offe 1986) as our characterization of the then-current stage of the accumulation process. Put simply, earlier PEers had interpreted the increasing monopolizations and state interventions of the first half of the twentieth century as signs of increasing control and organizations. Offe suggested that in the second half of the century, this process was being reversed. For example, what from one perspective appeared to be a centralizing tendency, the rise of transnational corporations, could from another be seen as decentralizing, leading to a world political economy beyond the systematic influence of either nation state or single corporation. In this situation, the consequences of a major technological development like computerization were less controllable than might otherwise have been the case.

While "new international division of labor" and "disorganized capitalism" helped describe some of what was going on, they didn't provide an account for the more innovative developments we also experienced. Given the volatility of the reproduction of actual social formations at the time, the diversity which was the hallmark of the correlates of computerization manifest in Sheffield was predictable. These correlates were much more a consequence of the characteristics of the specific social situation into which AIT was introduced than the technical nature of the equipment. To understand the connection between computerization and culture change, we must recognize that various social groups are battling over how computerization is understood as well as how it is used physically. In terms of political economy, the dynamics of social formations like that of Sheffield are clearly still bent to the imperatives of the reproduction of capital, but how people perceive themselves and their lives are also important. The symbolic or ideological role of computing is as significant as its material or physical role.

The limited effectiveness of the computer initiatives of local governments in the Sheffield region, and the more extensive effects of the national government, were also related to numerous factors. Some are technical, like the nature of available computer power; some are social, having to do with the breaking up of establish patterns in working class neighborhoods and villages; and some are semiotic or ideological, having to do with the extent to which humans' will to confront the forces shaping their lives are drained by images of domineering machines. Our study of Sheffield suggested that the best predictor of any specific computing initiative's correlates was the groups in society whom they mobilized and whose interest they served. For that moment at least, those groups remained the ones characteristic of previous labor social formations, owners/controllers of means of production and those whose survival depends on being able to sell their labor power.

In contrast, chapter 5 discussed data suggesting that we may be entering into a fourth stage of the capitalist labor process, in which the wellspring of value added is the collective performance of the workforce. Now, the successful organization is held to be the one able to realize capital by getting its workers to participate most actively while at the same time convincing customers of the genuineness of workers' performance. These forms of participation eventually confront the conflict inherent in all attempts to promote worker control which remain subjugated to the reproduction of capital, and trade unions less tied to collective bargaining might find here some new terrain on which such a social unionism for the contemporary era might be built. Social activism on these grounds, combined with the social experiments which decouple income from labor, are indicative of a very different political economy.

Conclusion

In the NNCP, the most important determinant of whether users had effective impact on system development was neither the degree of commitment of designers nor the effect of trade unions. Rather, it was users' preexisting power in the organization's labor processes. I encountered something similar in my first field research on early 1980s organizational computing in the Upper Mohawk Valley, New York. The most important determinant of what happened "when the computers came" was the quality of labor/management relations at the time of their arrival. Good relations correlated with effective, noncontroversial computing, whereas poor relations meant little effective use of the new technology, and often more intractable because more densely mediated problems. In fact, at the time of this writing most ISD is really system *redevelopment*: the expansion or modification of a preexisting electronically mediated information systems, not the development of new ones. Even systems which may be thought of as replacing existing ones are built on the practices characteristic of the old.

This chapter's "thick descriptions" have documented the continuing relevance of national patterns of industrial relations, policy, and culture as mediators of the social construction of computing, as having substantial impact on the structural implications of "really existing" computing. However, it has also offered examples of how new TANs can also be associated with new reproductive dynamics. Most AIT systems today are erected on the same base of Microsoft products, purchased "off the shelf," so there is less scope for user-influenced, custom developed systems. One could identify today (1999) as one of relative electro-mechanical autonomy, one in which certain de-skilling, time-and-effort saving tendencies of AIT systems seem likely to be manifest, especially given the way their direct creators and adopters talk. To argue differently would be to claim that technologies have no politics.

Still, the meaning of the loss of, for example, Nordic uniqueness, is complicated by another commonality, the international changes in thinking about ISD. Interest in "soft" system development, JAD (Joint Application Development), CSCW, even the humane face of BPR continues to grow. Thus, Nordic practice appears less distinctive because the ISD world has become more like Scandinavia. In like manner, one could fashion an argument, based on the structural characteristics of capitalism as a political economy, for the relative power and autonomy of capitalistic social relations, the Braverman perspective.[10]

But there is also a third interpretive possibility, what Barbara Andrews and I actually saw in Sheffield. The most important moment in terms of what actually happened when the computers came was not the technology *qua* machines, social relations in the abstract, nor the iron laws of the market. What was important was how the technology was perceived and which potentials actually were appropriated by the people in the relevant social relations. While social relations clearly marginalized some constructions, and economics and mechanics certain others, there was still a broad range of interpretive flexibility in the actual performance of AIT actor networks.

Such interpretive flexibility need not mean "anything goes." Cyberspace structuralistics need not be forced to choose between N-C economic/PE technological determinisms and postmodern anti-structuralism. One can be subtle about causation without abandoning it altogether. AIT is, in institutionalist/substantivist PE terms, better viewed as a terrain of contestation than as an ineluctable, independent force. Technologies do have politics, but like all politics, they are subject to multiple, contradictory forces, and their role in particular situations depends on multiple, often conflicting constructions. If one accepts the notion that capitalism is an inherently anarchic Political Economy—indeed, as argued by Aronowitz and DiFazio as well as Offe, that the brief period of Keynesian-induced "stability" in world capitalism appears to be over—then these contradictory forces and conflicting constructions are likely to continue to "produce" conflict in the future.

A SUMMARY OF THE LIKELY STRUCTURAL FEATURES OF CYBERSPACE

Cyberspace ethnography's alternative PE perspective can contribute to formulating policies relevant to creativity, innovation, and job creation. With the era of Fordist "machino-facture" out of which it is emerging, proto-cyberspace PEs share a number of features:

1. the commodity circuit—that is, the realization of profit through exchange of produced values, or the reproduction of capital—as the central element in the creation of social wealth;
2. shifting labor and product markets, reflecting changes in the commodity circuits specifics;
3. conflict between labor and capital over the division of the surplus value created by production of commodities;
4. jobs involving roughly comparable levels of substantive skill;
5. a close connection between ownership of successfully reproducing capital and broader social influence, especially in formal politics.

There are also important political economic dissimilarities between Fordism and the emerging stage:

1. the emergence of AIT as a primary site for the realization of capital, and thus of AIT workers as both relatively privileged and powerful, at least for a time, as individuals;
2. a decline in the social power of older working class social forms—trade unions, local communities, and class-based political parties—to influence the appropriation of surplus value and therefore the general distribution of social wealth;
3. a decline in the power of nations to influence the social correlates of capital reproduction;

4. the displacement of international structures (such as the Bretton Woods system of international financial control) for system "steering"—for avoiding the kind of general crisis like the overproduction accumulation crisis which led to the Great Depression of the 1930s; and

5. a world political economy in which crises and disturbances are spread more quickly from social formation to social formation and economic sector to economic sector.

Finally, there are significant areas of ambiguity:

1. whether the commodity form will continue to be extended into more areas of social life, including new areas of social life "created" by the commodity circuit, than it is withdrawn from, as by "community computing";

2. whether labor or the "job" will remain as central to realization of value, or whether non-wage mediated forms of work will become relatively more important; and

3. whether AIT workers will ultimately develop an identification with other workers.

THE POLITICS OF CYBERSPACE STRUCTURALISTICS

Contemporary anthropology is increasingly uncomfortable with notions like "tradition" and "custom" in accounting for characteristic practices. Rather, we stress the role of imagination in the production and reproduction of culture; how, in the face of constantly changing circumstances, humans/cyborgs use the conceptual tools available to imagine narratives of shared purpose and strive to embody these imaginings in new TANs and other social relationships.[10]

If contemporary social formations are to manage the structural tendencies toward conflict and disintegration identified here, alternative social dynamics capable of mobilizing the efforts of as many humans/cyborgs as possible must be imagined (Sclove 1995). (The basic grounding of any notion of democracy, this is arguably the evolutionary lesson to be drawn from the experience of complex human social formations.) Cyberspace is an important trope in the contemporary cultural imaginary, ethnographers having demonstrated the powerful hold of cyberspace imaginings on social groups—building friendships, establishing non-place bound communities, and in mobilizing ad hoc political networks—even in the face of repeated technological failure. As such, cyberspace offers an important basis for imagining alternative futures. What is the likelihood of that new potentialities for social power and new practices for its exercise will emerge in a full-blown cyberspace?

As Davidson is clearly aware from his perspective as an advocate of community computing, there are some important ways in which AIT has been used against dominant powers with macro-social potential, even consequences. The personal computer in its earliest "Apple" form was such a deliberate social intervention. The group of quasi-students who thought it up and produced early prototypes were motivated at least in part by the political desire to provide individuals with computing capabilities comparable to those of large bureaucracies, both public and private (Siegel 1986). The Internet provided Sub-commandante Marcos with means to communicate a Zapatista perspective on events to an international audience. A 1996 threat to U.S. National Science Foundation funding of social, economic, and behavioral research from the congressional leadership was blunted by an email campaign.

AIT is not inherently liberatory, "ineluctably" anything. While to say that information "wants" anything, like to be free, is dubious, there definitely are people who choose to keep information from others. Such choices are illuminable by relating them to class power relations; as these relations shift, so will the success of the attempts. A complexified technology discourse, one disciplined by empirical sensitivities, makes it more difficult to handle technology in the sweeping historical narratives loved by grand social theory, whether Structural/Functional, Marxist, or N-C. Among the advantages of treating technology as flexible, a point of contestation is that this perspective justifies active, practical intervention into the cultural constructions taking place, not just rides for those forced to hitchhike on an information highway.

It is difficult to imagine how these cyber-imaginings will counterbalance the increasing power of capital to promote its own reproduction, irrespective of social consequence, as long as the basic political economic relations described here prevail. The tremendous potential of AIT remains the captive of a structure which means that the vast majority find their life chances determined by the size of their income, this income itself determined ultimately by an increasingly inegalitarian, unstable distribution of social power. Indeed, cyberspace may only emerge as a distinct way of life when access to the means of subsistence is no longer mediated by the job. However, many recent changes (such as the end of "Welfare as we know it" in the U.S., contraction of the social wage in Europe, and of anything like a stable political economy in much of the Third and Fourth Worlds) run counter to this development.

Thus, a structural analysis of cyberspace suggests that access to a really different future, the bringing of what can be imagined into real life, depends upon policies which achieve a better balance in the social power of groups and organizations. Through promoting networks of viable multicultural social formations, rather than simple use of ever more elaborate artifacts, policy will best promote innovation and creativity, with or without jobs.

Cyborgs@cyberspace? has presented this ethnographer's perspective on what we know about a potentially new way to be human. Weighted toward my own research experience in cyberspace, this book has not pretended to be a general summation of the field. Still, it has argued for placing specific cyberspace problems in the context of a shared research problematic, testing the idea of a "Computer Revolution." It has also exemplified the value of one approach to that problematic, organizing it around issues which articulate most directly at the different levels of sociocultural integration, from the entity to the structural.

[7]

Knowledge in Cyberspace and the Practice of Ethnography

I have acknowledged, but not chosen, another way to cast the general cyberspace problematic, as a set of general conceptual issues. Several of these—information, democracy, work, and technology—have been addressed at various points and at some length. In this chapter, I wish to focus on two additional, underaddressed issues. One is the character of knowledge in cyberspace, including the notion of cyberspace as a "Knowledge Society," and the other is "practice"—how we cyberspace ethnographers can articulate our knowledge *of* cyberspace with involvement *in* its construction in a manner that is ethically defensible.

The Knowledge Question in Cyberspace

I first became aware of the "knowledge question" early in proto-cyberspace. In 1971, Barbara Andrews and I were on the staff of New University Conference (NUC), "a [U.S.] national political organization of graduate students and faculty working in, around, and in spite of institutions of higher education." NUCers were educational radicals, critical of the ways traditional, hierarchical, teacher-centered pedagogies contributed to educational underdevelopment, especially for women, minorities, and working class people. We attended the annual exhibition and meeting of the Association for Educational Communications and Technology (AECT) to learn more about the new computerized teaching machines. They were advertised as giving the learner more control over her education, but some teachers saw the machines as automation; after all, they were promoted as "teacher proof."

The "demos" and claims of the machine makers were impressive, but, having already worked with computers while at Stanford and the University of Chicago, I knew there was often a large gap between claim and "in use" performance. We searched out teachers actually using the machines. They told us (Andrews and Hakken 1977) that computer teaching machines were helpful in very precise areas of learning, like medical terminology, but that where consistency was not of overwhelming importance, the machines were of little value. They were repeatedly compared with language labs.

Within a few years, these early machines disappeared, and aggressive talk of "computerized teaching" was replaced by moderate talk of "computer-*assisted* learning." Yet "knowledge machine" rhetoric similar to that of the AECT has been a reoccuring CR theme: "The exponential growth of knowledge necessitates the use of technology"; the implied threat to teachers to again be left in the dust "because the 'Internet Train' is leaving the station"; or opaque slogans like "Faculty Empowerment through Student Use of the Internet."

Characterizations of cyberspace as a "knowledge society" are now common. "Knowledge" takes a central role in Davidson et al. (1994), "knowledge workers" constituting the new revolutionary class because of their centrality to production. In the OECD *Jobs Study* (1994), knowledge production is also the key ("magic"?) link in the technology/job creation chain. However, the knowledge leading to growth is produced by "Research & Development"; it does not come from workers. Since these latter are merely a medium for applying knowledge generated elsewhere, "Basic education should be practical and universal; the education-to-workplace transition should be streamlined through cooperation with industry; and workers should be given incentives to constantly hone their skills" (U.S. Chamber of Commerce 1995).

While the *Jobs Study* itself makes passing reference to how education should aim to achieve "other fundamental social and cultural objectives . . . as well as . . . extending and upgrading workers' competencies" (p. 47), only initial education, school-to-work transition, and work-related skills are discussed further. One does not proceed very far into discussions about knowledge in cyberspace without confronting diverse claims about whose knowledge is most central to creation of the "knowledge society." Like both computopians and compputropians, however, advocates share a questionable Modernist conception of knowledge. The *Call* for the Oslo conference restricts "innovation" *by fiat* to the realm of the economic, defining it as "the creative process through which additional economic value is extracted from the *stock* of knowledge" (emphasis added).

Educationists see narratives that treat knowledge as "stock" as based in a "banking" concept of learning. Under this conception, "knowledge" is a discrete, bounded, measurable, inert, uniform commodity; for example, a thing whose primary importance is that it can be drawn upon as a factor for expanding production. (This is called the "banking" theory because the role of the teacher is to treat the learners' minds as deposit boxes in a bank vault—to be opened, crammed full of as many "units" of knowledge as possible, slammed shut, and locked quickly, lest any spill.) In contrast, much contemporary education pursues Non-Modernist "constructivist" approaches (see Mathews 1998) in which learning is a cooperative activity and knowledge does not exist independent of the learning situations in which it is produced and reproduced.

ALTERNATIVE PERSPECTIVES ON CYBERSPACE KNOWLEDGE TALK

Perhaps because of the high social value associated with it, "knowledge" is a semiotic arena particularly vulnerable to techno-hype. Formal education is the institution to which Americans have increasingly assigned the task of accomplishing social change (as articulated by George Counts [1969] in *Dare the Schools Change the Social Order?*). Perhaps the reason why computers have continually been described as "mechanical brains" is that American heads are so easily turned by technicist "thinking machine" rhetoric. It has been thus very difficult for educational hucksters to avoid projecting education as the highway to cyberspace.

As a trope capturing the socially innovative, cyberspace "knowledge-talk" strongly parallels that about information. Because there are fundamental ambiguities regarding the way these two terms are used, posing empirical questions about knowledge is also as difficult.

On Sinding-Larsen's musical analogy, the knowledge resulting from computer-mediated thinking *may* be changing as drastically as music was transformed by the use of formal systems of notation. In 1996, however, Diana Forsythe depicted a very different kind of cyberspace talk about knowledge. She was describing a computer-based self-diagnostic system for people who wondered if they had migraines. The system prompts the "user" to describe her symptoms and is programmed to repeat precisely the symptoms typed in, whatever they are, as the proper indicators of migraine!

This ontological legerdemain was legitimated by the developers as "promoting user confidence in the system" to "increase the likelihood of patient compliance." Yet while the system is *capable* of recommending a wide range of therapeutic options, it is programmed to include only those therapies that the physician or clinic running it prefers. Again, this selection takes place *without the user knowing it,* while the system is described proudly as one that "increases control by the patient!"

The doubtful ethics of such computing indicates why some feel that, far from a "knowledge society," cyberspace may indeed be the era of "mythinformation." Contained within the normal notion of "cyberspace as knowledge society," however, is the implication that Cyberians do knowledge not just differently, they do it better—as if cybernauts have leapt a quantum from "normal-" to "super-knowledge." This perspective on knowledge in cyberspace is legitimate *only* if we can specify empirically:

- How the new devices and techniques for handling information significantly change knowledge;
- How the different knowledges actually, not just potentially, transform human activity substantially; and
- Why these transformed activities are justly described as "better" than those they displace.

DECONSTRUCTING KNOWLEDGE TALK IN CYBERSPACE

Very little empirical attention has been given to the cyberspace knowledge question. Part of the reason talk of "knowledge society" seldom moves beyond sloganizing is that the multiple notions of knowledge used are never acknowledged, let alone differentiated. On a "simple" Modernist conception like that of the OECD, knowledge is unproblematic, quantifiable, packagable, and objectifiable; its creation can be planned and predicted, etc.

Other "knowledge society" talk has a postmodern Einsteinian quality, where "more" means "different." Far from being abstract, on this view knowledge is localized and difficult to describe, let alone quantify. Rather, it is situated (Suchman 1987; Dahlborn and Mathiessen 1993), a position most developed within feminist standpoint theory (for example, Harding 1991; Hartsock 1983). As on the constructivist view,

> We may require a different way of thinking about knowledge. Rather than thinking that knowledge is in the minds of individuals, we could alternatively think of knowledge as the potential for situated activity. On this view, knowledge would be understood as a relation between an individual and a social or physical situation, rather than as a property of an individual (Greeno 1988).

On such a conception, a "body of knowledge" separate from a social relationship or collectivity of knowers is meaningless. Experience in cyberspace itself—such as the disengagement of space from place—is identified as a major factor promoting such antipositivist knowledge discourses (see Lyotard 1984). As if an extended commentary on the old programmer's excuse, "garbage in, garbage out," computing is "information" *as opposed to* "knowledge" technology. While the net may be full of information, only a group of concretely situated cybernauts can determine its reliability. For hyperrealist Jean Baudrillard (1975),

AIT renders commonsensical notions of "reality" obsolete, since both the real and the "unreal" only exist in constructed representations. On analogy with the early computer game "Space Invaders" (or, if you prefer, *Star Wars*), hyperreality is to reality as hyperspace is to "real" space.

That the content of culture is often contested was used in chapter 4 to critique Dennett's model of consciousness. The hyper-realists in effect extend the contestation, suggesting that our representations of what is are in some profound sense disciplined hardly at all by the empirical, as in Baudrillard's famous contention that the Gulf War only existed on television. On their view, cyberspace obviates further development of knowledge in a conventional Modernist sense. Cyber-knowledges are plural, encouraging multiple voices, and multiculturality.

On the one hand, marketing of computers evokes the positivist, progressivist, "bankable" concept of knowledge of "simple" Modernism. On the other, they draw on non-Modernist, relativist "train leaving the station," transformative talk that contradicts positivist conceptions. As Benjamin Woolley puts it in his examination of *Virtual Worlds* (1992), "The significance of virtual reality . . . is that it directly confronts the question: what is reality?"[1]

The popular discourse over knowledge in cyberspace implicitly assumes *both*

1. A vastly expanded version of previous forms of knowledge, its production being automated, technologized, etc., *and*
2. A de-centered, near hallucination which gives pride of place to paradigm shifts in the very character of knowing, rejects previous ways of knowing, and rethinks knowledge in profound, fundamental ways.

Moreover, these two incompatible knowledge discourses are mixed in practice, often unwittingly.

The increased volume of knowledge talk is not paralleled by an increased complexity of understanding. When evoked simultaneously, as in much current science fiction, the effect is schizophrenic. These conflicting answers to the knowledge question in cyberspace suggest that a dramatic complexification of talk about knowledge is needed before empirical research can be effective.

RECONSTRUCTING CYBER-KNOWLEDGE TALK

As indicated above, the CR assumption that knowledge in cyberspace is socially transformative adds to the confusion. The Modernist and Postmodernist perspectives discussed differ only on the character of the mechanism: On the modern approach, change follows from new *disembodied* knowledge, while in the Postmodern, knowledge is differently *embodied* in the new.

However, as in the "same technology" reading of the CR outlined in chapter 2, anti-change readings of both modernist and postmodernist approaches to knowledge in cyberspace are also possible. On a positivist *anti*-transformation reading, knowledge (verified information) continues to accumulate, as it has at least since the Renaissance, but with no particularly profound social consequences.

Similarly, an alternative reading based on Postmodernism stresses how it is our *understanding* of knowledge, rather than knowledge itself, that changes in cyberspace. Knowledge itself has always been situated; once blinded by Modernism, we now see more clearly the situatedness which has been and will always be. The understanding of knowledge developing in the current era is more mature, more accurate, but it is not a new *kind of* knowledge, are there no new *roles for* it, nor does our understanding change the nature of previous knowledges. So, at least in regard to knowledge, "cyberspace" is not all that different; we just understand better what it is. Contemporary knowledge is *even more* continuous with past knowledge, because we no longer misrepresent it.

To be non-self-contradictory and therefore usable, discussion of knowledge in cyberspace should aim to establish only one of four possible general claims:

1. That cyberspace is a different, knowledge society, because the accumulation of an increasing quantity of knowledge has led to a qualitative social transformation (Modernist Transformity);
2. That cyberspace is a different, knowledge society, because recognition of the fragmentation of knowledges and related phenomena have forced a new way of being in the world (Non-Modernist Transformity);
3. That there is as yet no distinct cyberspace "knowledge society" in any important sense, because, while knowledge is accumulating, such accumulation has been characteristic of modern society for some time without leading to fundamental break (Modernist Continuity); or
4. That there is as yet no distinct cyberspace in any important knowledge-related sense, because while a change in basic understanding of knowledge is characteristic of contemporary society, the character of knowledge has not changed in general, only our understanding of what knowledge is (and has always been; Non-Modernist Continuity).

One must be able to specify which claim is valid before being able to use the phrase "knowledge society" meaningfully, let alone talk about knowledge as "the prime factor of production" in cyberspace.

A Cyborg Anthropology Alternative:
Realist Actor Network Theory

In keeping with my situated skepticism, I find the Non-Modernist continuity alternative (#4) currently most plausible. Nonetheless, I believe empirical research on knowledge in cyberspace should be conducted in a manner that could conceivably justify the other alternatives. However, without knowing what we mean by "knowledge," having a serviceable knowledge construct, can we conclude anything at all about the character of knowledge in cyberspace?

To avoid this logical paradox, I offer the following "rethinking" of Actor Network Theory. ANT has a justifiably importance in social studies of technoscience. Although originally skeptical of it as theory, I became convinced of ANT's analytic value through the work of scholars like Ann Saetnan (1993) and Vicki Singleton (1993), who use ANT to illuminate developments in particular technologies in ways which foster comparison. Yet ANT remains controversial and has achieved little analytical cumulation. A reconstruction of ANT along realist (RANT) as opposed to textualist (TANT) lines could change this; it is outlined below and briefly illustrated in relation to the creation of international information infrastructures (IIIs).

STRENGTHS OF ACTOR NETWORK THEORY

ANT developed initially to provide a more satisfactory answer to the question, what is a technology? Rather than answer in the terms of the popular culture's equation of technologies with machines, ANT argues for conceptualizing technologies as actor networks (TANs), complexes of relationships among human and nonhuman—artifactual, organizational, and other life-formal—entities (see Callon 1986). From the perspective of ANT, the construction of a particular technological network or "system" is an active process. "Competing" actants-would-be-actors recruit other potential network participants into coalitions. Successful recruitment has to do with contextually relevant rhetorics and power and cannot be reduced to either transcendent external "reality" or internal "agency" alone. While not necessarily systemic, stable TANs have discernible trajectories. These trajectories are strongly influenced by the agency of those entities who/which become actors, active agents in the production and reproduction of the network.

Methodologically, ANT developed out of the attempt of STS scholars to free themselves of presentist or "Whiggish" readings of the history of technoscience, to be more "Kuhnian." To the extent that they refuse to explain the past in terms of the present, such studies are methodologically relativist. On ANT it is equally improper to privilege one type of actant—the human—over others in terms of their potential and actual agency; that is, their capacity to be "actors" as well as actant entities. Hence, another important ANT methodological premise is the potential for nonhuman agency.

CRITIQUES OF ANT

What is it that limits the value of actor network theory, and what might be done to expand its generalization value? Some of the responsibility for the failure of ANT to lead to cumulative knowledge of cyberspace can be traced to forms of its practice overly affected by Postmodernist presumptions. Textualism—the notion that social interaction is essentially linguistic or is only graspable linguistically—is a common postmodern position. It is sometimes justified ontologically but more generally, epistemologically. In a textualist reading, all that is available are various accounts—stories—of events; there is no way to operationalize the asking of questions about the correspondence between any given story and the events which it purports to represent.

Steve Woolgar (1993) and Keith Grint (1991), for example, approach technology as purely the production of situated texts. Since there are no grounds for preferring one interpretation over any other, social study of technology can only be interpretive rather than empirical. For example, explicit in Grint's attempt to write a sociology of work is the deep rejection of any structural theory and therefore ethnology: Because each experience of technology is constructed through the interpretations of specific text constructors, no generalizations about work beyond its diversity can be made. Since any actor network can only be apprehended semiotically, all attempts to identify similarities among forms of work—Bravermanite, structural/functional, Marxist, organizational cultural—fall before a radical relativism.

Rob Kling (1992a,b) identifies one difficulty that follows from such a theory in his polemic with Grint and Woolgar (1992) in the pages of *Science, Technology, and Human Values*. The critique, which Kling shares with Langdon Winner (1992) and others who refer to themselves as "political constructivists," is that radical interpretivism marginalizes the study of power and exploitation—such as whether new computing technology will tend to support community resistance to those organizations that use it to marginalize workers and peasants.

Textualist presumptions similarly limit an analyst's ability to intervene at the level of policy. Textualist ANTs cannot easily move beyond the limits of the particular case. As separate narratives, they fall before the standard criticism of abstract functionalisms, which ultimately amount merely to the claim that things are the way they are because, if they weren't, they'd be different.

In a critique similar to that of the political constructivists, Steve Brown and Nick Lee (1993) identify in ANT an implicit liberal politics of agency. In their desire to dethrone the presumption that agency is exclusively human, ANTers have a priori substituted a radical democracy of agency. Yet this inverted agency presumption is just as much an essentialist master narrative as the Modernist limitation of agency to the human.

A GENERAL ANT

A general theory of techno-science knowledge would allow us to differentiate analytically what it is that makes

1. Some actor networks stable and others transitory;
2. Some capable of living up to their promotional hype and others incapable;
3. Some realize their potential for new forms of activity and others not;
4. Some create new alliances and others only reuse old;
5. Some elicit new forms of agency and others not; and
6. Some change the expressions of power and others merely replicate the pre-existing forms.

The search for such empirically grounded generalizations is a legitimate part of any disciplined investigation (in Scandinavian "*vetenskap*" or German "*wissenschaft*" versus Anglo-Saxon "science"). *Pace* textualism, ANT methodological premises do not preclude such generalization. To say that techno-science can be read as text does not mean that techno-science is "only" text. Thus, the way forward is to eliminate presumptive textualism from ANT.

The methodological rejection of presentism and human-only agency as initial analytic stances does not necessarily imply permanent analytic agnosticism. That is, even though the truthfulness of a particular techno-scientific proposition is not established merely by its historical acceptance, analysis of techno-science must in some way come to terms with reality, albeit one constructed in social ways. I believe techno-science studies best respond to current critiques via active construction of alternative scientific accounts, which means a more complex relationship with reality than that of textualism.

For example, several critics of textualist ANT have attempted to develop more sophisticated arguments for some relative privileging of human agency. Harry Collins (1993), for example, refers to RAT (repair, attribution, and all that) as among the essential agency activities that in practice primarily humans bring to TANs.

Textualist presumptions are an important target of Michel Callon and John Law's recent (1993) attempt at a more materialist rendition of ANT. They argue, for example, that the slogan that "everything is text; there is only discourse" is based on the faulty assumption that "because texts are opaque, there is *nothing* beyond the text." Instead, Callon and Law wish us to "imagine chains or networks of representation" which extend into the opacity.

AN ALTERNATIVE, REALIST ANT

In attempting to specify how to conceive of these chains, Callon and Law retain an implicit texualism. The networks, the "chains which make the things, the texts, and the people" remain "representational"; they are described as "chains of translation" (p. 10). Such textualism is not, however, essential to Callon and Law's overall approach. They go on at some length:

> [W]e need to avoid the trap of imagining that discourse is a closed universe. If we go that way, it leads us to a form of monist idealism. Instead we need to broaden this notion of signification or representation. To allow that representations come in all kinds of more or less hybrid material forms. Some of which have little to do with language.
>
> [T]here are other ways of producing signification than through the use of language. . . . [R]epresentation in language may be different and distinctive. But [other] representation, chains of translation in other material forms, are not [to be] treated as second class citizens (p. 11).

Since it is clear that what is "translated" is not just or merely a linguistic phenomenon, a term like "transformative linkages" might be more appropriate than "signification," "representation," or "translation," a position which I understand Callon to accept (personal conversation).

In any case, the general point is about the need for more consistently realist ANT. Recent forms of Marxist realism, most notably those associated with Roy Bhasker (1989), offer a philosophy that can fruitfully develop ANT. For example, Kate Soper (1993) has applied a Marxist realist problematic in her investigations of ecology as a social movement as well as a scientific discipline. Chapter 2 showed how Marxist realism provides a serviceable theory of causation.

Realist ontologies embrace the existence of an external reality beyond human discourse, while realist epistemologies hold that this reality is substantially open to empirical study. Unlike empiricism, the naive Modernist realism which underlies so much natural science discourse, the materialist realism of scholars like Bhasker, recognizes the role of human action, including discourse, in the construction of reality. Like Callon and Law, these forms of realism also reject ontologies of simple correspondence: "There isn't a reality on the one hand, and a *representation* of that reality on the other" (p. 11; emphasis in original).

Realists like Burrows (1987) avoid reductionism by distinguishing among various levels of reality. The empirical or "immediately grasped through the senses" level of external stimuli is distinguished from the "actual." This is composed of the structures that underlie the actions that stimulate. In turn, the actual is distinguishable from the underlying "really real" generative processes.

This deeply real level, while removed from the actual, leaves traces that are discernible in political economic structures.

In "reproductionist" Marxist realism (Hakken 1987), such levels are understood to be related dialectically in that, for example, certain developments at the level of the actual can have a cumulative impact on the underlying real generative processes. As malleably real, they are only relatively transcendent. Such a perspective is usable by the anthropologist attempting to evaluate claims about major social transformations like the CR (Hakken 1991).

THE BENEFITS OF RANTING

The analytic value of a realist ANT (RANT) can be seen in relation to the issue of nonhuman agency. The material consequences of their history, not just human interpretations of them, also explain why some artifacts become the focus of a complex network, actors in a TAN manifest at the actual level. Sufficiently stable, actual-level TANs may even impact the generative "real." This is the way technologies have "real" impacts—mediated by, but not reducible to, the discourses through which humans apprehend, and influence, TAN reproduction. In RANT, it makes sense to talk of the agency of nonhuman entities in TANs, that such networks can be transformed—not just translated—by nonhuman actors. Sufficiently materialist RANTs are the way for cyberspace studies to escape the limitations of textualism (in particular and philosophical idealism in general).

RANT is also an advantage when confronting an issue that is of particular concern to political constructivists, whether technologies have politics. On the one hand, overly rigid arguments that particular politics are strongly built into technologies—as in the case, for example, of what Langdon Winner calls *Autonomous Technology* (1977)—come close to rejecting basic constructivist insights: that technologies are both initially constructed socially, and that reconstruction occurs repeatedly. On the other hand, to minimize the extent to which technologies have particular trajectories amounts to embracing the "technology is neutral"—guns don't kill people, and so on—arguments of those who would marginalize the relevance of social process in the realm of technology.

On RANT, however, the relative degree of autonomy of any particular TAN can be analyzed in terms of its manifestations in the various moments of reality (empirical, actual, and/or generatively real) in which it is implicated. This perspective can be used to sharpen Harry Braverman's (1974) core insight regarding technology in capitalist workplaces. Empirically, capitalists tend to select technologies that enhance their class power while eroding workers' control. The result is an actual, secular tendency toward the degradation of work in the employment-based labor process. There are of course other reproductive dynamics in the workspace, such as workers' resistances, the materiality of physical substances, and the understandings of science and technology. These must all be considered in analyzing what is the underlying, generative, or real structure of work in any era, including cyberspace.

Bryan Pfaffenberger (1992) urges us to see the technological systems embedded in artifacts as the outcome of previous political struggles, but to see these struggles themselves as framed in symbolic, textual discourses. On this reading, technologies have material, determinant qualities precisely because they embody the momentum of previous human activity, momentum particularly difficult to change in the short run when an actual TAN—for example, a system of national highways—integrates widely dispersed practices. This view of technological momentum is not incompatible with a perspective which recognizes how current practices can lead to new apprehension of old technologies, the malleability of TANs strongly emphasized in the Nordic scholarship of Berg and Lie (1993). Still, as argued by Donna Haraway (1994), it is the limitations on human action constituted by such momentums that justify the attribution of "agency" to the nonhuman components of technology actor networks.

AN ILLUSTRATION: A RANT ON INTERNATIONAL INFORMATION INFRASTRUCTURES

On a technicist reading, the main problem in creating an "international information infrastructure" (III) is inventing the right equipment—faster switches, and transmitters capable of handling broader band width. On TANT, such readings are themselves explicable as a rhetorical strategy, but TANT provides no insight as to why they are dominant. Nor does TANT offer much on which to build less impoverished and sterile alternative policy approaches to IIIs.

In contrast, RANT directs attention to the actual experience of system developers, those actually working on the creation of these systems. When one confronts the problem of how to make information practices in one organization compatible with those in another—a basic problem in creating a broadly accessible network—one begins to see the extent to which the building of large information infrastructures demands *both* greater autonomy and increased standardization. RANT helps us see why: Before actual workers will actually take advantage of the capabilities of such media of communication, they generally need a concrete sense of its value to them, such as access to information in other organizations (Hakken 1993). For such senses to emerge, however, workers in different organizations need the autonomy to explore and develop their work collectively. Yet information can only be shared by machines if it comes in predictable forms.

To the technicist, this means standardization, a reading only reinforced by TANT, which expects hegemonic discourses. Technicism sees autonomy and standardization as antithetical, and similarly TANT sees them as mutually exclusive alternative texts. RANT, however, is better able to accept the necessity of both imperatives and thus support design solutions that address both simultaneously. Concepts like open system architecture, evolutionary system development, user participation in system development, and object-oriented design at a minimum provide names for the kinds of relationships which must inevitably be a part of real world solutions to the III problem. Such perspectives also increase our collective ability to address contexts of computing, like class, gender, and race/ethnicity, which extend beyond organizational boundaries.

The Practice Question in Cyberspace Ethnography

There are also practical reasons for being clearer about knowledge in cyberspace; for example, when trying to put a college course "on-line." Investigating changes in knowledge, ethnographers find themselves *participating in* as well as describing the cultural construction of cyberspace. What can one say in general about the practice question in cyberspace ethnography, especially about the ethics of such participation?

Any research connection to practice is ethically risky, because dominant social forces encourage constructions of "the practical" which reproduce their dominance, to which researchers can be subjected. Moreover, to avoid "Hawthorne Effects," ethnographers try to limit their participation to "normal" performances, not interventions. Possibly affecting the course of specially directed or overt efforts at cultural reproduction is of particular concern to an empirical discipline like anthropology that employs participation in cultural performance as a key method.

Because cyberspace is so notional—that is, the material constraints upon cultural practice are so highly mediated—it is even more difficult for the cyberspace ethnographer to participate actively in its performance and yet claim not to influence overtly its production. Thus, applied cyberspace anthropologists face particularly acute scientific as well as ethical challenges.

THE COMPLEX PROFESSIONAL POLITICS OF APPLIED CYBERSPACE ETHNOGRAPHY: AN EXAMPLE

In general, computer professionals agree that new AIT systems should "integrate the human and technical sides." The problems occur over how *in practice* to use knowledge of the social dimensions of AIT. I experienced just how treacherous this gap between rhetoric and practice is in a 1980s Disability Technology Project (DTP; a pseudonym). Its purpose was to develop a computerized system for people whose disabilities were so severe that they could not access most assistive technologies. DTP aimed to use a new generation of technology controlled through eye movement, based on helicopter night-flying hardware, to provide a general "front end" for access.

Writing the application, I designed the project to be "culture-centered" in two ways. One was the inclusion of an advisory panel of consumers with disabilities from a local Independent Living center; this involvement was an important consideration for the funding agent, the state technology foundation. A second form of culture-centered practice was the placement of an anthropologist (myself) as principle investigator (PI) on the project. I hoped to perform a traditional role in applied anthropology, that of a "broker" among multiple worlds:

- The consumers,
- The funding agency,
- The other academic staff of the project, a professor of electrical engineering technology and a graduate student and a professor in computer science
- The staff of the Independent Living center,
- The military agency supporting the project through access to facilities,
- The vendors supplying the hardware, and
- Potential future system vendors.

The project collapsed, due to difficulties that in retrospect were entirely predictable. The academic computer science/engineering staff conceptualized the project in strictly technical terms, the panelists being sources of inspiration rather than full participants. A long discussion at a panel meeting of various ways to approach the system was dismissed at the end by one academic staff member: "What is this project about, anyway; just talk, or are we serious about a system?"

The panelists with disabilities had been selected because they were experienced, knowledgeable users of computer-based disability technologies, but they performed "a lack of interest in technical details." Developing a "wish list" for what the system should do, they deferred to technical staff to decide what was possible. While the project depended upon their being "actors," panel members eventually adopted a "dependent" role complementing the "expert" presumptions of the technologists.

Just how untenable my role had become was revealed in a controversy over an interim report. Unable to get input from the other academic staff, I had drafted the report more or less on my own. My draft, based on brief conversations and numerous assurances that we were effectively meeting project objectives, was denounced as "worthless." One staff person refused to discuss the "blatant errors" of the working draft to correct them because such a document "should not be written by someone from Arts and Sciences." A discussion over whether the technical objectives of the project were being met—talk which seemed to me to involve disagreement among the technical staff—was cut short, implying that such discussion was inappropriate within the presence of someone not technically qualified. Ultimately, two interim reports were submitted, one "technical" and one "nontechnical," and I resigned as PI.

ANTHROPOLOGY OF VS. ANTHROPOLOGY IN COMPUTING

To answer the practice question in cyberspace ethnography, one should begin with assessment of the already considerable experience of cyberspace ethnographers, including those in anthropology. In order to do so, however, one must first distinguish between study of the anthropology *of* cyberspace and a narrower discussion of the uses of cyber-artifacts *in* anthropology—such as using computers in anthropological data gathering, analysis, or communication. In the 1980s, discussion of the latter overwhelmed that of the former, and my attempts to promote the former were often misapprehended as an interest in the latter. While I did not wish to denigrate computing in anthropology, I did wish to legitimate a separate, cultural issue that was being displaced by them.[2]

APPLIED VS. BASIC RESEARCH IN THE ANTHROPOLOGY OF COMPUTING

By 1995, however, the anthropology of computing/cyberspace was getting attention. At the annual AAA meetings, sessions on CMC, community computing, cyborgs, and techno-science seemed to be everywhere; indeed, the meeting theme was "New Communities, New Modes of Communication." Because an anthropology *of* computing has finally differentiated itself from computing *in* anthropology, the applied anthropology of computing/cyberspace can now be differentiated as a special form of computing or cyberspace anthropology.

While differentiating between basic and applied perspectives has long been a part of academics, the value of such differentiations is being currently questioned. First, any such distinction tends to be supportive of elitism. The differentiation between science and technology first articulated by the Greeks, for example, paralleled that between a free member of the polis and a slave. Within anthropology, the basic/applied distinction continues to carry a similar invidious social evaluation and is thus to some extent suspect.

A second critique of the basic/applied distinction builds on STS-inspired ethnographies and histories of science, a common trope of which is demonstration of the deep dependence of science on technology. It turns out in practice to be much more difficult to differentiate scientific from technological activity than is presumed in the standard science narrative, where *de novo* scientific discoveries are only later given material form in technology. Because instead most scientific "discoveries" depend upon use of preexisting artifacts to construct new "facts" (see Traweek 1988), presumptive science/technology or basic/applied distinctions are more ideological than real. The term "techno-science" is to be preferred precisely because it avoids the presumptive priority of science over technology.

A third element of the critique, again drawing from STS, is that the differentiations actually made in practice between "basic" and "applied" are quite arbitrary and serve primarily bureaucratic, hierarchical purposes. Indeed, C. Wright Mills' characterization of the "practical men" of American business, and their academic sycophants, as "crackpot realists" (1959) neatly highlights some implications of standard "practicalist"rhetorics. As part of a more general questioning of the privileged position which science claims in contemporary social reproduction, all three critiques further complicate understanding of the role of applied knowledge in cyberspace.

RECONSTRUCTING THE BASIC/APPLIED DISTINCTION

Still, their general knowledge of cyberspace, which allows them to give cyberspace imaginings an empirical grounding, means basic ethnographers have something of value for those more active in its construction. Indeed, making sure that they have something to say is essential to maintaining access to the field site. Moreover, just as time for basic research, in general or practice settings, is of value to the practitioner, respect and time for practice applied research and cyberspace practice are equally important for good basic research.[3] Cyberspace ethnography, in short, needs a balanced development of its basic and applied aspects.

Teaching in a Bachelor of Arts degree program with an applied focus, I regularly focus student attention to applied perspectives as distinct from basic ones, and visa versa. To do this while also acknowledging the problems and critiques cited here, I have been compelled to replace the simple basic/applied distinction and expand it to differentiate among four ethnographic activities with different objectives:

- Basic research,
- Basic applied research,
- Practice applied research, and
- Practice.

In basic ethnography, the primary interest is in learning something about the world of human/cyborg action, what its dynamics are like independent of any specific deliberate interventions other than to learn. Most traditional anthropological ethnography is framed in this manner. The NNCP, for example, aimed to learn about the way computing is culturally constructed by comparing this activity in Norway and Sweden.

In my typology, "practice" is the opposite of basic research; it is activity intended to intervene in—rather than merely to learn about—individual, group, or social formation reproduction. However, all ethnographers, including those with basic orientations, often find themselves in practice settings. This is because such settings offer good entree into the cultural practices they wish to study, especially the activities in which they wish to participate most actively. "Basic-oriented applied research" is activity intended primarily to test or in some other way contribute to basic rather than practical (or professional) understandings, but it happens to be actually located within somebody's "interventions."

An example of basic applied research would be Barbara and my work while in Norway on education for Participatory Design. Our interest was not primarily to improve such education. Rather, we wished to test our understanding of differences between computing in the United States and in Norway by comparing and contrasting the ways educators trained students interested in similar careers. If asked, we would have hoped that what we learned would have practical value for educators, but getting knowledge of this type was not our chief motivation. Much of the research of anthropologists in high tech organizations—that of the ethnography group at Xerox PARC—is basic applied research.[4]

In contrast, "practice applied research" aims primarily to help interveners to obtain practical goals, as by separating out more effective from less effective strategies. Much evaluation research falls into this category. Such practice-oriented research often involves formalizing the tacit knowledge of practitioners in a field. Barbara and I attempted to get such knowledge in our interviews with Norwegian systems developers about user involvement in ISD.

An example of my fourth activity, "practice" or "direct intervention in social reproduction," is the RSSAIT project. While I did learn something about how *not* to practice cyberspace ethnography, my main object was different: to help the Oneida County Department of Mental Health use advanced information technology to develop a new system for service delivery.

A cyberspace ethnographic discourse vigorous in all four arenas but particularly with a clear take on practice issues will promote less schizoid research (and researchers!) and will have the most to say to both the project manager and the social critic. Separating these four moments from each other is not always easy,[5] but when, as in the NNCP, they are *not* muddled together, they can relate symbiotically. It is when they are not differentiated—when we try to treat practice-oriented applied as if it were basic-oriented—that we become confused about practice.

AN ILLUSTRATION: THE APPLIED CYBERSPACE ETHNOGRAPHY OF INFORMATION SYSTEM DEVELOPMENT

The key demonstration arena of these propositions is cyberspace ethnography in Information System Development (ISD), the richest arena of applied cyberspace ethnography, both basic- and practice-oriented research as well as ethnographic practice.

Ethnographically Informed ISD Practice

Nordic ISD's ethnographic sensibilities draw much from the participatory "action research" tradition, in which researchers and "subjects" attempt to construct a collaborative relationship. In the late 1960s, the Norwegian Computing Center joined the Norwegian Work Research Institute (Arbetforshnings Institut, AFI) in a set of action research projects with iron and steel trade unionists. Australian Fred Emery and Norwegian Nils Thorsrud ran these in the British Tavistock socio-technical tradition. These famous projects are often described as demonstrating, besides the threat to social equality which AIT represents, the potential for expanded social democracy that can follow from worker participation in technological decision-making in the workspace. Political activists in the mid-1970s used the results of the iron and steel trades projects to push for major work environment legislation in Norway, Denmark, and Sweden.

This legislative success led to three "second generation" participatory projects—Utopia in Sweden, Demos in Denmark, and Florence in Norway. All were intended to build on while pushing the limits of the new legislation, and all became icons in what is now described around the world as the "Scandinavian" approach to ISD. Of these projects, Florence was the most ethnographic. Named for Florence Nightingale, its purpose was to design a patient tracking and data system for a busy ward in a large urban hospital. In addition to two feminist graduate students in computer science, Gro Bjerknes and Tone Bratteteig, the project leader at the Norwegian Computing Centre, Kristin Nygaard, recruited a social anthropologist, Henrik Sinding-Larsen, onto the Florence team. In addition to its industrial democracy dimensions, the project came into existence at a time when feminist scholars had critiqued the role of techno-science in the reproduction of gender. Thus, the team also hoped to design the system to address power inequities between the largely female nursing staff and the largely male medical doctors. The three active researchers believed that their capacity to build a good system depended upon having a deep understanding of the work of the ward. Gaining this understanding, like all ethnography, depended upon establishing strong relationships with ward staff, and establishing such relationships depended upon confronting directly the power issues in the work and always implicated in ISD. The system ultimately developed, despite numerous hardware, staffing, and organizational issues, has been cited as demonstrating both the liberatory potential of user involvement in ISD and the technical superiority of systems in which users have substantial impact on design. Florence represents a particularly strong example of practice-oriented applied cyberspace ethnography.

As efforts to incorporate study of existing user practice directly into ISD, demonstration projects like Florence spawned practice-oriented ISD ethnography. An awareness that ISD is dialectical (Bjerknes 1993; Dahlbom and Mathiessen 1993) supported this relational posture. ISD professionals like those in the "information technology in practice" (ITIP) group at the Norwegian Computing Center had long seen the frame of individuals with single machines as too narrow. They broadened the conception of system development, to be more interactive through time, as in "iterative" system development. Moreover, they recognized that the most difficult problems in system development derive more from group/organizational rather than individual ergonomic, let alone technical, factors. In their view, the history of information technology is less about how IT changes organizations than how IT systems manifest organizational change.

Lucy Suchman's work is an example of a related U.S. tradition of ethnographically sensitive ISD. Built on a communications-informed (see Terry Winograd and Fernando Flores 1986) reading of ethnography, Suchman played a key role during the 1980s in bringing the Scandinavian work, especially Florence, to American attention. In *Plans and Situated Actions* (1987), Suchman demonstrates the poverty of cognitive science models of technical human action, arguing instead that human–machine interaction is not transcendent but "situated" in particular social constructions of the moment. Suchman argues that cognitive science models that presume decisions based on premeditated understandings systematically misapprehend communication and action. Julian Orr's work (1996) makes similarly useful cultural contributions to work practice in technologically rich environments.

Such orientations have become institutionalized in Xerox Palo Alto Research Center (PARC) ethnography. PARC was founded by Xerox Corporation as an exercise in creative but still product development-oriented RD. Anthropology was only one source of the innovative approach at PARC. Perhaps the key element of PARC ethnography has been respect for the autonomy of the researcher. Slowly, PARC ethnographers developed a well-articulated and documented case approach to ISD which first legitimated and then expanded this respect. Suchman has had a major role in convincing designers of the value of detailed understandings of real work in context. Under her leadership, a growing group of ethnomethodologically oriented cultural anthropologists and linguists have documented initial work practices and how these change with new technology.

Equally central to the Suchman perspective is a broad participatory rather than narrow, efficiency-oriented approach to issues of use. In machine-oriented ISD, humans are compared to information processing machines with programs, control systems, and established routines. In the situated action alternative, humans and machines are collaborators. PARC ethnography has had a founding role in Computer Supported Cooperative Work, where systems support groups of workers in accomplishing a broad range of tasks, as opposed to controlling workers in the execution of tasks dictated in detail from above.

Even if a machine model continues, unfortunately, to dominate most public discourse, PARC anthropologists like Orr, Jeanette Blomberg, Susan Newman, and Susan Irwin Anderson have helped create a situation in which major business policy initiatives—as in, for example, Business Process Reengineering (BPR)—have been forced to confront more cultural orientations.

Further, through work in organizations like Computer Professions for Social Responsibility, the PARCers have also demonstrated that high-profile work in a product development organization is compatible with activism in relation to the broader social dimensions of technological change and collective intervention to address them. In addition to building a continuous body of projects at PARC, the approach of Suchman and her colleagues has inspired the actual systems development work of other units in Xerox and in other organizations, like the Institute for Research on Learning and NYNEX Science and Technology. Within the Association for Computing Machinery in the United States and the Europe-based International Federation for Information Processing, it is now a common practice to draw attention to the importance of "the human element."

Such both basic and practice-oriented applied research is thus an important way in which cyberspace ethnography intersects with ISD. It produces what I call "culture-centered computing" (1991), or the use of a cultural perspective as a basis for intervention when the computers come. As consultants, Adam Koons and Ken Novak (1992) introduce a computer system that improves quality of production and work life in a Cameroon telecommunications facility. The practicing computing anthropology of David Novick and Wynn (1992), Suchman's with Randell Trigg (1991), and Patricia Sachs (1995) often addresses development of computing artifacts and systems under the rubric of Participatory Design (see Muller et al. 1991). PD has gradually evolved into a full-fledged alternative approach to ISD. Jeanette Blomberg is another anthropologist who does CSCW, developing systems that enhance the ability of groups to work collectively.

The initial user-oriented research projects convinced ISD theorists like Pelle Ehn (1988) to describe his preferred approach as anthropological, for example, as design oriented to and built around the actual work of the workers (but see Hakken 1990). More recently, ethnography has been integrated into usability testing as well, to help understand the work of professional system developers as well as providing insight in both the "old" and the new, computer-mediated work processes. Incorporating an ethnographic moment into ISD makes sense, because some mechanism must be found to transfer user knowledge of the work process into the system. One finds, for example, considerable discussion about ethnography in systems development today, skill with ethnography being advertised as important for at least some jobs with Microsoft.

Differences and Effective Ethnographer/Professional ISD Collaboration

The integration of ethnography into the practice of ISD is only partial, however. While the PARCers have succeeded in developing a number of tools with which to document both computer-mediated and non-computer-mediated work processes, their demonstration of viable methodologies has not been paralleled by extensive analytic influence. As in sociology, techniques of micro-observation based on ethnomethodology have not led to a substantial change in general understanding or of issues with policy relevance, like the extent to which computer mediation does or does not transform the labor process. In an even more relevant applied sense, while the PARC tradition has documented the important tacit knowledge of especially female workers, this knowledge has seldom been mobilized effectively to defend these workers' stake in the labor process. Nor has the cyberethnographic tradition at PARC easily found a comfortable place in mainstream product development; indeed, its practitioners have often resisted "crossing the line" and are perceived to be hesitant about "getting their hands dirty." Perhaps it is the way PARCers articulate their commitment to participatory methods of research that has emphasized the pessimistic picture of usability in Human-Computer Interaction studies. These are framed as approaches to be avoided rather than practices to be influenced (Allwood and Hakken n.d.).

While the research tradition at NR has involved crossing the line into development of actual systems, this experience has not always been happy. One problem in Florence was a dispute over the basis of claims to knowledge. The issue arose most strongly over which of the team members—the feminist researchers or the anthropologist—was the better understander/defender of the interests of the female nurses, a clash over whether situated, gender/politics-based or discipline-based knowledge claims had priority.

A related conflict emerged over the issue of producing a functioning information system. The ethnographer's general tendency to recognize, even to glory in, the ambiguity of practice collided head-on with the developers' professional imperative to standardize representations as a necessary prerequisite to using machines to mediate human activity. While the developers wanted the ethnographer to share fully responsibility for arriving at the best possible system in the given circumstances, the ethnographer opted for the role of *project therapeut* or project therapist. Even in Florence, where there was an unusually high degree of commitment and control, achieving an adequate level of coordination between the ethnographic and professional practice moments was a major difficulty.

As demonstrated by Forsythe (1993), much ISD continues to be based on technicist formal models. It fails because it misses important social aspects of human interaction, such as the informal aspects of work.[6] Lucas was one of the first to make this argument from within computer science in his attempt to address *Why Information Systems Fail* (1975). Enid Mumford's Tavistock-based "socio-technical approach" to development (1979) was an advance over "machine-centered" approaches, but it remained marked by a tendency to take organizational structure as a given rather than as a dynamic element itself subject to change.

Collaboration or Colonization?

James Nyce and Jonas Loewgren (1995) think the typical ISD appropriation of ethnography is much too narrow. Ethnography has only been used to describe action and behavior, but not for analytic perspectives on system development, what they call "foundational analysis." This latter "starts with questions about categories, meaning, and intention" (p. 39) in order to move beyond description. Nyce and Loewgren are equally critical of the few ethnographers who publish in the HCI/usability literature, who "also seem to ignore foundational issues" (p. 41). Many view the cost-related preference for "quick and dirty" rather than long-term ethnography as another important limitation.

Thus, willingness to "integrate the human and technical sides" does not in itself provide sufficient guidance on how to do ethnography in ISD. Indeed, cyborg anthropology would suggest that, because it implies the bringing together of distinct entities, approaching the issue as one of integration is to misframe the problem.

The decennial "Computers in Context" (CiC) conferences in Aarhus, Denmark, provide a good indicator of the state of ethnographic ISD. These conferences have been a public demonstration of the commitment of at least some Nordic, European, and American informaticians to the notion that theirs is not just a technical practice. Because it is a social activity, ISD should include users and other professionals who specialize in understanding social relations.

The changes in tone from one CiC conference to the next also offer a useful indicator of just how much (or how little) educators and leading practitioners in the field expect a social perspective to accomplish. The 1975 Conference reflected the militancy of broad public agitation for co-determination and other laws, which were expected to direct technological development. The 1985 Conference stressed development of specific programs, whereas the third, 1995 conference took as its title "Joining Forces in Design." Its underlying theme was the necessity to professionalize systems development. What is expected clearly changes over time, and it is thus hard to specify the permanent ethnographic impact on ISD practice.

Continuing Epistemological Differences Hamper Culture-Centered Computing

Views differ today on how well anthropologists and computer professionals work together in ISD. Henry Lundsgaarde (1992) sees himself as a full participant. My difficulties on the Disability Technology Project were far from unique, however. How can one explain lingering difficulties in constructing effective collaborations?

Narrow professionalism is one possible explanation, as in the claim that the writing of an interim report on technical matters can only be done by a person credentialled technically. From this perspective, problems of collaboration are comparable to trade union disputes over job demarcation, overlaid by academically conflicting knowledge claims. Such difficulties can be overcome at least in theory by selecting personnel more confident of their position and motivated more broadly.

Yet the staff on the Disability Technology Project, like those on Bader's and Nyce's educational initiatives, was credentialled and highly motivated. An alternative explanation draws on a linguistic reading of C.P. Snow's famous "two cultures" distinction (1969): Problems are essentially failures of communication which follow from differences in the way people use words. Such problems can be overcome through more effective translation between "technical" and "humanistic" language, the restating of equivalent propositions in appropriate technical jargons.

However, the problems described here were not primarily differences in jargon. Attempts to find equivalent language, of which there were several, were not fruitful. Attempts to present an argument for culture-centered computing to my technological institute colleagues generally encounter two linked responses. One is, "Oh, we already do that, by setting up user groups," and so on. The other is to see culture-centered computing as a thinly veiled political agenda, a sociological (read socialist) attack on the academic power structure, military domination of RD spending, etc. Often, it feels like colleagues just don't see the point; we're talking about different things, not just using different words.

Despite several years of working on implementation of systems for educational computing, Bader and Nyce (1991) argue that difference in epistemologies severely limit collaboration; the problems are as much philosophical as professional and linguistic. Culture-centered practice may be incompatible with current design practice because the framing of this practice systematically misconceives it as purely about artifacts. Since this framing is preconscious, the aspects of the computing process they impact are mostly inaccessible to examination. Forsythe found herself having to repeat the same critique of epistemological presumptions while trying to use ethnography to build effective AI systems. Blomberg and Suchman (1992) are notable for the extent to which their work supporting technology development for pretechnologized labor processes has included a nuanced critique of its politics.

Extensive study of system development in both Scandinavia and the U.S. has led Suchman, for example, to suggest that epistemological differences radically undermine much ostensibly collaborative ISD (for example, CSCW) in workspaces. She argues that only approaches that systematically raise episte-mological presumptions for examination, and that actively attempt to co-construct an epistemology shared by users and developers, have the potential for effectively supporting cooperative work. She finds models for such activity in certain forms of feminist practice.

Austrian Ina Wagner has had similar experiences (Egger and Wagner 1993). Projects to provide sophisticated on-line communication support have been blocked by powerful groups. For example, a system to schedule surgery in a teaching hospital was blocked by the surgeons, who were unhappy with hav-ing their whereabouts becoming common knowledge. Wagner and Suchman reject systems that force rigid formalizations of practices, offering alternatives that support rather than undermine the constant negotiation characteristic of relations between professions in a hospital or law office. The alternatives in-volve automating awareness of decision point relationships rather than the de-cisions themselves. Such systems create opportunities to discuss power, rather than hiding it in automated applications. Information systems focus, rather than replace, human action.

Guidelines for Ethnographically Informed ISD

In sum, those anthropologists most visible in ISD are generally skeptical of their professional influence on most ISD. My post hoc examination of at-tempts at interdisciplinary cooperation in ISD like Florence helped explain why this is so. By and large, the discourses on ethnography in ISD among pro-fessional systems developers remain distinct from those among anthropological ethnographers. Feminist standpoint theory can be helpful in accounting for these dynamics, but the problems incorporating such theorizing into practice remain daunting.

Still, applied cyberspace ethnography allows projection of some program-matic notions about how best to do holistic ISD:

1. Development work should be preceded by broad analysis, involv-ing the frank discussion of both workers and managers about pre-existing organizational dynamics. Particular attention should be given to separating out truly needed information from "needs" which are simply institutionalizations of the reproduction patterns encouraged by occupational cultures.
2. Because of the dangers of the "dazzle" effect—presuming that the best solutions are the most technological—models of information needs should at first be formulated independent from computer options.
3. Consideration of computing options should only begin after all groups involved have requisite knowledge, and decision-making

should be "culture-centered" and collaborative. This means taking into account the broader social dynamics within which individuals and organizations choose goals and the strategies for achieving them.

4. Prototypes should be developed and tested under real conditions, and redeveloped through several iterations.

Policy Implications of Applied Cyberspace Ethnography

The preceding section addressed applied cyberspace ethnography in particular workspaces. Other practice issues arise at the level of policy.

CULTURE-CENTERED COMPUTING IN SHEFFIELD, ENGLAND

The culture-centered AIT initiatives undertaken here during the 1980s (Hakken 1991) were part of a broader policy of New Municipal Socialism (NMS). On the standard neo-classical approach to local government, policy should only address how to divide that portion of the social surplus which can be diverted for public services without undue impact on the reproduction of capital. That the regional social formation can reproduce adequately is taken for granted. In contrast, institutionalist NMS presumed that the capitalist political economy is in "systemic crisis" and that the local state must also find means, in production as well as consumption, to overcome this problem. By combining an activist local state with new structures for popular participation, the Sheffield and other local authorities were to exercise, in the words of its political leader, "genuine democratic control of total national resources" (Hakken with Andrews 1993).

The attempt to promote new technologies while controlling their consequences was identified by city political leaders as a central arena in which to try NMS: "The challenge for the City Council and the people of Sheffield then, is how to gain control of the ways in which new technology is being introduced in order to protect jobs; how to identify those technologies, skills, and areas of research already present in the city which have growth potential for job-creation in the future; and how to attract and graft on those technologies skills which could help to diversify opportunities and broaden the economic and employment base of the city" (quoted in Hakken with Andrews 1993).

Eventually, the Sheffield AIT program included:

1. With regard to the private sector, the use of local authority grant and loan funds to "develop within Sheffield the technology-based industries which preserve skills and jobs, and draw on Sheffield's resources of knowledge and expertise to develop new employment";

2. The encouragement of a network of AIT-oriented local services, including a product development center, a microsystem center, and a program to develop community computing;

3. Strategic promotion of new information technology within Council departments, including conversion of the Council's own "Computer Panel" into an "Information Technology Panel" to oversee development and implementation of an internal Council AIT strategy;

4. Promotion of both general new technology skills and awareness of potential social consequences through training, education, research, sponsoring of conferences, etc.; and

5. Development with trade unions representing Council workers of a model technology agreement including "no redundancy" (lay-off) and "prior approval"—no implementation without prior trade union negotiation—clauses.

Such computerization policy depended in specific ways upon the success of the Council's general NMS strategy:

- use of loans/grants to encourage socially responsible new technology depended upon a substantial pool of available municipal capital;
- effective development of a technology network implied a proactive planning role for the Council in the local economy;
- successful internal promotion of AIT and development of an effective IT strategy meant effective Council control of the operation of Council Departments;
- promotion of skills and awareness required an effective system for publicity, education, and popular participation; and
- effective operation of the Technology Agreement was only possible with a high level of management/work force cooperation.

ACCOMPLISHMENTS AND SHORTCOMINGS OF NMS/AIT POLICY

Sheffield AIT policies had some positive correlates. For example, case studies of Sheffield businesses indicated only moderate technology-related disemployment; technology-related skill levels even rose in some areas, while they fell in others. Sheffield organizations, particularly worker cooperatives, manifested some quite unique approaches to computerization. A network of technology training, advice, and promotion centers was initiated and developed, giving credence to the idea that Council program officers knew what local economic intervention could accomplish. NIT applications spread, albeit slowly, through

Council departments; some described Sheffield as a leading local authority in this area. Consultation through "Planning for Change," the Technology Agreement, was institutionalized in some departments. Innovative approaches to training, such as the Women's Technology Training Workshop, received national recognition.

In short, Sheffield demonstrated the possibility of a political response at the local level to AIT, not merely a technological one. Technological education was not only about preparing the Sheffield working class for new technology jobs; it also aimed to promote an effective, collective political response to industrial transformation. "Though 'new technology' often evokes feelings of uncontrollable change, we had paradoxically been able to plan our intervention much more systematically in this field than others" (a 1983 Sheffield pamphlet, quoted in Hakken with Andrews, 1993).

In contrast, however, a 1986 pamphlet assessing Sheffield local policy made no reference to AIT policy. When Barbara and I tried in the latter year to talk with Council program officers about AIT policy, they often said it didn't exist. A leading program officer argued that the five initiatives could not "be described as a coherent computerization policy. In the early days we did consider attempting to develop such a thing, but it was quite clear that . . . we lacked the resources to achieve this" (Hakken with Andrews 1993).

With regard to the private sector, the program of municipal capital grants and loans to encourage socially useful incorporation of new technology was largely abandoned, and there was little to suggest that the program ever had much effect on private sector use of new technology. Other attempts to develop a more interventionist role in the local economy for the Council had foundered on a number of difficulties, including the inability of the Department of Employment to develop a meaningful program of research on the local economy. Instead, research activity focused primarily on meeting short-term, agitational needs, such as writing pamphlets in campaigns against the closing or privatization of nationalized steel works located in Sheffield.

Nor did the technology network have a noticeable effect on community politics. Innovative training programs reached only a tiny proportion of the workforce and had only a marginal impact on other parts of the training system, such as the national state-run Industrial Training Boards. A set of conferences on "New Technology: Whose Progress?" was abandoned in the face of a lack of interest in the local trade union community. New technology courses were never popular in the local TUC education scheme, and a Trades' Council discussion group on new technology collapsed.

In sum, a high initial policy profile was given to AIT, but initiative was lost, leading to frustration. By 1986, the Chair of the Council Employment Committee acknowledged that council initiatives in this area would henceforth be restricted more or less to what could be accomplished internally, within the

Council Departments. Yet even here activities proceeded very slowly. The original Council Technology Agreement was the focus of a bitter strike in 1983; after this strike ended, the new "Responding to Change" agreement was implemented unilaterally by managment. Industrial action brought to light some embarrassing facts about council AIT policy, such as the extreme Taylorist conditions endured by data entry clerks in the Treasury Department. While the systems implemented have brought improved service in some areas, in others they ossified preexisting bad information practices.

Council AIT programs focused almost exclusively on questions of hardware rather than the social impacts of computerization. Indeed, a 1987 Council presentation on office automation presumed an axiomatic connection between new information technology and improved quality of worklife. The presentation ignored the negative experience that many council workers had already had with AIT. One knowledgeable officer described the Council's approach as "cobbled together and irrational." Another program officer found herself defending "reactive" planning, saying "each new implementation feeds into the strategy and helps us develop it." AIT development was more or less uncoordinated, implemented separately by chief officers in each Department. AIT tended to be "application," not "information" driven—that is, people saw themselves as implementing discrete types of systems, such as word processing or electronic filing, rather than beginning with a notion of maximizing the sharing of the kinds of data required for general organizational purposes.

The IT Panel, the political/administrative vehicle which was supposed to oversee the progressive NIT policy, remained primarily a "talking shop," partly because it was never given spending authority. The Council's inability to plan contributed to the development of increased skepticism about what could be achieved in terms of progressive AIT. In a 1987 interview regarding AIT policy, the new Leader of the Labour Group on the Council chose to justify policy development strictly in terms of improved service to citizens, not quality of work life or influencing private sector practice.

ALTERNATIVE PERSPECTIVES ON AIT POLICY

While policy based on applied cyberspace ethnography is possible, and one can point to real projects—in British local governments, Scandinavian nations, and U.S. communities—where it is applied well, such policy has seldom has broad impact. What follows are some suggestions to remedy this situation:

Replace Hardware-Oriented Information Technology Policy with Network-Oriented Information Policy

Compu*ting* policy need not be compu*ter* policy. Too much public AIT policy is preoccupied with hardware, with too little regard for how machines fit into evolving technology actor networks, let alone their longer-term social correlates. The initial Clinton proposals for a national information infrastructure, like the "infobahn" ideas from Bildt in Sweden, were almost all about hardware—the "roads" themselves and how to make money off building them, not the reasons for using them.

As Ivar Solheim of the NR argues (1992), it is information policy, policy to promote more effective use of information, rather than information technology policy, which is needed. Similarly, network- rather than artifact-oriented policy focuses on what blocks the sharing of information and removing it. Such more strategic orientations have meant a switch for those concerned with disability technology in Sweden away from promoting local production of particular artifacts and toward making open, universal design standard in European AIT.

Replace "Searching for the One Best Way" with "Multiculturalism"

Guessing which hardware architecture is most likely to become the proprietary standard has proven to be very risky in AIT. Artifacts evolve rapidly and in unexpected ways because of the unpredictability of the end-use situation and the tendency for powerful institutions to influence human behavior as strongly as any techo-logic. Indeed, the AIT world continues to be, in anthropological perspective, deliciously ambiguous. How should policy come to terms with in such a world?

As argued by Hanseth (1997), a strategic approach to standards need not mean a mindless, Taylorite commitment to standardization. We should prepare for diversity rather than reinforce prior structurings, whether secure-merely-because-familiar nostrums, centralized national policies, or domineering transnational corporations. We need to support arrays of possibilities, grounded in recognition that there may just not be "one best way." Following Wallace's model of culture, the proper role for policy is to support development of AIT mazeways capable of handling the likely broad diversity of information practices. The proper metaphor for ISD, contend Sumner and Stoltze (1995), is what American carpenters call a "toolbelt," a device which fits around the waist and thus makes an array of frequently used tools accessible. Policy should aim to facilitate translation across diverse practices, to help establish open standards.

To be effective, such a multicultural AIT policy must be articulated with the specifics of each workspace, which presupposes better workplace ethnography. This is a point where the Scandinavian tradition of action research is particularly relevant (see Qvale 1992). Older approaches, even TQM, BPR, and the other applied organizational culture movements, promote Positivist uniformity and thus simplistic understandings of work. Newer organizational narratives see diversity as an AIT advantage and resource, monoculturalism as a drawback.

For example, the Swedish pop music industry is, in relative terms, quite successful, although not as much as the American one. At the risk of being simplistic, one could describe these industries as follow diverse strategies, one "cultureless," the other "culturefull." For the Swedes, the approach has been to develop an "international" style, to the point where most American teenagers have only a vague idea that groups such as "Roxette" or "Ace of Base" are Swedish. American pop music, in contrast, continues to mine rich seams of ethnic experience, especially African American. Better connections to the points where culture is generated are an ultimate source of the greater viability of the American product in the marketplace. American ISD, like the Swedish music industry, is vulnerable because its abstract pursuit of "one best way" interferes with connecting to real ethno-genesis.

Appropriately Balance the National and the Global

A multicultural approach to AIT justifies flexible national policies to support networking among diverse initiatives. One should expect each national AIT discourse to be distinct. This distinctiveness can be an important resource in developing programs that promote national well-being as well as marketable products. Besides, such national narratives must be mastered because they structure what is possible to think and therefore what policy can be conceived, let alone implemented.

At the same time, because of the marginalization of the nation, national policies must be developed deftly. Successful, nationally distinctive strategies will be based upon an accurate assessment of real practice rather than complex self-mystifications. Concomitantly, there is obvious need to maintain a global, rather than a national, information infrastructure built on open standards. For those on the Net, communication is as easy, even if more mysterious, with the person on the other side of the world as it is with the guy down the hall. Further, the Net is a veritable wellspring of innovation, including, but not limited to, that which supports capital reproduction, precisely because it is perceived to be a free space in both economic and artistic/cultural senses. Actually, of course, it is paid for by various institutions, many of which are publicly supported. It seems likely that the best role for the Internet is to remain free. Quite a bit of money is being made out of creating tools for access to this free space; perhaps, like national parks, the Internet should stay that way, not only because this is more ethical, but because it is also wealth-creating.

Openness of Access as Essential to Verifying Information

With an article or book, one has known procedures, the cultural practices surrounding what it takes to get into these particular forms of print, to help judge information quality. Faced with a document from the World Wide Web, however, one doesn't have a set of conventions allowing equivalent inferences regarding veracity. A key intellectual issue on the Internet, and perhaps in cyberspace generally, is how to verify information. This, rather than securing "intellectual property rights," is the root source of the need for an effective theory of knowledge in cyberspace.

In this as in so many other regards, full use of AIT requires creativity, but creativity in cyberspace may be even more a collective community as opposed to an individual activity. The policy problem with regard to innovation is how to create a participatory framework for evaluating the new forms that information takes in cyberspace. The Internet's governance provides a model for doing this, through ad hoc, essentially self-appointed protocol committees whose members share a commitment to maximizing access, and therefore open standards. This is also perhaps our best model of/for the nonhierarchical global institution required by a multicultural world.

Strike a Proper Balance of Social Power

If creative workplaces require participation, then we should be very concerned, from a policy perspective, about the decreasing scope for the real participation of those less powerful, whether nations, classes, genders, or minority groups. Perhaps the most important role of social policy with regard to AIT is indirect, to promote forms of social formation reproduction in which all groups have the power to participate effectively.

Ethics

Given that many applied cyberspace ethnographers are employed by corporations and thus have managers, one source of the marginalization of their work is suspicion about research subordinated to the reproductive needs of capital. Cyberspace ethnographers tend to strike extreme poses, of either subservience to, or loathing for, managers. Some in, for example, the Committee on the Anthropology of Science Technology, and Computing in the AAA's General Anthropology Division have resisted participation of those involved in practice-oriented projects. They feel cyberspace ethnography could be compromised by such projects, either through incorporation into a management-oriented perspective—which compromises both objectivity and the ability to be critical—or through a more general limiting of one's capacity to pursue the most pressing intellectual, as opposed to practical, issues. Such concerns have long been characteristic of social sciences (as opposed to business studies). The relevance of such concerns is underlined by those who, like Lucy Suchman, herself a manager, have pledged not to participate in projects which result in workers losing their jobs.

While it is certainly the case that basic research also raises ethical issues, practice-related research raises them most directly. This is because practice-oriented ethnography by definition involves intervention in people's lives. Ethical challenges are also greater for applied cyberspace ethnographers because it is they who are most likely to find themselves working collectively in teams in the workspace, even though the experience is not always salutary, as described earlier. In such teams, the anthropologist, the social scientist in practice the most committed to "single handed" research, may be less able to exercise an ethical influence.

At the same time, it is important to realize the value of legitimate practice-oriented applied research, as in program evaluation. Being able to keep the primary research objective straight helps when considering the ethical implications of our actions. In regard to the ethical responsibilities of the applied cyberspace ethnographer, the following points seem in order:

1. It is important for professional organizations to foster a vigorous discussion over ethical issues, which means fostering a disciplinary culture in which ethical discourse is lively and thick (Hakken 1990);

2. Codes of conduct like those of the AAA and the National Association for the Practice of Anthropology are important devices in summarizing disciplinary consensuses over past experiences. Indeed, such codes are especially useful to those employed in the private sector. They need articulated guidelines with which to defend themselves against particular examples of pressure to engage in questionable activities such as surreptitious research;

3. Such codes should not be expected to provide detailed guidelines for all situations, the search for categorical imperatives having been largely abandoned by professional philosophy. Consequently, the action of collectives is of greater ethical significance than that of individuals—as in, for example, the work of those attempting to develop an information policy for the AAA, or those active in Computer Professionals for Social Responsibility.

Indeed, it may be more difficult for everyone to act ethically in cyberspace. As noted in chapter 4, the increasingly opaque character of AIT-mediated representations such as "objects" decoupled from place makes it harder to know the implications of the action alternatives available to us. Mark Slouka (1995) argues that, to the extent that we no longer share a common "real life" experience, we become less able to develop a serviceable sense of the impact of our behavior on others, a precondition for ethical action. Equally problematic is the blurring of the boundary between the real and the imagined, a boundary he feels is also necessary for effective ethical action. Separating out the implicit claims of the different forms of cyber-knowledge talk is essential to any meaningful articulation of cyber-ethics. As agency is distributed to more entities, both cyborgic and nonhuman, Modernist notions which limit ethical agency to the strictly human are less applicable.

These can all be taken as reasons for anthropological cyberspace ethnographers to participate in construction of cyberspace by applying their knowledge of it. Discussion of what happens when you try to apply the abstract perspectives to concrete situations is one of the real contributions we can make to these formidable challenges. In the long run, the capacity of applied cyberspace ethnographers to exercise a proper ethical sensibility will be largely determined by the nature of the knowledge that we have to apply. And, since cyberspace is a so thoroughly deliberate act of imagination, there is less reason for "Hawthorne" sensitivities. These are just some of the reasons to give special emphasis to the ethical dimensions of cyberspace anthropology.

Empirical Results: What We Can Say about Cyberspace

Cyborgs@cyberspace? has reached the following conclusions about what cyberspace is really like:

WHILE THERE HAS NOT YET BEEN A GENERAL COMPUTER REVOLUTION, THERE IS EVIDENCE OF A FOURTH STAGE IN THE LABOR PROCESS

What we know about cyberspace so far does not *yet* empirically justify drawing a sharp boundary between its social dynamics and the current type of social formation. At none of the levels of sociocultural integration discussed in the preceding chapters do the data currently support

[8]

Conclusions

the widely shared Computer Revolution notion. Still, the character of social practices like labor, activity for which people are paid wages, has changed rapidly at the same time as computers have been introduced into work processes. If we are not to explain this correlation causally by a CR, how are we to account for it?

First, effusive, prolix CR talk must be deconstructed into more precise notions about the possible social transformations that *might* be associated with computerization: A species transformation, a fundamentally new type of human social formation, a new stage in the current social formation type, or no change of real significance. There is little data to support the first two, and ethnographic prudence suggests adhering to last. Yet considerable data are consonant with the third proposition— that we are currently experiencing an important shift within the same social formation type, from a social formation based on one stage of the labor process to one based on another. Machino-facture, the most recent stage in the labor process, has involved replacing skilled labor with machines wherever possible. Machino-facture is associated with mass production, mass consumption, and working class suburbanization.

The current period of proto-cyberspace involves in some workspaces a retreat from manic mechanization and a re-emphasis on groups' capacities to create and perform culture as the prime source of value. As a fully separate stage, the chief role of computing would likely be to facilitate cultural performance in production. Broader social formation dynamics might include accelerated decoupling of social life from place, developments equally urban and ex-urban.

The empirical conflicts characteristic of AIT-mediated work sites seem to show contradictions between the older, replacement role of technological artifacts of machinofacture and the newer role supportive of "cyberfacture." Still, it is too early to conclude that new forms of labor like virtual work or telecommuting constitute a new mode of employment society. They could also be compatible with a "machinofacture of the mind" analysis, reversion to "division of labor" manufacture with its socially bifurcated urbanism, or even "putting out" ruralism.

THE CURRENT ROLE OF AIT IN SOCIAL FORMATION REPRODUCTION IS BETTER UNDERSTOOD AS MORE SYMBOLIC/IDEOLOGICAL THAN "TECHNOLOGICAL"

Cyberspace ethnography documents extensive changes in contemporary social formation reproduction, and several of these changes correlate with and therefore may have something to do with AIT. Moreover, I personally accept the continued relevance of causative discourse, of trying to account for the change/AIT connection. Contrary to the CR perspective, however, the social changes cannot usefully be described as in any simple sense *resulting from* AIT; they demand more holistic causative explanations.

If there is no convincing argument that we are already in a CR, how does one account for the widely shared belief that this is the case? The most important specific roles of AIT in social formation reproduction to date are not "technical" in the sense in which that term is usually employed—that is as a force largely external to social reproduction, implicit in phrases like, "the juggernaut of technological innovation." Rather, at several levels of socio-cultural integration, AIT has had an obvious and significant role as symbol or ideology.

Emphasis on the specific socio-ideological power of AIT emerged from consideration of attempts to *apply* knowledge of cyberspace ethnography practically. While the technical effect of AIT artifacts on organizations is often overestimated, the reverse is the case for these semiotic effects. AIT is pervasively cultural, irrespective of its technical efficiency or effectiveness.

For example, the most important organizational "impacts" of AIT in practice follow from its role as a lever with which to promote organizational change. Workers will often respond negatively to organizational change for its own sake. Often, one finds organizational change *successfully, albeit technically inappropriately, brought about when justified by* the need to adopt AIT. This is the "Midas' touch" of applied cyberspace ethnography. It is tempting to use AIT as a wedge for organizational change, but too often overpromotion of what AIT can deliver on its own produces a backlash. The ease with which AIT can be used to accomplish quite separable objectives in practice is a primary source of the considerable ethical responsibility that devolves on those of us who promote its adoption.

AIT ALSO PLAYS AN IMPORTANT ROLE SIMPLY AS A COMMODITY

It may well be that capitalists introduce information superhighways for essentially the same reasons they supported the interstate highway system, as means to "prime the pump." Like building, computing is directly involved in production. While such uses are often shortsighted, meaning wasted off-ramps to economic (or technological) "nowheres," they also create space for those able to provide socially valuable, alternative forms of, points of origin for, and destinations for information (see Hanseth, Thoresen, and Winner 1993).

Arguably, however, an even greater structural relevance of AIT to the reproduction of capital may be not as process but as products to be sold, or commodities. Building information infrastructures helps maintain computing as an effective site for the realization of capital. Recent growth in the value of the U.S. stock market, for example, is very heavily concentrated in "the technologies." If Americans were to cease collectively to believe that the future of technologies is bright, the consequences could be severe. To question the value of "more bells and whistles" or "all singing, all dancing" hardware is virtually unpatriotic. Dependent upon the technologies for the reproduction of capital, the U.S. social formation is semiotically wedded to "high tech" irrespective of its efficiency or effectiveness in the workplace.

Linguists tell us that, because all language is ultimately based in metaphor, people easily substitute their submerged imaginary representations of the world for their actual experience. For Americans, this is particularly true with regard to technology. Implicit performances of technological imaginings, truly fetishized commodities, may be an important source of the social persuasiveness of CR's technicist metaphors.

WE MUST COME TO TERMS, ESPECIALLY IN POLICY, WITH AN ACCELERATED DECOUPLING OF SPACE FROM PLACE

Several meanings of "space" and "place" overlap. However, the former term typically gives primacy to social relations, as in the statement, "I need more space in this relationship." In contrast, the latter points primarily to geographic referents, in the sense of "locus."

A tendency for social spaces to become less tightly tied to particular physical locations has long been recognized in social thought. In the late nineteenth century, Ferdinand Toennies (1887) constructed a sociological contrast between earlier *Gemeinschaften* ("communities" based primarily on local family and landed estate ties) and the new *Gesellschaften* ("societies" based on contract). On all of the levels discussed, similar decouplings accelerate as we approach cyberspace. One finds, for example, a substantial complexification of the business of constructing manageable personal identities or intimate relationships as one "lives" more in de-placed spaces. Similarly, one is increasingly involved in more "imagined communities" disconnected from neighborhoods, streets, or villages.

This empirically noticeable decoupling has important implications for those concerned about the increasing difficulty of sustaining democratic social processes. If democracy is largely dependent upon localized, face to face relationships, its viability in cyberspace is highly questionable. Alternatively, one can conceive of and construct democratic social relations which, while less tied to place, can still be based in substantial spaces, as in civic computing. Identifying and fostering non-place-bound but still democratic relations is a substantial policy problem in the construction of cyberspace.

Analytic Conclusions

In addition, some conclusions about how to explain cyberspace data are also warranted:

RETHINKING THE UNITS OF SOCIAL ANALYSIS

A rethinking of several ethnographic and ethnological concepts and tools is necessary for constructing a proper understanding of proto-cyberspace, among them cyberspace itself. Rather than being merely a glitzy term for the conceptual space "occupied" by a computer user, "cyberspace" can refer to the broader social totality evoked by "Computer Revolution" talk, as a label for the purported new way of life or social formation. "Cyborg" can also be assigned a broader meaning, not just as a fictional symbol evocative of the technological bizarre but as a label for the characteristic carriers of virtually all culture.

MODELS FOR UNDERSTANDING CYBERSPACE CULTURE MUST HIGHLIGHT THE COMPLEXITY OF ITS (RE)PRODUCTION

A recurrent finding of both basic and applied research on cyberspace is that one can account for the emergent patterns only by recourse to multiple practices. This contrasts strongly with the presumption of unidirectional determination typical of "tech talk"—that science discovers, technology gives scientific knowledge material form, and humans adapt. Rather, to understand them, AIT innovation and the multiple facets of techno-related social change must be contextualized by broader patterns of social formation reproduction.

Analyses of technology in use, especially AITs, often stress the large gap between the intentions of designers and the practices of users. A particularly striking example of this gap is the Internet. Originally designed for rapid, one to many dissemination of the results of military, often secret, research, it was quickly appropriated for interactive communication about, among other things, science fiction. France's Minitel, a public system of terminals placed in millions of homes, experienced a similarly unplanned developmental trajectory. Intended basically for dissemination of official information, the system has been transformed by many users into a many-to-many system for personal communication, something like Use-net in the United States.

One methodological implication of this generalization is the need to study techno-science in its use as well as its development context if we wish to understand its cultural construction fully. Further, the multiplicity of the production and extended reproduction/transformation of techno-cultural entities means their patterns will likely be contested, involving not only differences in perception but also actual differences across different actors and situations. Analytically, this means utilizing conflict rather than functional models of reproduction.

Paradoxically, diversification of determinations necessitates construction of more unitary analytic fields. Coming to terms analytically with the CR requires thinking of techno-science as a unity rather than separating science and technology as distinct practices. Distinguishing between them may sometimes still be appropriate, but, as far as understanding cyberspace is concerned, it is the extent to which technology and science are essentially the same thing that needs to be stressed. An easy example is the field known in the U.S. as computer science. Like other sciences of the artificial, it in practice has much more to do with the design of programs to run machines (engineering, if not "pure" technology) than with exploration of fundamental natural "laws." The need to focus on technology in use rather than technology as a thing in itself further marginalizes the study of science as a distinct cyberspace practice.

The need to think in unitary terms about techno-science is an additional reason to avoid constructing analyses of cyberspace around traditional topical areas, whether science, technology, work, democracy, information, knowledge, or practice. Besides fostering false interpretive divisions (as between science and technology), a topical division merges analysis of phenomena that operate on analytically distinct levels (such as the very different implications for democracy of community computing on the one hand versus globalization on the other).

LABOR THEORIES OF VALUE HAVE A PLACE IN INTERPRETIVE MODELS OF CYBERSPACE

Classical Political Economy was based on a labor theory of value, the idea that the value of commodities derived primarily from the work of hired laborers. This theory was the basis of the widely shared belief that there was a secular tendency of the rate of profit to fall. The neo-classical revolution substituted a capital theory of value, justified on the notion that entrepreneurship would only occur with a return to capital. If value can be traced to capital, and capital can take many forms ("knowledge," "R&D," or "social"), then profits are, in theory, infinite, and capitalism can go on forever.

Cyberspace ethnography supports renewed interpretive interest in labor theories of value (LToVs). The weak argument for LToVs, one justifying the supplementing of capital theories with labor ones, is the re-emergence in proto-cyberspace of what Sweezy labeled "realization crises" (1963). Having taken advantage of the globalization of the division of labor, authoritarian states, and anti-union policies to cheapen labor, international capital periodically finds it difficult to sell its products profitably, because too few can afford to buy them. Undermining Fordism has negative implications for capital as well as labor, a more equitable return to which, justified by an LToV, is a necessity of capital reproduction.

The strong argument for LToVs builds on the empirical observation of the possible emergence of a cyber-cultural stage of the labor process. The distinctive newness of this stage would be its historic rejection of Taylorism. Forms of computing which build on the collective aspects of skill (such as CSCW) "empower" rather than de-skill labor and degrade work further. To foster such forms is to recognize labor as a key source of value.

On an expanded "fourth stage" view, AIT enables capital to carry out a strategic retreat in the class struggle. While overtly dependent upon collective labor, capital still tries to control the labor process. Through fostering an individuated "techno-"consciousness in each worker, indirect control is substituted for direct control of the worker's body. Ideally, the worker does spontaneously what is in the interest of capital. A matrix organizational structure, one in which work is done in teams but individuals are rewarded, is an increasing form for managing the emergent contradictions. The spread of collective bonuses and group stock ownership plans, however, can also interfere with mental individuation. This conflict, a new form of the classic Marxist contradiction between the social and technical relations of production, may turn out to be the basic contradiction in cyberspace.

NONPROGRESSIVE EVOLUTIONISM

Good metaphors release interpretative creativity, while bad ones subvert it. Industrial robotics began to develop impressively only when designers freed themselves from the notion that a robot had to look like a human being to perform similiar functions. Similarly, evolutionary biology, so much at the base of physical anthropology, has had to free itself of the metaphor of a progressive "great chain of being." As described by Gould (1981), an important leap in explanatory power took place when biologists recognized that evolution and progress were not the same thing; that evolution, like history, has no telos or goal.

A similar shift is needed in our thinking about current social changes, which are not necessarily important. Also, while social change may be a good thing, it isn't necessarily so. The movement away from a mass production, mass consumption Fordist society may be toward utopia, but it may also be toward an even more commoditized society. Paradoxically, because it may no longer depend less upon workers, it may also be a limited consumption, mass marginalization society.

In the broad sweep of cultural evolution, traumas are increasingly traced to internal, self-induced contradictions (information overload?) rather than external (climatic) forces. Breaking with the "evolution equals progress" trope, Gould and his colleagues point out that species destruction is as likely to come from overadaptation as from failure to adapt. The species with the best prospects for long-term viability is that which contains the greatest diversity in its internal gene pool. In cultural evolutionary terms, this helps explain why cultures develop as mazeways for handling diversity, not uniform "sememes."

It is the adaptationist, Social Darwinist tone of the OECD master narrative which most disturbs. Projecting deterministic techno-economic forces, such Neo-Classsical narratives adopt the rhetorics of presumptive inevitability. Particular types of social formations are based on particular technologies—for example, Marx's overstated epigram about the water wheel and feudalism, the steam engine and capitalism. Yet anthropologists often make the contrasting point: that particular technologies are based on particular culture types. Consequently, we are suspicious of discourses that seem to infer causation from mere correlation—such as the argument that, because in some situations AIT *is associated with* job creation, it is the *cause* of job creation.

Rhetorical CR hype has a clear cultural rationality, its own "logic." As in the *Jobs Study*, however, where new technology is seen as automatically requiring greater substantive skill and therefore more education, this logic obscures. Some in higher education repeat this mantra, while at the same time developing new technologies intended explicitly to represent, and thereby eliminate the need for, worker skill. In general, the picture underscores a basic point of political economy, that social developments are closely connected to social power.

NON-MODERN CONCEPTIONS OF TECHNO-SCIENTISTS

Chapter 2's critique of the CR view traced its popularity to the technicism of Modernist dualism. Modernism continues to hinder understanding of and in techno-science. A meaningful rejection of Modernism entails more than merely traversing the terrain Sancho Panza–style, offering an occasional dissent to fundamentally unreconstructed practice. Unfortunately, this is the role for social studies of techno-science outlined in Jay Labinger's "Science as Culture: A View from the Petri Dish" (1995). Albeit a metaphor which reverses roles—the techno-scientist in the Petri dish, and the STSer peering into the microscope—the Petri dish perspective severely limits Labinger's vision. Sociocultural study of techno-science is only perceivable to Labinger if it fits into the categories of "normal" science, as critique of social "distortions." Reproducing the narrow dualism, the categories "scientist" and "STSer" can only be complementary.

Rather than accepting everyday scientific practice as necessary, STS demands that we recognize the multiple ways in which "really existing techno-science" reproduces highly questionable cultural and philosophical premises. These include the masculinist practices of what Fuller (1992) calls "epistemological chicken."

Labinger fails to see the broader potential contribution of STS to day-to-day practice. So that our maps of it become substantially less systematically distorted, STS calls us to deconstruct the manner in which the terrain of techno-science itself has been culturally constructed. A reflexive view of the techno-scientific enterprise is a necessary prerequisite to effective STS/techno-science collaboration. I can have no interest in "collaboration" which projects a self-satisfied view of techno-science while denigrating other scholars, as in Labinger's disparaging "sociologist" story.[1]

Both in the Petri dish and looking through the microscope, I apply STS in techno-science. I do so as a scientist of the anthropological sort, not alone but with techno-science colleagues who share a critique of scientism. Refusing to limit myself to either actant or actor, an impossibility for Labinger, I am what Haraway calls a monster. While I take exception to the narrow role for critique which he projects, I am hopeful that Labinger and other "techno-scientists of good will" can be prodded to move with STSers to engage in a positive (but not positivist) reconstruction of science. Indeed, his initial premise is quite accurate: There are few occasions when the bridges between the "two cultures" of natural science and social studies carry much traffic.

On the Science Question, or Reconstructing Techno-Science Practice

Coming to terms with cyberspace not only stimulates some new uses of old tools, it also necessitates new approaches to the fundamental conception of techno-science. As the social formation most intimately connected with science, it is logical that inquiry into the dynamics of cyberspace would stimulate such a rethinking.

THE SCIENCE QUESTION IN TECHNO-SCIENCE

The phrase "science question" refers to such foundationist critiques of the conception of scientific activity. Modernism and technicism are embodied in both scientific practices and artifacts, especially in engineering and computer science as in the myths of the independence of science from technology or of a radical disjunction between the natural world, the domain of objective science, and the social world, the domain of practice. These critiques seriously undermine the standard "scientistic" narrative taught in most schools—its positive, progressive character, its privileging of laboratory methods, and its presumptions of value freedom and objectivity. Termination of the super-conducting super-collider is indicative of the declining power of this standard narrative.

Encouraged by A.N. Whitehead's trenchant deconstruction of the scientistic character of scientific practice, criticism of Modernism emerged early in twentieth century philosophy of science. The science question was reposed historically by Stephen Toulmin (1990), theoretically by Bruno Latour (1987), and of course by Thomas Kuhn (1978). The intellectual basis of the critique has been broadened by figures within science like Goedel and Heisenberg.

Equally important to the emergence of the science question is the emergence in the 1960s of a social critique of techno-science. This critique developed within feminist and ecology social movements and was articulated within "natural" science by the radical science movement. More recently, scholars within the various strands of STS have developed convincing philosophized (Feyerabend 1975), sociologized (Latour and Woolgar 1979), and ethnographied (Traweek 1988) accounts of scientific ways of knowing, accounts which reveal important disparities between scientific ideology and practice. Along with the radical critique of techno-science associated with humanistic Postmodernism, these developments obviate self-promotional presentations of science as an unalloyed good.

A PRACTICE-BASED ARGUMENT FOR RECONSTRUCTING SCIENCE

Given these critiques, why should one try to reconstruct science as a practice, rather than rejecting it altogether? Techno-science is so deeply embedded as a performance moment in such a broad range of contemporary social activities that it is unlikely to disappear any time soon. Indeed, many of the pressing social issues which humans face, from AIDS to environmental degradation, have so intimately involved techno-science in their social construction that it will likely be involved in both their apprehension and ultimate resolution.

THE INCAPACITY OF TECHNO-SCIENCE TO RECONSTRUCT ITSELF, OR STS TO RECONSTRUCT SCIENCE

The necessary reconsideration of science is unlikely to take place within a "natural" science left to its own devices. Among the reasons for this pessimism is the continuing dominant position of scientistic narratives and practices in much of higher education. A second is the importance of positivist science myths to the natural science enterprise, the notion of the "natural" being one of the key myths (Ingold 1995). Third is the integration of "really existing" science and its mythic texts into the selling of commodities and therefore the reproduction of capital; these myths are central to notions of science as "the prime productive factor" in the "information society." The myth of progressive science is still very powerful: in May 1995, budget-cutting U.S. congressional

Republicans still sought a three percent *increase* in NSF funding for basic natural science research (to be financed by shutting down funding for social, behavioral, and economic science).

Rather than coming to terms with the critique, most natural scientists, the
publicly accepted high priests of scientism, chose to deflect them and attack the
critiquers. Witness the promotion and popularity of Gross and Levitt's *Higher
Superstition* (1994), the most visible form of the "backlash" against STS, or the
New York Academy of Sciences conference on "The Flight from Science and
Reason."

Nor is STS on its own effectively promoting the necessary general rethink.
Indeed, the vulnerability of STS has led some ethnographers (see Diana
Forsythe 1994) to shrink back from the implications of its challenge to scientism, instead identifying the construction of cultural understandings of science
as ideographic and therefore a nonethnological activity. Steve Fuller spells out
the problematic implications of such retreats:

> The problem . . . is that case studies can always be accepted "on their
> own terms" but ultimately [be] dismissed as lacking clear implications
> for the grand narrative of scientific progress. Since [STS] practitioners
> have been loath to develop their own counter-narratives of the history
> of science, there is no alternative macro-context in which to situate the
> case studies, and hence prevent them from simply being reduced to di-
> versions from what scientists regard as the main story (1995:23).

In sum, the necessary reconstruction of techno-science requires more developed counter-constructions, aimed toward a more general counter-context or
"paradigm" in the properly Kuhnian sense.

CYBORG ANTHROPOLOGY AS A BASIS FOR SUCH A "COUNTER-CONSTRUCTION"

Reconceptualized along cyborg lines, informed by cyberspace ethnography, and
using the RANT theory of chapter 7, anthropology has the capacity to lead this
general reconstruction of techno-scientific practice. However, just as there is a
science question in techno-science, there is a substantial science question in
U.S. anthropology. That is, the diversity of views with regard to the place of a
"scientific" perspective in anthropology is so broad as to cast doubt on the
value of the current mission statement of the AAA—"to advance anthropology
as the *science* that studies humankind in all its aspects" (emphasis added). We
do not "all know what science is."

A more effective discourse on techno-science, plus effective alliances with
techno-scientists around applied and practice issues, could turn this anthropological diversity into an asset.

The "Anthro" Science Question and the "Science" Science Question

While the diversity of views on science in anthropology has obvious roots "domestic" to anthropology itself, the science question in anthropology needs to be viewed in the context of the broader science question in science. The most visible problematizers of the "science" perspective in anthropology—including those who, inspired by the "literary turn," critique ethnography as an "Occidentalist" narrative, or those who, after Kathleen Gough (1968), question the "objectivity" of a discipline which is the "child of imperialism"— would appear to have little common ground with problematizers of the scientistic perspective in science. Nonetheless, in the Western world, knowledge is conceived as unitary, and as long as "science" is perceived as the form of knowledge *par excellence,* anthropology is affected by any change in the cultural assessment of science. Moreover, one form of American anthropological knowledge, physical or "biological" anthropology, is tied directly to the natural science narrative, while the methodology of another, archaeology, is similarly tied to physics in its "scienticity." Also, much funding for anthropological research is tied to "science" narratives.

Fortunately, anthropologists have discovered techno-science as a legitimate field of cultural inquiry. As anthropologists become more visible in STS, the anthropological and STS projects become increasingly intertwined. Indeed, ethnography is now arguably the preferred approach in STS (ironically, just as ethnography encounters the reflexivist critique in anthropology). Discussions over scientific traditions in non-Western contexts are also a major theme in STS, an important part of the case for science as part of, not separate from, social reproduction. Thus, the fates of anthropology, STS, and techno-science itself are now linked to construction of a general answer to the science question.

A Cultural Road to Reconstructing Science

United States anthropology is actually well placed to help the reconsideration of science. Unlike sociology, political science, and economics, U.S. anthropology was less affected by post-World War II positivist scientism. Excepting both extreme positivists and antitechnologists, the breadth of the field has made the notion of a single, privileged epistemological narrative less "operationalizable." As that branch of science most clearly trying also to be one of the humanities, four/five field Americanist anthropology has never fit easily into the "science program" dominant in the American Academy; indeed, we are badly stretched by those who would split the sciences and the arts. Ethnography is methodologically more similar to "natural history" than quantifiable hypothesis testing. Ethical sensitivities as well as a tradition of identification with one's "people" obviated adoption of the experimental method and its ethical relativism.

Indeed, science critics often invoke ethnography, the chief episteme of sociocultural anthropology, as an example of a "nonscientific" methodology. When feminists talk concretely about feminist epistemology, for example, they often outline practices which bear close resemblance to ethnography; for example, invoking studies of how culture is embodied against the alienated white male authoritative narrator so characteristic of scientific discourse (Rothschild 1983).

During the long reign of Modernism, anthropologists often felt lost in the borderlands between the "hard" sciences and the "soft" humanities. "Post-positivistically," based on a legitimate claim to work from within both science and the humanities, anthropologists are uniquely placed to move the project of non-Modern science forward. An anthropologist who does STS is not bound by the "either scientist or humanist" dualism of techno-science. With both "natural"(inhuman?) and "human" (unnatural?) science colleagues who share a critique of scientism, she has often been consciously non-Modern.

Rethinking Anthropology

However, major parts of the anthropological project must themselves be rethought if it is to lead the reconstruction of science. In addition to reconstructing a shared conception of science, another area of needed change is in our ambivalence toward technology. As described in chapter 3, we habitually insist on treating science as part of the sacred (cultural) while too easily adopting CR rhetorics. Such ambivalence also obstructs achievement of a level of mastery sufficient to serious study of techno-science.

To overcome such difficulties, it is necessary to recast the object of study, to no longer draw the boundary of the field's object at the human skin but treat humans and their technologies as unitary entities. A range of anthro-techno-science concepts (such as cyborgs and Creolized Objects) can help to do this. Such steps to put technology more at the center of disciplinary concern will of themselves help anthropology take leadership in a reflexive reconstruction of techno-science.

Less Talk, More Action

While rethinking anthropology technologically will be difficult, it should on the whole be less difficult than a general recasting of science. Still, anthropologists who perceive a crisis of representation have already shown us that we have much to learn from better understandings of the way metaphor works, while at least some archaeologists are already finding inspiration in STS.

In carrying out their own acts of reconstruction, anthropologists can connect with those in techno-science sympathetic to their efforts. In ISD, a number of practitioners have come to doubt the value of naming their field "computer science," preferring the less scientistic "informatics." As they recognize the need for integrating users more effectively into the system development process, and how problems in system development often have more to do with social than technical factors, they look to social science for practical partnerships, accepting "ethnography of work" as essential to system specification. In field studies of and practice with information system developers, I have learned that we can construct equality as scientists of the artificial.

Epistemological differences between systems developers and anthropologists remain significant. Still, the existence of at least some such "across-the-two-cultures" links means that prospects for making alliances in rethinking the relationship of social and natural science are better here than in many other disciplines. There are other obvious points for shared projects, as between development anthropologists and social movement-oriented technologists, or between health anthropologists and socially oriented health practitioners.

Implications of a Cyberspace Ethnography-Based Reconstructed Techno-Science Practice

The meanings of terms like "cyborg" and "cyberspace" are plastic and have changed considerably. Like all good advertising copy, flashy language can hide more than it reveals, lulling us into thinking we understand when all we really have is a label for ignorance. Having only our distinctions to monger, we are vulnerable to the *bon mot* or merely engaging story. Can the appropriation of seductive, volatile cyberspace rhetorics really help ethnography?

I have spent thirty years in anthropology studying culture in contemporary societies, roughly the last half of this focusing on the relationship of AIT to social change. My main goal has been to separate out what can reasonably be said and be grounded empirically from the nonsense that abounds in regard to this subject. Since part of my activity has involved legitimating the study of this relationship within anthropology (not always an easy task), I have tried to organize my colleagues in this field, so I pay even closer attention to their work than usual (Hakken 1993). Much of their cyber-rhetoric, such as the CR notion, is extremely loose, with roots in Western technicist rhetorics that automatically attribute any social change to technology. Bryan Pfaffenberger argues that cyberspace rhetorics are particularly contrived. Aware of the limitations of technicism, many cybernauts deliberately choose rhetorics celebratory of cyberspace anyway.

In short, my empirical bent makes me suspicious of cybertalk, especially the hype associated with the catchy phrases, the fey, contrived, "shi-shi" forms of technoid, postmodern enthusiasms. Most of my published work is in fact skeptical of the CR hypothesis. The widespread presumption of massive social change, and uses of the cybertalk associated with it, increase chances of mistakenly assuming the accuracy of the terminology without proper investigation. Difficulty with formulating a specific sense of analytic problem and failure to understand complex technologies adequately can be the result.

CYBORGS@CYBERSPACE? THE RHETORICS OF CYBERSPACE ETHNOGRAPHY

A reluctant cybernaut, why do I choose to "talk this talk" (at least some of it) anyway? First, much of General Anthropology—such as notions about the transition from horticulture to agriculture—rests upon theories about technology and fundamental social change. Many of the technology-related concepts used to describe likely future practices—"cyborg," "cyberspace," the new ways of thinking about "information"—provide rich labels for the practices anthropologists wish to investigate. Anthropologists take seriously the term "popular" among our natives. This is understandable, considering that, in an important sense, the only wares they have to flog in the academic marketplace are concepts. Use of cybertalk fosters attention to ethnographic perspectives on problems of broad public interest, like those of new communities (such as hackers and monsters) and new modes of communication (national information infrastructures, MOOS, MUDS). There is tremendous popular interest in cyberspace, and my professional ethics code urges me to speak out on matters where my expertise is relevant.

Second, as an empirical social scientist who normally spends his time trying to describe and analyze what is happening in the world, taking up cyberrhetorics prods me to go beyond the descriptive to assess what *should* be imagined in cyberspace. Any new way to be human is difficult to name before it is fully here, but cyberspace seems to be accepted as a provisional label for the virtual "space" where the new life way is being explored/created, especially by youth. It's helpful to have a name for the space where its patterns are first manifest.

Similarly, through the cyborg construct anthropology can combine a critical appreciation of existing anthropology of technology, empirical study of the social correlates of the new forms of AIT so obviously central to constructing cyberspace, and attempts to apply this knowledge to the development of new technology. Cyberspace anthropology could provide practical guidance to those currently creating cyberspace through their actions.

THE POLITICAL POTENTIAL OF ETHNOGRAPHICALLY REFLEXIVE CYBORGS@CYBERSPACE

My student generation of the 1960s believed that new ways of life would develop through a deliberate social transformation, one inverting existing images of age, race, gender, and class. Currently, discussion of cyberspace and technology has tended to replace these earler rhetorics of freedom. Especially among the young, cybertalk constitutes the prime terrain for liberatory rhetorics, and it is on this terrain, wherever it is, that a humanistic science like anthropology should be located. Humans/cyborgs can be made conscious of their responsibility for the worlds they create, and liberatory impulses remain a prime resource in our attempts to imagine collectively a future that we can embrace. To abandon the cultural construction of cyberspace to those whose rhetorics obscure their intent is to evade this responsibility. My personal walkabout in cyberspace has given me glimpses of a truly different world, and I wish to share them.

In her "Cyborg Manifesto" (1991), Donna Haraway identifies the cyborg of science fiction as an entity worthy of techno-scientific as well as literary study. Several humanist STS scholars have taken up Haraway's suggestion (see Dery 1994). While not often excited by their work,[2] I find the reading of science fiction itself, especially its cyber-varieties, both pleasurable and suggestive. Science fiction writers have found in the cyborg an image which transcends the limits of current social relations, and one can find in some of their work (Piercy 1991) clues to an alternative techno-science practice. *Cyborgs@cyberspace* has used the cyborg discourse as an alternative way to conceptualize existing AIT practices. While we apply cyborg talk to different data, Haraway and I share an appreciation of how it promotes suggestive cyberspace imaginings.

Contemporary anthropology is very aware of the extent to which culture is invented and thus the importance in this process of an active imaginary. Contemporary humans/cyborgs *could* be in the midst of an imagining process leading to a new, cyberspace way of life, and it is certainly the case that cyberspace has a powerful hold over contemporary imaginations. A more effectively imagined cyberspace could itself be a part of creating a social formation with profoundly different dynamics. However, to get us to a really new way of being, current cyber-imaginings are *as yet* neither sufficiently deliberate nor collective.

Cyberspace ethnography promotes more deliberate ways of looking. It facilitates a more general encounter of social thought with cyberspace. Through careful, disciplined study of "really existing" proto-cyber-behavior, it makes possible future patterns more visible. Desirable power relations in a more full-blown, future cyberspace can be grounded with some confidence on these patterns. An expanded cyberspace ethnography would sustain a more grounded imaginary which itself could be an important component of the deliberate creation of cyberspace.

GROUNDING CYBERSPACE IMAGININGS IN PRESENT PROBLEMS

Of what practical value are such envisionings? Can we increase their relevance to the kinds of questions dealt with by those actively engaged in the creation of new technologies? It is surely wrong to demand that the value of an intellectual activity be reckoned primarily in terms of its utility, yet just as surely one can legitimately inquire after applicability. The ultimate intent of an ethnographically led cyberspace studies, the proper techno-science of the future, is to ground the process of imaging cyberspace on both a rich empirical understanding of what is actually taking place and to articulate ethically informed intellectual rules of thumb to guide further imagining.[3] I believe it also to be a responsibility of cyberspace ethnography to explore diligently what the empirical study suggests regarding how best to imagine the future—to help create cyberspace, not just be created by it.

If some alternative courses of development appear to have more applicability, demonstrations of this applicability can be used to argue for these courses. Demonstrations of "practical" value are of increasing importance to those like myself who find themselves confronting hostile colleagues, "natural" scientists, engineers, and technologists whose inclinations to be dismissive of STS are encouraged by the current "backlash."

The proto-cyberspace practices described in *Cyborgs@cyberspace?* may be precursors of fully developed cyberspace. Because of the role of imagination in reproducing social formations, however, they cannot be simply extrapolated into the future. Our discourse over cyberspace cannot be a merely passive one—even more than the nation, cyberspace must be imagined actively.

Because its imaginings can affect the future, cyberspace ethnography has a distinct moral charge. We study what is not because it will tell us what will be in any simple way, but because in understanding what is (and what has been) we can learn ways of imagining that discourage practices that should be hindered, as ways that help us set goals we can attain.

References Cited

Adams, Robert McC. 1996. *Paths of Fire: An Anthropologist's Inquiry into Western Technology.* Princeton, NJ: Princeton University Press.

Allwood, Carl M., and Tomas Kalen. 1993. "User-Competence and Other aspects When Introducing a Patent Administrative System: A Case Study." *Interacting with Computers* 5:167–191.

Allwood, Carl M., and David Hakken. n.d. "Deconstructing 'Use': Problems of Diverseness in Discourses on 'Users' and 'Usability' in Information System Development and Reconstructing a Viable Use Discourse." Unpublished manuscript.

Althusser, L., and Etienne Balibar. 1970. *Reading Capital.* London: New Left Books.

Anderson, Benedict. 1983. *Imagined Communities: Reflections on the Origin and Spread of Nationalism.* London: Verso.

Anderson, Jon W. 1995. "'Cybarities,' Knowledge Workers and New Creoles on the Information Superhighway." Paper presented to the AAA/CRA workshop on Culture, Society, and Advanced Information Technology, Washington, D.C.

Andersen, Kim Viborg, and Kenneth L. Kraemer. 1994. "Information Technology and Transitions in the Public Service: A Comparison of Scandanavia and the United States." *Scandinavian Journal of Information Systems* 6(1):3–24.

Anderson, S. Irwin. 1993. "Working the Structure and Structuring the Work: Life in a Large Engineering Organization." Paper presented at the annual meeting, American Anthropological Association, Washington, D.C.

Andrews, Barbara, and David Hakken. 1977. "Educational Technology: A Theoretical Approach." *College English* 39(1):68–108.

Anonymous. 1981. "From Tikal to Tucson: Today's Garbage is Tomorrow's Artifact." *Anthropology Newsletter* 22:3.

Armstrong, D. F., William Stokoe, and Sherman E. Wilcox. 1995. *Gesture and The Nature of Langauge.* Cambridge: Cambridge University Press.

Aronowitz, Stanley, and Philip DeFazio. 1995. *The Jobless Future: Sci-Tech and the Dogma of Work.* Minneapolis: University of Minnesota Press.

Attewell, Paul, and James Rule. 1985. "Computing and Organizations: What

We Know and What We Don't." *Communications of the ACM* 27. 1184–1192.

Baba, Marietta. 1988. "Innovation in University-Industry Linkages: University Organizations and Environmental Change," *Human Organization* 47(3):260–269.

———.1992. "Anthropological Research in Major Corporations." *Central Issues in Anthropology* 7(2):1–17.

———, with Donald Falkenberg. 1991. "Anthropology and Engineering in the Socio-Technical Systems Paradigm." Paper presented to the annual meeting, American Anthropological Association, Washington, D.C.

Bader, Gail, and James Nyce. 1991. "Theory and Practice in the Development Community: Is There Room for Cultural Analysis?" Paper presented at the annual meeting, American Anthropological Association, Washington, D.C.

Bansler, J., and Phillip Kraft. 1994a. "The Collective Resource Approach: The Scandinavian Experience." *Scandinavian Journal of Information Systems* 6(1):71–84.

———1994b. "Privilege and Invisibility in the New Work Order: A Reply to Kyng." *Scandinavian Journal of Information Systems* 6(1):97–106.

Barnes, Annie. 1986. *Black Women: Interpersonal Relationship in Profile*. Bristol, IN: Wyndham Hale Press.

Baudrillard, J. 1975. *The Mirror of Production*. St. Louis: Telos Press.

Bell, Daniel. 1973. *The Coming of Post-Industrial Society*. New York: Basic Books.

Benedict, Ruth. 1934. *Patterns of Culture*. New York: New American Library.

Berg, Anne-Jurunn, and Marete Lie. 1993. "Do Artifacts Have a Gender? Feminism and the Domestication of Technical Artifacts." Paper presented to the CRICT conference, Brunel University.

Bernal, J.D. 1965. *Science in History*. London: C.A. Watts.

Bhaskar, R. 1989. *Reclaiming Reality: A Critical Introduction to Contemporary Philosophy*. London: Verso.

Bijker, Wiebe, Thomas Hughes, and Trevor Pinch. 1987. *The Social Construction of Technological Systems*. Cambridge, MA: MIT Press.

Bjerknes, G. 1992. "Dialectical Reflections on Information Systems Development." *Scandinavin Journal of Information Systems* 4:55–78.

Bjerknes, Gro, and Tone Bratteteig. 1995. "User Participation and Democracy: A Discussion of Scandinavian Research on System Development." *Scandinavian Journal of Information Systems* 7(1):73–98.

Bjerknes, Gro, and Bo Dalhbom, eds. 1990. *Organizational Competence in System Development: A Scandinavian Contribution*. Lund, Sweden: Studentlitteratur.

Bjerknes, Gro, Pelle Ehn, and Morten Kyng, eds. 1987. *Computers and Democracy: A Scandinavian Challenge*. Aldershot: Avebury.

Bjorn-Andersen, Nils, Enid Mumford, and Helga Novotny, eds. 1982. *Information Society: For Richer, For Poorer*. Amsterdam: North Holland.

Blauner, Robert. 1964. *Alienation and Freedom*. Chicago: University of Chicago Press.

Blim, Michael. 1992. "Small-Scale Industrialization in a Rapidly Changing World Market." In Rothstein, Francis A., and Michael Blim, eds., *Anthropology and the*

Global Factory, pp. 85–101. New York: Bergin and Garvey.

Blomberg, Jeanette, and Lucy Suchman. 1992. "Field Studies of Work and Co-Design." Paper presented to PDC'92, The Participatory Design Conference, Cambridge, MA.

Boone, Margaret, and John Wood. 1992. *Computer Applications for Anthropologists.* Belmont, CA: Wadsworth.

Bott, Elizabeth. 1957. *Family and Social Network.* New York: The Free Press.

Bourdieu, Pierre. 1978. *Outline of a Theory of Practice.* Cambridge: Cambridge University Press.

Braa, Joern. 1993. *Health Management Information Systems in Mongolia: Present Situation and Future Possibilities.* Oslo: Norwegian Computing Centre.

Braverman, Harry. 1974. *Labor and Monopoly Capital.* New York: Monthly Review Press.

Brown, Stephen, and Nick Lee. 1993. "The Unexplored Country: Actor Network Theory and Otherness." Paper presented to the Surrey Conference in Theory and Method, University of Surrey.

Burrows, R. 1987. "Some Notes Toward a Realistic Realism." Paper presented to the British Sociological Association Conference on Science, Technology, and Society, Leeds University.

Calhoun, Craig. 1995. *Critical Social Theory.* Cambridge, MA: Blackwell.

Callon, M. 1986. "The Sociology of an Actor Network: The Case of the Electric Vehicle." In Callon, M., ed., *Mapping the Dynamics of Science and Technology,* pp. 19–34. London: MacMillan.

———, and John Law. 1993. "Agency and the Hybrid Collectif." Paper presented to the Surrey Conference in Theory and Method, University of Surrey.

Casey, Geraldine. 1992. "High Tech Across the Border: Women in Puerto Rico Confront the Internationalization of Clerical Work." Paper presented to the annual meeting, American Ethnological Society, Memphis, TN.

Castells, Manuel. 1989. *The Informational City: Information Technology, Economic Restructuring, and the Urban-Regional Process.* Oxford: Basil Blackwell.

Chomsky, Noam. 1965. *Aspects of a Theory of Syntax.* Cambridge, MA: MIT Press.

Clawson, D. 1980. *Bureaucracy and the Labor Process.* New York: Monthly Review Press.

Clifford, James, and George Marcus, eds. 1986. *Writing Culture: The Poetics and the Politics of Ethnography.* Berkeley: University of California Press.

Collins, H. M. 1993. "RAT-think." Paper presented to the Surrey Conference in Theory and Method, University of Surrey.

Cooley, Michael. 1982. *Architect or Bee?: The Human/Technology Relationship.* Boston: South End Press.

Counts, George. 1969. *Dare the Schools Build a New Social Order?* New York: Arno Press.

Dahlbom, Bo. 1990. "Using Technology to Understand Organizations." In Bjerknes, et al., eds., *Organizational Competence in System Development,* pp. 127–147. Lund, Sweden: Studentliteratur.

―――, and Lars Mathiessen. 1993. *Computers in Context: The Philosophy and Practice of Systems Design.* Cambridge: NCC/Blackwell.

Damasio, Antonio. 1994. *Descartes' Error: Emotion, Reason, and the Human Brain.* New York: Avon Books.

Davidson, Carl, Ivan Handler, and Jerrry Harris. 1994. "The Promise and the Peril of the Third Wave." *cy.Rev* 1:28–39.

Davis-Floyd, Robbie. 1995. "From Technobirth to Cyborg Babies: Reflections on the Emergent Discourse of a Holistic Anthropologist." Paper presented to the annual meeting, American Anthropological Association, Washington, D.C.

Dennett, Daniel. 1991. *Consciousness Explained.* Boston: Little, Brown.

Dery, Mark, ed. 1994. *Flame Wars: The Discourse of Cyberculture.* Durham, NC: Duke University Press.

Dobres, Marcia-Anne. 1995. "Prehistoric Cyborgs?—Or Thoughts on How to Weave Ancient Technosocial Webs in the Present." Paper presented to the annual meeting, American Anthropological Association, Washington, D.C.

Downey, Gary. 1991? "CAD/CAM Saves the Nation? Toward an Anthropology of Technology." Unpublished manuscript, Center for the Study of Science in Society, Virginia Polytechnic Institute and State University, Blacksburg, VA.

―――. n.d. "Steering Technology Development through Computer-Aided Design." Unpublished manuscript.

―――, Joseph Dumit, and Sarah Williams. 1995. "Cyborg Anthropology." *Cultural Anthropology* 10:264–269.

Dubinskas, Frank, ed. 1988. *Making Time: Ethnographies of High-Technology Organizations.* Philadelphia: Temple University Press.

―――. 1991. "American Individualism and Engineering Teamwork." Paper presented to the annual meeting, American Anthropological Association, Washington, D.C.

―――. 1993. "Modeling Cultures of Project Management." *Journal of Engineering & Technology Management* 10(182):129–160.

Eggan, Fred. 1954. "Social Anthropology and the Method of Controlled Comparison." *American Anthropologist* 56:743–760.

Egger, E. and I. Wagner. 1993. "Negotiating Temporal Orders. The Case of Collaborative Time Management in a Surgery Clinic." *Computer-Supported Cooperative Work. An International Journal* 1:255–275.

Ehn, Pelle. 1988. *Work-Oriented Design of Computer Artifacts.* Stockholm: Almqvist & Wiksell.

Ellul, J. 1964. *The Technological Society.* New York: Alfred A. Knopf.

Engels, Freidrich. 1961. *Scientific and Utopian Socialism.* New York: Pathfinder.

Erickson, Ken. 1995. "Reskilling the Jungle: Multilingual Craft Knowledge in a High Plains Boxed-Beef Factory." Paper presented at the annual meeting, American Anthropological Association, Washington, D.C.

Escobar, Arturo. 1994. "Welcome to Cyberia: Notes on the Anthropology of Cyberculture." *Current Anthropology* 35(3):211–231.

Evans, Michael, and H. Russell Bernard, 1987. "Word Processing, Office Drudgery, and the Micro-Computer Revolution." In Bernard, H. Russell, ed., *Technology and Social Change* pp. 239–258. Prospect Heights, IL: Waveland Press.

Fabian, J. 1991. "Ethnographic Objectivity Revisited: From Rigor to Vigor." *Annals of Scholarship* 8(3-4):381–408.

Ferne, Georges. 1989. *Science and Technology in Scandinavia*. London: Longman Group.

Feyerabend, Paul. 1975. *Against Method*. London: Verso.

Fleck, J. 1994. "Knowing Engineers?: A Response to Forsythe [Responses & Replies]." *Social Studies of Science* 24:105–103.

Forester, Tom, ed., 1985. *The Information Technology Revolution*. Cambridge, MA: MIT Press.

Forsythe, D. 1992. "Artificial Intelligence as a Cultural System." Paper presented to the annual meeting, American Anthropological Association, San Francisco, CA.

———. 1993. "Engineering Knowledge: The Construction of Knowledge in Artificial Intelligence." *Social Studies of Science* 23(3):445–477.

———. 1994. "STS (Re)constructs Anthropology." *Social Studies of Science* 24(1): 113–123.

———. 1996. "Representing the User in Software Design." Paper presented to the Workshop on Simulating Knowledge, Cornell University.

Frates, J., and W. Moulderup. 1983. *Computers and Life: An Integrative Approach*. Englewood Cliffs, NJ: Prentice Hall.

Freeman, Carla. 1990. "The New Era of Home-Based Work: Directions and Policies." *Anthropology of Work Review* 11(4):1–5.

Friedman, Andrew. 1989. *Computer Systems Development: History, Organization, and Implementation*. New York: Wiley.

Fugelsang, Lars. 1995. *Technology and New Institutions: A Comparison of Strategic Choices and Technology Studies in the United States, Denmark, and Sweden*. Copenhagen: Academic Press.

Fuller, S. 1992. "Talking Metaphysical Turkey about Epistemological Chicken, and the Poop on Pidgens." Paper presented to the annual conference, Society for Social Studies of Science, Gothenburg, Sweden.

———. 1995. "Two Cultures II: Science Studies Goes Public." *EASST Review* 14(1): 21–25.

Gallie, J. 1993. "Ritual." Paper presented to Department of Social Anthropology, University of Oslo.

Garfinkel, Harold. 1984. *Studies in Ethnomethodology*. Cambridge: Polity Press.

Garsten, Christina. 1994. *Apple World*. Stockholm: Stockholm University Studies in Social Anthropology.

Gatewood, John. 1991. "My PC and Me: Personal Computers and Academic Routines." Paper presented to the annual meeting, American Anthropological Association, Chicago.

Gersheny, J. 1978. *After Industrial Society: The Emerging Self-Service Economy.* London: Macmillan.

Geertz, Clifford. 1966. "Religion as a Cultural System." In Banton, Michael, ed., *Anthropological Approaches to the Study of Religion,* pp. 1–46. London: Tavistock.

Gibson, William. 1984. *Neuromancer.* New York: Ace Books.

Giddins, Anthony. 1987. *Social Theory and Modern Sociology.* Stanford, CA: Stanford University Press.

———. 1991. *Modernity and Self-Identity.* Stanford, CA: Stanford University Press.

Glenn, Natalie, and Roz Feldberg. 1979. "Proletarianizing Clerical Work: Technology and Organizational Control in the Office." In Zimbalist, Andrew, ed., *Case Studies on the Labor Process,* pp. 51–72. New York: Monthly Review Press.

Glimell, Hans. 1989. *Aatereroevra datapolitiken!* Linkoeping: Universitetet I Linkoeping Tema Teknik och social foeraendring.

Goffman, Erving. 1959. *The Presentation of Self in Everyday Life.* Garden City, NY: Doubleday Anchor.

Gough, K. 1968. "Anthropology: Child of Imperialism." *Monthly Review* 19(11):12–27.

Gould, S. J. 1981. *The Mismeasurement of Man.* New York: W.W. Norton.

Gramsci, A. 1971. *Selections from the Prison Notebooks.* London: Lawerence and Wishart.

Gray, Chris H., ed. 1995. *The Cyborg Handbook.* New York: Routledge.

Greenbaum, Joan. 1995. *Windows on the Workplace: Computers, Jobs, and the Organization of Office Work in the Late Twentieth Century.* New York: Monthly Review Press.

———, and Morten Kyng, eds. 1991. *Design at Work: Cooperative Design of Commputer Systems.* Hillsdale, NJ: Erlbaum.

Greeno, James. 1988. *Situations, Mental Models, and Generative Knowledge.* Palo Alto, CA: Institute for Research on Learning.

Gregory, Kathleen. 1983. "Native View Paradigms: Multiple Cultures and Culture Conflicts in Organizations." *Administrative Science Quarterly* 28:359–376.

Grint, Keith. 1991. *The Sociology of Work: An Introduction.* Cambridge, England: Polity Press.

———, and Steven Woolgar. 1992. "Computers, Guns, and Roses: What's Social About Being Shot?" *Science, Technology, and Human Values* 17(2):366–380.

Gross, Paul, and Normal Levitt. 1994. *Higher Superstition.* Baltimore: John Hopkins University Press.

Habermas, Juergen. 1997. "The Short Twentieth Century." Paper presented at Union College, Schenectady, NY.

Hakken, David. 1987. "Reproduction in Complex Social Formations: The Case of Sheffield." *Dialectical Anthropology* 12(2):193–204.

———. 1990. "Has There Been a Computer Revolution?" *Journal of Computing and Society* 1(1):13–30.

———. 1991. "Culture-Centered Computing: Social Policy and Development of

New Information Technology in England and the United States." *Human Organization* 50(4):406–403.

———. 1993a. "Computing and Social Change: New Technology and Workplace Transformation, 1980–1990." In Durham, W., ed., *Annual Review of Anthropology* 22, pp. 107–132. Palo Alto, CA: Annual Reviews.

———. 1993b. "International Information Infrastructure: Social and Policy Considerations" *Telektronikk* 89(4):106–109.

———. 1994. "The Cultural Construction of Computing in the Nordic Countries: Results from the Nordic National Computing Project." Paper presented at the annual meeting, European Association for Studies in Science and Technology, Budapest, Hungary.

———. 1995. "The Cultural Reconstruction of Science: A Response to Labinger." *Social Studies of Science* 25(2):317–30.

———. 1997a. "Technology, Democracy, and Work: State-Mandated Worker Involvement in Decisions Regarding Advanced Information Technology in the United States, Britain, and the Nordic Countries," In Hakken and Haukalid, Knut, eds., *Technology and Democracy: User Involvement in Information Technology. TMV Skriftserie Nr. 26.*, pp. 9–30. Oslo: Center for Technology and Culture.

———. 1997b. "Cultural Attitude, Social Environment, and Innovation—An Anthropologist's View." In *OECD Proceedings: Creativity, Innovation, and Job Creation*, pp. 157–176. Paris: Organization for Economic Cooperation and Development.

———, and Johanna Lessenger, eds. 1987. *Perspectives on U.S. Marxist Anthropology*. Boulder, CO: Westview Press.

———, with Barbara Andrews. 1993. *Computing Myths, Class Realities: An Ethnography of Technology and Working People in Sheffield, England.* Boulder, CO: Westview Press.

———, et al. 1991. *Oneida/Herkimer Human Needs Assessment.* Utica, NY: Greater Utica United Way.

Hall, Stuart. 1980. "Cultural Studies: Two Paradigms." *Media, Culture, and Society* 2:57–72.

Hammer, M., and James Champy. 1994. *Reengineering the Corporation.* New York: Harper Business.

Hannerz, U. 1992. *Cultural Complexity: Studies in the Social Organization of Meaning.* New York: Columbia University Press.

———. 1996. *Transnational Connections: Culture, People, Places.* London: Routledge.

Hanseth, Ole. 1997. "Information Infrastructures and Standardization Ideologies." In Hakken, David, and Knut Haukelid, eds., *Technology and Democracy: User Involvement in Information Technology, pp.* 73–92. Oslo: Center for Technology and Culture.

———, Kari Thoresen, and Langdon Winner. 1994. "The Politics of Networking in Health Care." Unpublished manuscript, Norwegian Computing Center, Oslo.

Haraway, Donna. 1991. *Simians, Cyborgs, and Women—The Reinvention of Nature.* London: Free Association Books.

_____. 1994. "Worldly Diffractions: Feminism and Technoscience." Paper presented to the annual meeting, Society for Social Studies of Science, New Orleans.

Harding, Sandra. 1991. *Whose Science? Whose Knowledge?* Ithaca, NY: Cornell University Press.

Harris, Marvin. 1980. *Culture, People, Nature: An Introduction to General Anthropology.* New York: Harper and Row.

Hartsock, Nancy. 1983. *Money, Sex, and Power: Toward a Feminist Historical Materialism.* Boston: Northeastern University Press.

Harvey, David. 1989. *The Condition of Postmodernity.* Oxford: Basil Blackwell.

_____. 1995. "Cartographies of Knowledge: Space, Time, and Public Discourses in Contemporary Capitalism." Paper presented to the annual meeting, American Anthropological Association, Washington, D.C.

Heath, Deborah. 1994. "Recombinant Fieldsites: Chimeric Ethnography and the Co-production of Technoscientific Research." Paper presented to the annual meeting, American Anthropological Association, Atlanta, GA.

Helmreich, Stefen. 1996. "Refiguring 'Nature' and 'Culture' in Ethnographic Engagement and Argument with Artificial Life Scientists." Paper presented to the annual meeting, American Anthropological Association, San Francisco.

Herrnstein, Richard, and Charles Murray. 1994. *The Bell Curve.* New York: The Free Press.

Hess, David. 1992. "Introduction: The New Ethnography and the Anthropology of Science and Technology." In Hess, David, and Linda Layne, eds., *Knowledge and Society: The Anthropology of Science and Technology,* pp. 1–26. Greenwich, CT: JAI Press.

HEW (US Department of Health, Education, and Welfare). 1972. *Work in America (Report of a Special Task Force to the U.S. Secretary of Health, Education, and Welfare).* Washington, D.C.: Government Printing Office.

Hobsbawm, Eric. 1994. *The Age of Extremes: A History of the World, 1914–1991.* New York: Vintage.

Hochwald, Eve. 1982. "Women, Technology, and Workplace Equality in the Newspaper Industry." *New Political Science* 9/10:137–142.

_____. 1991. "Women's Workplace Culture and Political Activism in the Newspaper Workplace." Paper presented to the annual meeting, American Anthropological Association, Washington, D.C.

Ingold, Tim. 1993. "Tool-Use, Sociality and Intelligence." In Gibson, E. Kathleen, & Tim Ingold, eds., *Tools, Language, and Cognition in Human Evolution,* pp. 429–446. Cambridge: Cambridge University Press.

_____. 1995. "'People Like Us': The Concept of the Anatomically Modern Human." *Cultural Dynamics* 7(2):187–214.

Jacobs, Jane. 1961. *The Death and Life of Great American Cities.* New York: Random House.

Jarvie, I.C. 1964. *The Revolution in Anthropology.* Chicago: Henry Regnery Co.

Joans, Barbara. 1992. "Outlaws and Vigilantes in Cyberspace." Paper presented to the annual meeting, American Anthropological Association, San Francisco.

Jones, Stephen. 1995. *Cybersociety: Computer-Mediated Communication and Community.* Thousand Oaks, CA: Sage.

Jules-Rosette, Bennetta. 1990. *Terminal Signs: Computers and Social Change in Africa.* Berlin: Mouton de Gruyter.

Kautz, Karlheinz. 1993. *Theories of Evolution and Their Relation to System Development.* Oslo: Norsk Regnesentralen.

Kidder, Tracy. 1981. *The Soul of a New Machine.* New York: Avon Books.

Kiel-Slawik, Reinhardt. 1995. "From Mechanization of the Brain Towards an Ecology of the Mind: A Personal Perspective on Contextualizing Design in Informatics." Paper presented to the decennial conference on Computers in Context, Aarhus, Denmark.

King, A. 1982. "Introduction: A New Industrial Revolution or Just Another Technology?" In Fredrichs, G.,and A. Schaff, eds., *Microelectronics and Society,* pp. 1–35. New York: New American Library.

Kling, Rob. 1980. "Social Analyses of Computing: Theoretical Perspectives in Recent Empirical Research." *Computing Surveys* 12(1):61–110.

———. 1992a. "Audience, Narratives, and Human Values in Social Studies of Technology." *Science, Technology, and Human Values* 17(2):349–365.

———. 1992b. "When Gunfire Shatters Bone: Reducing Sociotechnical Systems to Social Relationshps." *Science, Technology, and Human Values* 17(2):381–385.

Knudsen, Trond. 1993a. *Conception of Knowledge, Work Organization, Roles and Tasks in Three Systems Development Teams.* Department of Information Science, University of Bergen.

———. 1993b. "The Scandinavian Approaches." In Bansler, et al., *Proceedings of the 16th IRIS,* 29–38.

Komito, Lee. 1995. "The Impact of Groupware on a Face-To-Face Community of Practice." Paper presented to the annual meeting, American Anthropological Association, Washington, D.C.

Koons, Adam, and Ken Novak. 1992. "The Ethnography of a Computer Workplace in Cameroon." In Boone, Margaret, and John Wood, eds., *Computer Applications for Anthropologists,* pp. 27–48. Belmont, CA: Wadsworth Publishing Co.

Kraft, Philip. 1979. "The Industrialization of Computer Programming." In Zimbalist, Andrew, *Case Studies on the Labor Process,* pp. 1–17. New York: Monthly Review Press.

Kroker, Arthur, and Michael A. Weinstein. 1994. *Data Trash: The Theory of the Virtual Class.* New York: St. Martin's Press.

Kuhn, Thomas. 1970. *The Structure of Scientific Revolutions.* Chicago: University of Chicago Press.

Kunda, Gideon. 1992. *Engineering Culture: Control and Commitment in a High-Tech*

Corporation. Philadelphia: Temple University Press.

Kusterer, Ken. 1978. *Know-How on the Job*. Boulder, CO: Westview Press.

Kyng, Morten. 1994. "Collective Resources Meets Puritanism." *Scandinavian Journal of Information Systems* 6(1):85–96.

Labinger, Jay. 1995. "Science as Culture: A View from the Petri Dish." *Social Studies of Science* 25(2):285–306.

Lamphere, Louise. 1979. "Fighting the Piece Rate System: New Dimensions of an Old Struggle in the Apparel Industry." In Zimbalist, Andrew, *Case Studies on the Labor Process*, pp. 257–276. New York: Monthly Review Press.

———, ed. 1992. *Structuring Diversity: Ethnographic Perspectives on the New Immigration*. Chicago: University of Chicago Press.

Lane, Harlan. 1989. *When the Mind Hears: A History of the Deaf*. New York: Vintage Books.

Latour, B. 1987. *Science in Action*. Cambridge, MA: Harvard University Press.

———. 1993. *We Have Never Been Modern*. Cambridge, MA: Harvard University Press.

———, and Steve Woolgar. 1979. *Laboratory Life: The Social Construction of Scientific Knowledge*. Beverly Hills, CA: Sage.

Layne, Linda. 1997. "Studying Up, Down, Around and Through: Reflections on the Anthropology of STS." Paper presented to the first Workshop of the Committee on the Anthropology of Science, Technology and Computing, Troy, NY.

Lenk, K. 1982. "Information Technology and Society." In Fredrichs, G., and A.Schaff, eds., *Microelectronics and Society*, pp. 261–296. New York: New American Library.

Levins, Richard, and Richard Lewontin. 1985. *The Dialectical Biologist*. Cambridge, MA: Harvard University Press.

Levitan, S. A., and Johnson, C. M. 1982. "The Future of Work: Does It Belong to Us or the Robots?" *Monthly Labor Review* 105(9):10–14.

Lewis, Oscar. 1960. *Tepotztlan: Village in Mexico*. New York: Holt, Rinehart, and Winston.

———. 1966 "The Culture of Poverty." *Scientific American* 215(4):3–9.

Lincoln, Yvonna. 1992. "Virtual Community and Invisible Colleges: Alternation in Faculty Scholarly Networks and Professional Self-Image." Paper presented at the annual meeting, American Anthropological Association, San Francisco.

Lindqvist, S. 1984. *Technology on Trial: The Introduction of Steam Powered Technology into Sweden, 1715–1736*. Uppsala: Almqvist & Wiksell.

Lucas, Henry. 1975. *Why Information Systems Fail*. New York: Columbia University Press.

Lundsgaarde, Henry. 1992. "Knowledge Engineering and Ethnography." Paper presented to the annual meeting, American Anthropological Association, San Francisco.

Lyons, John. 1981. *Introduction to Theoretical Linguistics*. Cambridge: Cambridge University Press.

Lyotard, François. 1984. *The Postmodern Condition*. Minneapolis: University of Minnesota Press.

Madsen, Ole L., Boger Moeller-Pederson, and Kristen Nygaard. 1993. *Object-Oriented Programming in the Beta Programming Language*. Workingham, England: Addison-Wesley Publishing Company.

Malinowski, Branislaw. 1922. *Argonauts of the Western Pacific*. New York: E.P. Dutton.

Marcus, George, and Michael Fisher. 1986. *Anthropology as Cultural Critique: An Experimental Moment in the Human Sciences*. Chicago: University of Chicago Press.

Markussen, Randi. 1994. "Dilemmas in Cooperative Design." In Trigg, Randall, Susan Irwin Anderon, and Elizabeth Dykstra-Erickson, eds., *PDC'94: Proceedings of the Participatory Design Conference*, pp. 59–66. Palo Alto, CA: Computer Professionals for Social Responsibility.

Marx, Karl. 1871 (1967). *Das Kapital*. New York: International Publishers.

Marx, Leo. 1964. *The Machine in the Garden*. London: Oxford University Press.

Massey, Doreen. 1984. *Spatial Divisions of Labor: Social Structures and the Geography of Production*. London: Macmillan.

Mathews, Michael, ed. 1998. *Constructivism in Science Education: A Philosophical Examination*. Dordrecht: Kluwer Publishers.

Mead, George Herbert. 1962. *Mind, Self, and Society*. Chicago: University of Chicago Press.

Mead, Margaret. 1928. *Coming of Age in Samoa*. New York: New American Library.

Michaelson, Karen. 1995. "Community Networks and the Interplay of Space and Place in Cyberspace." Paper presented to the annual meeting, American Anthropological Association, Washington, D.C.

Mills, C. Wright. 1959. *The Sociological Imagination*. New York: Oxford University Press.

Mitchell, J. Clyde. 1969. *Social Networks in Urban Situations*. Manchester: Manchester University Press.

Muller, Michael. 1991. "Cooperative Work, Community Knowledge, and Computers." *Belcore Exchange* 7(6):8–12.

Mumford, Enid. 1979. *Designing Secretaries*. Manchester, U.K.: Manchester Business School.

Nash, June. 1987. "Corporate Hegemony and Industrial Restructuring in a New England Industrial City." In Hakken, D. and J. Lessinger, eds., *Perspectives in U.S. Marxist Anthropology*, pp. 231–258. Boulder, CO: Westview Press.

———, and Maria-Patricia Fernandez-Kelly. 1983. *Women, Men and the International Division of Labor*. Albany, NY: SUNY Press.

Nielsen, J. Flohr, and N.J. Relsted. 1994 "A New Agenda for User Participation: Reconsidering the Old Scandinavian Prescription." *Scandinavian Journal of Information Systems* 6(2):3–20.

Noble, D. 1984. *Forces of Production*. New York: Alfred A. Knopf.

Novick, David, and Eleanor Wynn. 1992. "Participatory Behavior in Participatory Design." Poster presented at PDC'92, The Participatory Design Conference, Cambridge, MA.

Nyce, J. M., and Jonas Loewgren. 1995. "Toward Foundational Analysis in Human–Computer Interaction." In Thomas, P. J., ed., *The Social and Interactional Dimensions of Human–Computer Interfaces,* pp. 37–46. Cambridge: Cambridge University Press.

Nyce, James, and Herbert Stahlke. 1996. "Belief, Community, and Technology on the Internet." *Practicing Anthropology* 18(2):33–35.

Offe, K. 1986. *Disorganized Capitalism.* London: Polity Press

Oldenburg, R. 1991. *The Great Good Place.* New York: Paragon House.

Organization of Economic Cooperation and Development. 1994. *The OECD Jobs Study: Facts, Analysis, Strategy.* Paris: OECD.

Orr, Julian. 1996. *Talking About Machines: An Ethnography of a Modern Job.* Ithaca, NY: Cornell University Press.

Pape, Tom, and Kari Thoresen. 1992. "Evolutionary Prototyping in a Change Perspective: A Tale of Three Municipalities." *Office, Technology, and People* 6(2-3):145–170.

Parsons, Talcott, and Edward Shils, eds. 1951. *Toward a General Theory of Action.* New York: Harper and Row.

Perrin, C. 1988. *The Moral Fabric of the Office: Organizational Habits vs. High-Tech Options for Work Schedule Flexibilities* [Working Paper, Alfred P. Sloan School of Management], Cambridge, MA: MIT Press.

Pfaffenberger, B. 1988. "The Social Meaning of the Personal Computer: Or, Why the Personal Computer Revolution Was No Revolution." *Anthropological Quarterly* 61(1):39–47.

———. 1990. *Democratizing Information: Online Data-Bases and the Rise of End-User Searching.* Boston: G.K. Hall.

———. 1992. "The Social Anthropology of Technology." *Annual Review of Anthropology* 21. 491–516.

———. n.d. "The Second Self in the Third World." Unpublished manuscript, University of Virginia.

Pfeiffer, J. 1987. "How Were Cities Invented?" in Hunter, David, and P. Whitten, eds., *Anthropology: Contemporary Perspectives,* pp. 79–84. Boston: Little, Brown.

Piercy, Marge. 1991. *He, She, and It.* New York: Fawcett Crest.

Piore, Michael, and Charles Sabel. 1984. *The Second Industrial Divide: Possibilities for Prosperity.* New York: Basic.

Putnam, Robert. 1995. "Bowling Alone: America's Declining Social Capital." *Journal of Democracy* 6(1):65–78.

Quale, T. U. 1992. "Om premissence for en evaluering." *Forskningspolitikk* 16–17.

Rabinow, P. 1992. "Serving the Ties: Fragmentation and Dignity in Late Modernity." In D Hess, David, and Linda Layne, eds., *Knowledge and Society: The Anthropology of Science and Technology,* 9:169–187. Greenwich, CT: JAI Press.

Radcliffe-Brown, A. R. 1952. *Structure and Function in Primitive Society.* Glencoe, IL: Free Press.

Read, Dwight. 1991. "Making Visible the Invisible: Computer Modeling of Hidden Structure." Paper presented to the annual meeting, American Anthropological Association, Chicago.

Redfield, Robert. 1960. *Peasant Society and Culture.* Chicago: University of Chicago Press.

Rifkin, Jeremy. 1995. *The End of Work: The Decline of the Global Labor Force and the Dawn of the Post-Market Era.* New York: G.P. Putnam's Sons.

Rheingold, Howard. 1993. *The Virtual Community.* New York: Harper Perennial.

Roberts, John, and Gary Chick. 1987. "Human Views of Machines." In Bernard, H. Russell, and Pertti Pelto, eds., *Technology and Social Change,* pp. 301–328. Prospect Heights, IL: Waveland Press.

Rose, Stephen. 1992. *The Making of Memory.* New York: Doubleday.

Rothschild, Joan, ed. 1983. *Machina Ex Dea: Feminist Perspectives on Technology.* New York: Pergamon Press.

Ruyle, G. 1987. "Rethinking Marxist Anthropology." In Hakken, D., and J. Lessinger, eds., *Perspectives on U.S. Marxist Anthropology,* pp. 24–56. Boulder: Westview Press

Sachs, Patricia. 1994. "Transforming Work: Collaboration, Learning, and Design." *Information Technology and People.*

Sacks, Karen. 1982. "Caring by the Hour: Women, Work and Organizing at Duke Medical Center." In Sacks, Karen, and Dorothy Remy, eds., *My Troubles Are Going to Have Trouble with Me,* pp. 172–192. New Brunswick, NJ: Rutgers University Press.

Saetnan, A. 1993. "Ultrasonic Tales: Gendered Controversies in the Construction of Ultrasound, Obstetrics and Pregnancy." Paper presented to the CRICT Constructivism and Feminism Conference, Brunel University.

Sahlins, Marshall. 1972. *Stone Age Economics.* Chicago: Aldine-Atherton.

Sandberg, Aake. 1994. *"Volvoism" at the End of the Road? Is the Closure of Volvo's Uddevalla Plant the End of a Human-Centered and Productive Alternative to 'Toyotaism?"* Working Paper #12, Center for Working Life, Stockholm.

Sandberg, Aake, Gunnar Broms, Arne Grip, Lars Sunstroem, Jesper Steen, and Peter Ullmark. 1992. *Technological Change and Co-determination in Sweden.* Philadelphia: Temple University Press.

Sapir, David. 1991. "Shareware and Computer Utilities for Dictionary Development." Paper presented to the annual meeting, American Anthropological Association, Washington, D.C.

Sayer, A. 1984. *Method in Social Science.* London: Hutchinson Press.

Schaff, A. 1982. "Occupation vs. Work." In Fredrichs G., and A. Schaff, eds., *Microelectronics and Society,* pp. 322–333. New York: New American Library.

Schneider, David. 1968. *American Kinship.* Englewood Cliffs, NJ: Prentice-Hall.

SCI-TECH-STUDIES. 1996. Discussion re: ethnography. Thu, 16 May 1996

10:53:49 ñ0400. X-ListName: Science & Technical Studies Discussion Group. archive URL: ftp://cctr.wukc.edu/list–archives/sts/.

Sclove, Richard. 1995. *Democracy and Technology.* New York: Guilford Press.

Scott, John. 1991. *Social Network Analysis: A Handbook.* London: Sage.

Sejersted, Francis. 1997. "Technological Development and the Right to Work." In *OECD Proceedings: Creativity, Innovation, and Job Creation.* Paris: Organization for Economic Cooperation and Development.

Serra, Artur. 1992. "Changes in the Academic Culture: The Computer University." Paper presented at the annual meeting, American Anthropological Association, San Francisco.

Shapiro, Dan. 1995. "The Limits of Ethnography: Combining Social Sciences for CSCW." In ACM, *CSCW '94 Proceedings.*

Shapiro-Perl, Nina. 1979. "The Piece Rate: Class Struggle on the Shop Floor." In Zimbalist, Andrew, *Case Studies on the Labor Process,* pp. 277–298. New York: Monthly Review Press.

Sherry, John. 1995. "Cooperation and Power." In Marmolin, H., et al., eds., *Proceedings of the Fourth European Conference on Computer-Supported Cooperative Work,* pp. 67–82. Stockholm, Sweden.

Shuler, Douglas. 1996. *New Community Networks.* New York: Addison-Wesley Publishing Company.

Siegel, Lenny. 1986. "Microcomputers: From Movement to Industry." *Monthly Review* 38:110–117.

Simons, G. 1986. *Silicon Shock: The Menace of Computer Invasion.* Oxford: Basil Blackwell.

Sinding-Larsen, Henrick. 1991. "Computers, Musical Notation, and the Externalization of Knowledge." In Negrotti, M., ed., *Understanding the Artificial,* pp. 101–125. London: Springer.

Singleton, V. 1993. "Actor Network Theory—A Useful Tool for Feminists Approaching Science." Paper presented at the CRICT Constructivism and Feminism Conference, Brunel University.

Slouka, M. 1995. *War of the Worlds: Cyberspace and the High-Tech Assault on Reality.* New York: Basic Books.

Smith, Keith. 1996. "Creativity, Innovation, and Job Creation." Paper presented to the OECD Conference, Oslo, Norway.

Snow, C.P. 1969. *The Two Cultures.* London: Cambridge University Press.

Solheim, Ivar. 1992. *Fra imitasjon til nasjonal innovasjon?* Oslo: NorskRegnesentralen.

Soper, Kate. 1993. "Feminism and Ecology: Realism and Rhetoric in the Discourses on Nature." Paper presented to the CRICT Constructivism and Feminism Conference, Brunel University.

Sproul, Lee, and Sara Kiesler. 1995. *Connections: New Ways of Working in the Networked Organization.* Cambridge, MA: MIT Press.

Stacey, J. 1987. "Sexism by a Subtler Name? Postindustrial Conditions and Postfeminist Conciousness in the Silicon Valley." *Socialist Review* 17(6):7–28.

Star, S. L. 1995. *The Cultures of Computing*. Oxford: Blackwell.

Stein, Maurice. 1960. *The Eclipse of Community*. New York: Harper and Row.

Stoll, Clifford. 1995. *Silicon Snake Oil: Second Thoughts on the Information Highway*. New York: Anchor Books.

Stolz, Markus, and Tamara Sumner. 1995. "Evolution, Not Revolution: PD in the Toolbelt Era." In *Proceedings of the Third Decenial Conference in Computers in Context*, pp. 30–39. Aarhus: Department of Computer Science.

Stone, A. R. 1995. *The War of Desire and Technology at the Close of the Mechanical Age*. Cambridge, MA: MIT Press.

Suchman, Lucy. 1987. *Plans and Situated Actions*. Cambridge: Cambridge University Press.

————, and Randall Trigg. 1991. "Understanding Practice: Video as a Medium for Reflecting and Design." In Greenbaum, J. and M. Kyng, eds., *Design at Work*, pp. 65–90. Hillsdale, NJ: Erlbaum.

Sweezy, Paul. 1963. *Theory of Capitalist Development*. New York: Monthly Review Press.

Thompson, E. P. 1963. *The Making of the English Working Class*. New York: Random House.

Toennes, Ferdinand. 1887 (1955). *Gemeinschaft und Gesellschaft (Community and Association)*. London: Routledge and Kegan Paul.

Toffler, A. 1983. *Previews and Promises*. New York: Bantam Press.

Toulmin, Stephen. 1990. *Cosmopolis: The Hidden Agenda of Modernity*. New York: Macmillan.

Traweek, S. 1988. *Beamtimes and Lifetimes: The World of High Energy Physicists*. Cambridge, MA: Harvard University Press.

Trigg, Randy, et al., eds. 1994. *PDC'94: Proceedings of the Participatory Design Conference*. Palo Alto: Computer Professionals for Social Responsibility.

Turkle, Sherry. 1980. "Computer as Rorschach." *Society* 172(12):15–24.

————. 1984. *The Second Self: Computers and the Human Spirit*. New York: Simon & Schuster.

————. 1995. *Life on the Screen: Identity in the Age of the Internet*. New York: Simon & Schuster.

United States Chamber of Commerce/Center for International Private Enterprise. 1996. January 4 Hypertext extension to "Generating Jobs, Raising Wages" [WWW document] URL http://www.cipe.org/e17/laborC_3_95.html.

Van Mannen, John. 1983. "The Fact of Fiction in Organizational Ethnography." In Van Maanen, John, ed., *Qualitative Methodology*. Newbury Park, CA: Sage.

Veblen, Thorstein. 1934. *The Theory of the Leisure Class*. New York: The Modern Library.

Wallace, Anthony F.C. 1970. *Culture and Personality*. New York: Random House.

Wallerstein, Emmanuel. 1976. *The Modern World System*. New York: Academic.

Weinberg, G. M. 1971. *The Psychology of Computer Programming*. New York: Van Nostrand.

Weizenbaum, Joseph. 1976. *Computer Power and Human Reason: From Judgement to Calculation*. New York: W. H. Freeman & Co.

Wenger, Etienne. 1991. "Communities of Practice: Where Learning Happens." *Benchmark*, Fall.

White, L. 1949. *The Science of Culture*. New York: Farrar, Strauss, and Giroux.

Whitehead, A. N. 1925. *Science and the Modern World*. New York: Mentor Books.

Winch, Peter. 1958. *The Idea of a Social Science and Its Relation to Philosophy*. London: Routledge & Kegan Paul.

Williams, Bernard. 1985. *Ethics and the Limits of Philosophy*. Cambridge, MA: Harvard University Press.

Williams, Raymond. 1989. *Resources of Hope: Culture, Democracy, Socialism*. London: Verso.

Winner, Langdon. 1977. *Autonomous Technology*. Cambridge, MA: MIT Press.

————. 1980. "Do Artifacts Have Politics?" *Daedalus* 109:121–133.

————. 1984. "Mythinformation in the High Tech Era." *IEEE Spectrum* 21(6):90–96.

————. 1994. "How to Criticize Technology Without Becoming a Luddite." Paper presented at the annual conference, Society for Social Studies of Science, New Orleans.

Winograd, Terry, and F. Flores. 1986. *Understanding Computers and Cognition: A New Foundation for Design*. Norwood, NJ: Ablex.

Wolfe, Alan. 1989. *Whose Keeper? Social Science and Moral Obligation*. Berkeley: University of California Press.

Wood, Stephen, ed. 1982. *The Degradation of Work?* London: Hutchinson.

Woolgar, S. 1993. *Constructivism and Feminism*. CRICT conference, Brunel University.

Woolley, Benjamin. 1992. *Virtual Worlds: A Journey in Hyped Hyperreality*. Oxford: Blackwell.

Wright, Eric Olin. 1979. *Class Structure and Income Determination*. New York: Academic.

Wynn, Eleanor. 1988. "Use of Anthropology in Information Technology." *Central Issues in Anthropology* 7(2):57–78.

————. 1991. "Taking Practice Seriously," in Greenbaum, J., and M. Kyng, eds., *Design at Work: Cooperative Design of Computer Systems,* pp. 45–64. Hillsdale, NJ: Erlbaum.

Zimbalist, Andrew. 1979. *Case Studies on the Labor Process*. New York: Monthly Review Press.

Zuboff, Shoshona. 1988. *In the Age of the Smart Machine*. New York: Basic Books.

Notes

Notes to Chapter 1

1. Other terms beside cyberspace—"Post-Industrial Society" (Bell 1973), "Information Society" (Lenk 1982), or "Cyberia" (Escobar 1994)—are also used to refer to this possible new type of social formation. While the former two are popular, they also mislead fundamentally (Stoll 1995). While the last means much the same as cyberspace, it has much less popular cache.

Similarly, there are other terms besides "AIT" for the artifacts/technical practices associated most closely with cyberspace—"high tech," "techno-science," "new information technology," "computer-mediated communication," "computer-mediated activity," or, most simply "computing." In this book, "AIT" is used because its connotations strike the optimal balance between generality and accuracy.

There are also many concepts—"computer revolution," "informating," "cyborgification"— to name the process by which use of AIT is supposed to produce the social preeminence of cyberspace. "Use of AIT" directs attention to potentially revolutionary ways of dealing with information while helping to correct a crucial misrepresentation of much cyberspace discourse, the idea that it is the first social formation that uses information extensively.

2. "Social formation" is the abstraction of preference in contemporary social thought with which to refer to social entities. This term does not give unwarranted priority to any one level, as is the case, for example, in standard uses of the term "society," which privilege the national level. From a "social formation" perspective, the basic questions are about how social entities are reproduced from one period to the next, whether more or less the same, modified somewhat, or fundamentally different.

3. Many of our contemporary difficulties in coming to terms with cyberspace are related to the way we think about culture, difficulties for which anthropologists bear major responsibility. In general, the difficulties turn on the presumptions of homogeneity which are part of the way anthropologists, especially in the United States, have used the culture concept. If it still makes sense to use the notion, it clearly needs to be rethought, a process encouraged by anthropological study of cyberspace.

4. In my view, "ethnography" refers to both: 1) executing revealing, extended field-based studies of a "people" or some more restricted aspect of its way of living, and 2) effectively communicating what was learned via fieldwork. As described in chapter 3, there has recently been a tendency to restrict attention only to the latter and ignore the former.

5. The change in the meaning of cyborg may be related to a development in robotics, the creation and marketing of feedback-based tools. A major conceptual breakthrough in this field occurred when designers gave up the presumption that in order to "do" a human task it was necessary for a machine to "look" like a human. As robots became less anthropomorphic, cyborgs became more "machino-morphic." These developments were symbolized in popular culture by the team of R2D2 and C3PO in the first *Star Wars* movie.

Notes to Chapter 2

1. Work anthropologists avoid the miscommunication which follows from trying to apply common research frames to incommensurate processes by basing their labels for eras on cross-cultural theory. Such miscommunications marr the discussion about how to characterize the modern social formation among sociologists. Giddens, for example (1987) discusses the heated exchanges between Marxist sociologists, who want to call the present era "capitalist," and Weberians, who prefer "industrial." "Capitalist" is too narrow because of the basic similarities between non-capitalist worker states like the Soviet Union was and capitalist social formations. Conversely, "industrial" as a label is confusing. It is sometimes used generally to refer to social formations in which much activity involves the production of commodities, but more frequently it is used narrowly to refer to a particular kind of commodity production, that which takes place in factories. Consequently, a term like "postindustrial" is equally confusing, used equally to refer to a new, post-commodity social formation and to a commodity social formation in which a presumed predominance of factory work is replaced by a predominance of "service" (see Bell 1973 and Gersheny 1978).

2. Much of the vast Futurist literature places great emphasis on computerization. Among those who tend to be computopians are Toffler (1983) and several other authors (see Forester 1985), as well as most of those coming out of the "Computers and Society" course curriculum in computer science (Frates and Molderup 1983). Although sociologists tend to be more pessimistic, or compputropian, there is clearly a procomputer position in sociology growing out of the work of scholars like Bernal (1965), Blauner (1964), and Bell (1973). The compputropians include Cooley (1982) and Simons (1986). Their views are interestingly related to Ellul (1964).

3. Pfaffenberger (1992) uses Thomas Hughes' concept of "technological system" to make similar points regarding the necessity of thinking of technology within a social context. "Actor network" as a concept has the advantage of not implying that the set of relations under examination are necessarily "systematic."

TAN theorizing does have problems. It can fall victim to David Schneider's critique of functionalism, the meager claim that things are the way they are because, if they weren't, they'd be different. That the scope of a network is difficult to specify theoretically is especially problematic for theory which, in its Callonian versions, attributes agency to nonhuman entities. Also, an obvious silence in the literature on TANs regards the problem of how one differentiates those networks which are related to basic social change, even evolutionary social change, from those which aren't. To say that the new technology actor network based on computing is significant, one needs standards of significance.

4. It is true that several famous anthropologists, like Margaret Mead, doubted the ability of anthropology to develop a general theoretical account for the multiplicity of human social forms. These arguments were developed primarily in reaction to nineteenth century evolutionism, and they were justified by their advocates primarily in methodological terms. After the Second World War, the pendulum within anthropology has swung again in an evolutionary direction. More anthropologists now accept the notion that, in addition to the profound differences in the cultural dynamics of different social formations, there are still some basic types which develop out of each other in an evolutionary, historical sequence. While careful to be critical of the shortcomings of particular theories of cultural evolution, or of naive applications of evolutionary frameworks, many anthropologists accept that the explanation of the changes in the fundamental ways of being human is a primary goal of anthropology.

5. The conceptual confusions here lead inevitably to analytic ones. For example, Stacey (1987) labels female workers in the Silicon Valley of California "quintessentially postindustrial" even though by her own description most of them work at unskilled factory jobs in the electronics industry, either on a "putting out," homework basis or on unautomated, repetitive, piecework based assembly lines.

6. The post-Braverman (1974) sociology of work has renewed interest in the theorization of the history of the labor process, the characteristic ways in which work and other activities mediated by the commodity nexus are executed in employment social formations. Among the most important findings of this scholarship is the demonstration that a change in the social organization at work, the introduction of a detailed division of labor, is much more important in creating the industrial revolution than the introduction of self-actuated machines. (Our historical fixation on machinery is yet another manifestation of technicism.) Important examples of the new sociology include Zimbalist (1979) and Clawson (1980).

7. U.S. anthropologists characteristically use the term "culture" to refer to that complex whole, including basic subsistence patterns, patterns of human interaction, and core symbols which are characteristic of the way a group of people live. Employment social formation anthropology uses the traditional anthropological notion of culture, but recognizes the characteristic forms of life shared by those in particular social strata in this formation, or their "class culture," as the appropriate unit of cultural analysis, rather than the patterns shared by those in a nation state (Bourdieu 1978).

Thus, forms of formal organization and networks of social relationships are as important a part of culture in this social formation as are shared senses of self-identity and patterns of symbolizing.

There are several reasons for focusing particularly on the working class. At least since Marx, many sociological studies have been oriented toward working class people, probably because most approaches see some connection between the specific experience of such people and the general dynamics of employment social formations. More specifically, much computer futurism has projected extensive change for working class people. As in the alternatives outlined initially, some have conceived of a liberation from onerous work through computerization as the most likely outcome, while others have imagined a vast expansion of unemployment, leading to an underclass of information poor working class people.

8. A technology-based label for this transformation would tend to overshadow the equally important role of new social arrangements in the causal drama. Because machine-mediated technologies were important in at least some stages (for example this would be at least a second, if not a third, "machine revolution"), a term which highlights a specific type of technology, cyber-facture, is more appropriate for these CR views than a general term like "technotronic."

Notes to Chapter 3

1. The current trend to use the term "ethnography" to primarily refer to writings based on such study rather than to the study itself follows from the postmodern argument that no text (ethnographic writing) has greater claim to veracity than any other. The dialectical realist philosophy which informs this book takes an different position: That, in attempting to answer important questions like the character of cyberspace, the inability to reach the absolute level of veracity implied in the Modernist project does not mean abandoning efforts to proceed as accurately as one can.

It is certainly true that even when doing fieldwork I have in mind the process of generating ethnographic text; field data are definitely affected by this aspect of the cultural construction of my purpose. At the time I am writing, however, I have in mind my field experiences. Thus, the quality of ethnographic writing is related dialectically to the quality of the fieldwork on which it is based, just as the fieldwork experience depends upon the worker's ability to give activities context; both are equally "ethnography."

2. The "computing in anthropology" discourse has considerable presence within the discipline, as in Boone and Wood (1992). Regular features appear in the *Anthropology Newsletter* on computing (for example, a column entitled "Soft.where"). There have been several efforts to organize a "computing in" section of the American Anthropological Association, none as yet successful. The AAA's "Committee on the Anthropology of Science, Technology, and Computing" has thrived, while the Committee on Advanced Technology as a Cultural Process of the Society for Applied Anthropology never established much momentum. (See also chapter 7.)

3. In an important paper on ethnographic epistemology (1954), Fred Eggan advocated the "method of controlled comparison" as a vehicle for handling the knotty ethnographic problem of how to generalize from specific concrete cases. In essence, Eggan's argument was to try to locate two very similar societies which shared a practice of interest, do field work in both of them, and try to figure out the connection between the practice in each and other similarities and differences. Since the occurrence of such similar social formations constitutes something like a "natural" experiment, controlled comparison should provide a basis for more confident generalizations.

In general, anthropologists follow Eggan's advice opportunistically; that is, they do controlled comparisons when the opportunity arises, as I believe it did with regard to Nordic computing. Our failure to adopt the practice more generally results less from a criticism of it than from the relative infrequency of the occurrence of such similarity in conjunction with the "right" problem. The Plains Indian societies that Eggan studied were, for a variety of historical reasons that he well understood, a particularly fruitful arena for controlled comparisons.

Notes to Chapter 4

1. Indeed, Borg is an implacable villain, a common characteristic of literary robotic/cyborgic creatures. This means their evocation typically involves substantial degrees of irony in cybertalk; see Dery 1995:6, and Haraway 1991.

2. On philosophy's side, this is partly due to recognition of the complex ways in which knowledge is socially constructed and the consequent limits of introspection as an analytic methodology. Philosophers are also becoming more sensitive to issues of cultural construction, especially the need for (and the difficulties in creating) cross-culturally valid constructs or mental tools. Through the turn to natural language and similar developments, philosophy has become more empirical, learning in the process more appreciation for the "real event" as opposed to the thought experiment. The critique of mainline philosophy as an elitist and Occidental project has added to this tendency. For all these reasons, philosophers are less inclined to invent abstract, personal "philosophical anthropologies" and more likely to address the data generated by the really existing discipline which goes by that name.

For its part, anthropology has become more philosophical. The direct influence of Winch (1958) during the rise of symbolist, semiotic conception of culture is one obvious example of philosophy's impact. Anthropologists are now as likely to cite as ultimate analytic sources Althusser, Derrida, or Wittgenstein as other anthropologists.

We have also developed a more reflexive awareness of our analytic language. Earlier in my career, I was attracted to sociological writing because it seemed an effective antidote to the simplistic empiricism/naive realism—such as implicitly assuming that the appropriate units of analysis are obvious, directly apprehended via the field encounter—characteristic of much anthropological writing. The deconstructive, postmodern turn in philosophy has added to our awareness of anthropology as an

Occidental enterprise and prompted a valuable examination of ethnography from a textual perspective.

3. The "Chinese room" thought experiment of philosopher John Searle is one of many arguments which attempt to reject the "strong program" in Artificial Intelligence: the idea that it is possible to model human intelligence more or less accurately on a machine. The "Monroe Room" is Dennett's counter.

Notes to Chapter 5

1. Mitchell and his colleagues tried to develop this insight into a general theory of networks. Unfortunately, their approach was overly abstract and had little further influence on the development of complex society anthropology. With the arrival of computers, there has been a revival of interest in formal models of social network analysis, especially the attempt to marry anthropological network analysis with digraphs and other mathematical tools (Scott 1991). I found these attempts of substantial initial interest in formulating my research on the networks creating and reproducing computing in the Nordic countries, but I was unable to use them for formal analysis (see Komito 1995). Network-related ideas have perhaps had more influence in theorizing (see Bott 1957) than in field methodology.

2. As in so many other areas of social thought, Anthony Giddens helps us understand this tendency. Under conditions of what he calls high modernity (1991), individuals are faced with the problem of living lives that are increasingly decomposing into multiple, increasingly distinct "spheres." Moreover, they must cope with this disembedding at a time when older authoritative narratives of society are rapidly loosing cache. As a result, individuals get less and less help creating a self-narrative which has coherence or a single "trajectory."

Under such circumstances, we appear to be less able to differentiate between our voluntary, close social relations and the broader networks in which we find ourselves irrespective of our choices. The difficulty analysts like Turkle, Stone, and Rheingold have distinguishing between micro- and meso-social relations in cyberspace is a psychological reductionism consonant with the condition which Giddens describes; it is also a failure of what Calhoun describes as the critical perspective. Moreover, the tendency to collapse meso and micro social relations into each other is associated with a declining sense that social action can lead to social change. Thus, the high modern individual is likely to confuse changing his spouse or friends with changing his social condition.

3. On a Marxist reading, the basic problem with "social capital" is that it is both a fetishized redundancy and an oxymoron. Like its obvious conceptual kin, the "human capital," of Blauner (1964) and the "cultural capital" of Bourdieu (1978), the term is an attempt to use an analogy to point out that there are "things" other than "monetary capital" which are important for social development. "Capital" however, as Marx explains at great length in *Das Kapital* (1871), is itself a social relationship, albeit one which people tend to talk of fetishistically, as if it were a distinct object. Capital in a

technical sense is reinvested profit, itself being surplus value, or the difference between the value of what workers produce and what they are paid. If invested profit fails to produce greater profit, capital ceases to exist. Workers only accept the exploitation of getting in wages less than the value of what they produce because they have no independent access to means of production. These are things over which capitalists have a monopoly, a transference from their feudal monopoly over access to land.

Thus, to think of capital as a "thing," or money, is to confuse its real source; to fetishize it, in the Marxian anthropological analogy. "Social capital" compounds the fetishization. The notion is oxymoronic in that "capital," being the appropriation of the value of the labor of many by an individual, is inherently "private," not social. It is redundant in that "social capital" would be a "social" social relationship.

4. Today, the eighteenth century Scottish Moralists like Adam Smith and Adam Ferguson are evoked primarily because they strongly articulated justifications for freeing the marketplace from state control—for example, Smith's idea that the "invisible hand" of the free market would lead to the greatest good for the greatest number. "Civil societarians" like Wolfe valuably stress how the Scots' free market arguments *presumed* a dense sociality and shared purpose as necessary preconditions of effective markets and "invisible hands." Inattention to non-market, non-state phenomena, the "third sector," is, in Wolfe's view, the fatal flaw in the social theory of militant marketeers like the contemporary "Chicago school" (1989).

To highlight these dimensions of civil society, writers like Wolfe choose to distinguish it from "the market." This contrasts with the practice of the Scots, who used "civil society" to label all the "social space" not occupied by the state, thereby encompassing within civil society relations of both sociality and of an economic, market sort. I follow the Scots' practice, conceiving of civil society as including *both* the often ignored "third spaces" (Oldenburg 1991) and the market. In employment-based societies, people's intermediate social relations almost always contain elements of both market mediation and diffuse solidarity. For example, as a college teacher I both engage my students in an abstract "pursuit of knowledge" and include them in the administratively mandated "body count" essential to justifying our institute's budget. Similarly, while students have one eye on "knowledge for its own sake," the other is on how "that piece of paper"—their degree—will improve their chances in regional job markets.

There are also policy reasons for considering civil and market relations together. Private organizations are now taken as the models which publics and private not-for-profits should try to emulate. Moreover, changes in all organizations are often presented as driven by AIT. Integrating an understanding of the actual role of AIT in organizational change with our understanding of the dynamics of non-market aspects of civil society would be of practical value. This is another reason for stressing the relative autonomy of levels rather than spheres of activity in discussing intermediate social relations.

5. It is precisely in regard to social movements that social theorizing in regard to community seems to have broken down. That is, in the 1960s and 1970s, at the same

time that community studies practitioners in sociology were announcing the eclipse of community, the rhetoric of community was being taken over by the new social movements of racial and ethnic minorities, women, gays/lesbians, and people with disabilities. As these latter have lost political effectiveness, their rhetoric of community, which retains its popular appeal, has been taken over by more conservative political groups, to the point where perhaps the strongest image of a "community" in the contemporary U.S. is that of the walled, exclusive suburban development.

While anthropologists continued to find community, they have in general failed to see it in political activity, perhaps as a consequence of models of culture which define it as "extra-" or "pre-political." It is only the emergence of debate over virtual communities which has rekindled a focus on the community as a theoretical object. Unfortunately, the tendency of "virtual communitarians" to dissolve the meso into the micro—that is, to invert the sixties political slogan, "the personal is political" into "the political is personal"—threatens once again to obscure the profound political issues at the heart of cyberspace.

Notes to Chapter 6

1. Because at least some macro-social relation-related processes include a popular component (e.g., mass elections), macro-social relations retain some aspects of voluntary, deliberate action, and are somewhat like meso-social relations. While for this reason one can distinguish macro social relations from structure as normally understood—as the kinds of things which preceed human action, go on, as it were, "behind our backs"—this differentiation has not been particularly important in my work. Macro-social relations and structure are dealt with together in this chapter.

2. Yet it can be argued that these presumptions have some negative consequences for the quality of Norwegian AIT actor networks. For example, strong pressure for participation may have impeded detailed documentation and analysis of actual patterns of computing, and thus a clearer perception of how it might be improved. These difficulties are compounded by the confusions over ultimate purpose so often a part of the action research on which much Norwegian IDS depends.

3. In his critique of nationalism, Benedict Anderson (1983) has demonstrated the important sense in which all trans-local social entities are based on collective "imagining," more or less deliberate creation of coordinated senses of identity and relationship. Cyberspace is like the national "imagined community" in that it is built on mental creations. At the same time, macro-social conceptions of cyberspace reject the presumption of the primacy of national identity, positing instead a more global sense of personhood. At their worst, cyber-rhetorics rehegemonize the worst aspects of nationalism at an even more reified, global "technotronically compelled" level. At their best, cyberspace imaginings offer a decentralized, network alternative to hegemonic nationalism.

4. There is reason to be skeptical of how much substantive impact will ensue from even conservative Swedish governments, given the imperative of merging with European Union structures. (It is interesting that one of the first acts of the new Social Democratic Prime Minister in 1994 was to move the computer off his desk!) The current popular model of corporate development is ABB, a transitional corporation formed by a merger of Swedish and Swiss organizations. ABB stresses corporate "good citizenship" as this concept is understood in each of the many national contexts in which it finds itself. Increased flexibility of capital flow across national boundaries in such a situation provides a powerful disincentive to all strong or controversial participative acts.

5. Answering such a question anthropologically is not an easy task. Most ethnographic discourses are grounded in a specific here and now, whether IRL or virtual, whereas most economic discourses are much more abstract, claiming to be about underlying processes characteristic of either several systems or "systems in general." This is one reason why this chapter is less about particular ethnography than the others. One of the accomplishments of the critical anthropology of the 1970s and 1980s (see Hakken and Lessinger 1986) was to demonstrate the structuralistics, often neo-classical, implicit in much ethnography. The ethnographer should attempt to make as explicit as possible the presumptions about general system characteristics, the political economic underpinnings of the framework, within which she works.

6. The actual *Jobs Study* policy recommendation is "enhance the creation and diffusion of technological know-how," although the narrative goes on to describe technological development as "the main force determining growth in productivity, employment and living standards in the medium and long run" (1994:44).

7. At various times, this black boxing has been identified as a flaw in neo-classical theorizing, related to their more general difficulty accounting for fundamental change. The tendency to perform CR rhetorics while failing to integrate these dynamics fully into their models is a shortcoming just as typical of anthropologists as of neo-classical economists (Hakken 1993).

8. I am as committed as I ever was to Marxist analysis of the dynamics of contemporary social formations; indeed, it would be difficult to identify a period in the history of wage/commodity-based social formations where capital had more power and hegemony. Any serious account of AIT must come to terms with capitalism as a political economy, and I believe that getting ourselves straight on AIT is essential to reconstructing a viable Marxist project.

9. It was precisely such shifts in labor market, long a feature of capitalist political economies, which was the ground on which Wood (1982) critiqued Braverman's deskilling hypothesis (1974).

10. The founding of the Society for the Anthropology of work was in part a response to the publication in 1972 of the HEW Report *Work in America,* which identified the American workplace in as a site of the "blue collar blues." This social trauma was traced to cultural factors, notably the mismatch between assembly line jobs and an

educated working class anticipating meaningful work. A generation of workplace ethnographers drew on Harry Braverman's work which, like the HEW Report, provided a socio-technical rather than strictly technical explanation for workplace dynamics.

Notes to Chapter 7

1. Much of Woolley's highly readable account of the philosophical puzzles and interesting, occasionally bizarre, practices of virtual reality devotees is highly recommended. In the end, however, he gets lost on the finer points of chaos theory and falls into the classic science journalism trap of hagiography, adopting an attitude of "trust them, they know what they are doing." He thus fails to establish a perspective for evaluating the claims of virtual realists.

2. In an interesting way, I now find myself contributing a bit to confusing the two again. I have recently joined efforts get the AAA to develop an information strategy, to think more carefully about how it can use CMC to influence its own fate as an intellectual and academic enterprise. It is perhaps on these grounds that those more concerned with applying cyberspace ethnography will be able to join hands with the "bits and bites" types. The change corresponds to the abrupt emergence of CMC as a legitimate field of broader cultural, including linguistic, study, as well as the growing fascination with cyborgs among anthropologists influenced by Science, Technology and Society (STS) and Donna Haraway–style feminism. Moreover, these interests were emerging from computing in anthropology, as in David Sapir's (1991) and John Gatewood's (1991) reflexive examinations of how computer-mediation changed both their anthropological practice and their lives, or Douglas Read's attempts (1991) to use computers to discover deep structure in culture.

3. Indeed, there will always be a tension between the more basic and more applied moments in social science within the context of a capitalist economy. This conflict can be understood and planned for, its most extreme forms avoided most of the time. Unfortunately, discussion of this conflict is too often obscured by the way it is framed. Thus, in anthropology, there is a tendency to treat the question of orientation as determined by who employs you; that academically employed anthropologists are "basic" researchers, whereas the non-academically employed are called "applied," but the meaning is really "practice-oriented." However, there is one thing of which I have been convinced by hanging out with Xerox PARCers, and that is that they do considerable basic research, while many so-called academic anthropologists are narrowly practice-oriented. (Suchman's more recent research is more practice oriented, however.) The important issue is not who pays you, but what is the tune you play, the fundamental orientation of the project: toward understanding some cultural process, or improving some practice.

4. Especially in fieldwork, two or more of these moments are often implicated in the same project. For example, one finds oneself in an interview formalizing tacit knowledge as part of trying to understand a basic cultural process. Indeed, as commu-

nicated by the phrase "participant observation," some degree of both "practice" and more detached observation is likely to be present in any ethnographic fieldwork. Moreover, even the most basic-oriented ethnographer has an ethical responsibility to focus on the practice implications of one's work (or policy); this is a prime motivation for the current chapter. One of the more unfortunate consequences of the elitism in anthropology is the tendency to assume that any research carried out for a private sector employer is necessarily practice-oriented and therefore not "basic." As a result, much basic-oriented applied research is ignored.

5. The difficulty here, it seems to me, lies in the tendency for the various moments to get in each other's way. A major difficulty on the Florence Project in Norway, for example, was a difference over the extent to which the ethnographer should share responsibility for producing an information system which "worked." As described in chapter 2, gaining entree to do research in technology settings, especially in a higher status professional role, often necessarily involves making certain knowledge claims of a professional and therefore "practice-oriented" sort. Having made such claims, it is difficult to be responsive to empirical actualities while defending the knowledge claims on which one's right to participate is based.

The solution to such dilemmas is not some rigid demarcation between the moments, but to manage them effectively. Indeed, I consider it one of the fortunate aspects of my career that I have been able to be involved in all in roughly equal proportions.

6. In a combative response to an article by Diana Forsythe (1994a), James Fleck (1994) critiques her for claiming that her ethnographer's view of work is superior to that of the engineers. In her response (1994b), Forsythe denies Fleck's claim, presenting herself as a relativist making no judgment in regard to whose view is more "accurate."

As is evident from personal experiences like that on the Disability Technology Project, I know well that which Forsythe describes as "a challenge familiar and often frustrating to cultural anthropologists: trying to discuss meanings constructed within a relativist framework with someone who talks like a positivist" (1994b:113). However, Forsythe's adoption of a purely relativist position is neither necessary nor helpful. Her work does make knowledge claims beyond merely the telling an interesting story: For purposes of creating a workable "expert system," Forsythe's critique *does* lay the basis for an approach superior to that of the engineers she describes.

Notes to Chapter 8

1. One final example of Labinger's non-reflexivity: restricting STS to "science," as opposed to "techno-science." Labinger asks rhetorically, "can anyone point to an example of an interaction between [Science as Culturers] and scientists [sic] that transcends the experimenter-subject relationship in any significant way?" (p. 4). There are—indeed, I am personally involved in—collaborative, nonhierarchical STS/techno-science interactions among some systems developers, both in Scandinavia and in the United

States. These interactions work because practitioners from both sides of the two culture divides share substantial parts of a world view. Reflexive techno-scientists and STSers learn to construct and be constructed by the substantial limitations of "practical" activity. (It is precisely because technologically oriented techno-scientists deal regularly with [socially constructed] real worlds that collaboration is easier for STSers with them than with scientifically oriented techno-scientists, who often need never "put their feet on the ground.")

Nonetheless, there are depressingly few examples of this sort of collaboration. The best parts of Labinger's comment draw attention to an important part of why this is so: obscure phrasings, Postmodern posturing, "in your face"isms which serve primarily to draw boundaries or impose personal agendas, in exactly the same manner as the techno-scientists we sniff at. The worst truth is not what Labinger's abstract describes as "the virtual total absence of any participation by practicing scientists" (p. 1), but rather that when they do participate, we have insufficient ideas about how to respond cooperatively.

2. This is primarily because of the problem I have being clear about the relationship between what is written and the IRL social processes which I take as the primary focus of ethnographic interest, whatever the particular social formation at hand. What writers of science fiction write, just as writers of ethnographic vignettes, is mediated by several factors, but a desire to reflect IRL as accurately as possible is not necessarily one among them. When the point, as in some experimental ethnography (see Clifford and Marcus 1986), seems to become the demonstration of the futility of attempts at accuracy, I am even less interested.

3. "Intellectual rules of thumb" is chosen as a deliberate alternative conception to the "design criteria" suggested by Sclove (1995) with regard to democratic technology and Schuler (1996) in relation to new communities. While I appreciate their projects and can even understand how their approaches may appeal to those with more positivist training, I also feel that the focus on such criteria can divert attention from the question of how to actually get somewhere worth going. This was essentially Engels' critique of Utopian socialism (1961).

Index

@ 4

Action Research 196

Actor Network Theory 185+, 246
  Critiques of 186, 247
  Realist 188
  Benefits of 189
  Strengths of 186
  (See also Technology Actor Networks 23+)

Advanced Information Technology (AIT) 1, 245
  Alternative Perspectives on 206
  Social Change, and
    Alternative Framework for Assessing Contribution to 23+
    Evolutionary Approach to 25+
  Transformative potential of 2

Agency 75, 78, 185
  Cyberspace cyborgs and 84
  People with disabilities 149
  Technology Actor Network and 23, 84

Anthropology, anthropological
  Applied vs. Basic Research in Computing 193
  Cyberspace Ethnography in 43+
    Examples of 47+
      Basic 47, 193+, 254
      Practice-oriented 52+, 193+, 254
    Hurdles Encountered doing 55+
    Issues in using to study cyberspace vs. other social formations 67
    Locating (siting) within 58
    Roots and Forms of 39+

Critique of ethnography within 63
Cyborg 71+
Ethnography, Distinctive Features of 43+
  Versus Other Forms of 43+
General 25
Of computing versus in Computing 44, 193, 248, 254
Philosophy and 249
Rethinking Anthropology 224
Science Question in 223
Technological Ambivalence of 64

Archaeology of language, illustrated 81

Artificial Intelligence 72, 250

Artificial Life 89

Bio-cultural perspective 78

Biological Anthropology 72

Capital 158, 218, 253
  (See also Social Capital)

Civil Society 104
  Cyberspace Meso-social Relations and the Destruction of 95
  Policy Issue, as a 104

Class culture 30, 247+

Collaboration, Anthropology and Information System Development 81

Communication and computerization in Professionalized Workspaces 114

Community 251-2
  Ethnography of Cyberspace forms of 97+
  US Computing 97
  Virtual, or Virtually No, Community? 126+

Community Computing 99
  Civil Society and 97
  Democracy and 106
  Ethnological Issues in Community
    Computing 104
  Jay County, Indiana 100
  In US 99
  Re-coupling with place via? 105
  RSSAIT and 99
  Eastern Washington State 102
Computer Revolution (CR) Thought 15+
  Absence of Empirical Study of 19
  Alternative to, an 23+
  Conclusions regarding 34
  Deconstructing 17
  Devolution, as 32
  Echoes of Technicism in 18–19
  Ethnocentrism in 20
  Elements of 15
  Has There Been a? 15+
  Identity and 87+
  Logical Flaws in 21–2
  Rhetorical Inflation of 18+
  Skepticism about 18+
  Social Problem, as a 17
  Social Revolution, as 27
  Source in Advertising of Much
    Rhetoric of 18
  Species Revolution, as 26
  Stage in the employment-type social
    formation, as a New 29, 120+
  Technology, CR as "just another" stage
    in 32
Computer Science 13, 41+
Computer Supported Cooperative Work
  (CSCW) 114
Computers, Computing, Computeriza-
  tion 16, 246
  Communication in Professionalized
    Workspaces 114
  Cyber-labor as a Social Activity: Ubiq-
    uitous Computing 121

Workspace Cultures and 108+
  National Aspects of 134+
  Cultural Aspects of 134+
    Second World Imaginings 136
    Third World Computing 138
Computopian 17
Compputropian 17
Conclusions
  Analytic 216+
  Complexity of Cyberspace 216
  Culture and 219
  Rethinking the units of Social Analysis
    216
  Labor Theories and Cyberspace 217
Consciousness 73
  Alternative Cyborgic Model of culture
    and 80+
  Critique of Dennett's Concept of 78+
  Cyborgic Model of 72+
  Dennett's View of, illustrated 76
  Folk" Model of, accounting for the 75
  Non-Cartesian Approach to 73
Creolized Objects 84
Culture 70, 245
  Alternative Cyborgic Model of 80+
  Conceptualizing Entities to Bear 71
  Contested Terrain, as 80
  Critique of Anthropological concept
    of 62
  Critique of Dennett's Concept of 79
  Cyborgic Entities and 78+
  Cyborgic Model of Illustrated 81
  Exploring Cyberspace Culturally 2
  Nation and 131
  Occupational in cyberspace 117
  Organizational
    In Cyberspace 115+
    Summary of Preliminary Studies of
      Computing and 120
  Relevance of in Any Complex Social
    Formation 62
  Computing and Workspaces 108+

Work Culture in Cyberspaced Scandinavia 111
Culture-centered Computing 47, 198
Cyberfacture, New Stage in the Labor Process 30, 120+, 173, 248
Cyberspace 1, 5, 216, 245
  Agnosticism regarding 5
  Continuity of Organizations in 117
  Cultural exploration of 2
  Ethnography of 37+
  Ethnography of Communities in 97+
  Gendering in organizations in 118
  Issues in the Ethnography of 7+
    Summary of 11
  Management Strategies in 118
  National/Cultural Differences in Constructing, Scandinavia 142+
  Occupational cultures in 115
  Organizational Culture in 115+
  Organizational Dynamics in 117
  Political Economy of 107, 164+
  Race/Ethnicity in organizations in 119
  Self-Identity in 87+
  Social Formation Type linked to Information, as a 28
  Social Relations in 93+
  Studies 2, 10
  Virtual Work in 119
Cyberspace Research, a Narrative of 12
Cyborg, Cyborgic 4, 68, 71, 246
  Alternative Model of Culture 80+
    Illustrated 81
  Anthropology, 71+
  Cyberspace Entities
    Actants, as 84
  Cultural Processes 78+
  More Creolized Forms of, as 84
  Mental Activity, A Model of 72+
Cyborgs@cyberspace (book) 1
  Intellectual Problem at the Center of 5
  Structure of 11
  Political Potential of 226

Data 21
Democracy
  Community Computing, and 107, 216
  Cyberfacture and 125
  Deskilling 253
  Disability 87, 149
  Identity in cyberspace and 88
  Macro-Social Relations and 176
  Objects in cyberspace, and 86
Eastern Washington State 102
Economics 158+, 215
  Changing Dynamics of in Employment Social Formations 158
  Neo-Classical Approaches to in Cyberspace 158+
  Substantive Political Economies of Cyberspace 169+
    Shoe workers in the Third Italy 170
    Cyberspace Political Economics in 1980s Sheffield 172
  Technicist Political Economics of Cyberspace 161, 164+, 253
    Third Wave Workers of the World, Unite! 164
    Critique of the Historical/Evolutionary Moment 168
Education, computerized Teaching Machines and 179–80
Email, Netiquette: and Professionalism at NR 108
Empirical Data on AIT and Social Change, Initial 33+
Employment Social Formation Type, New Stage in 30
Entity 69+
  Conceptualizing a Culture-Bearing 71
  Conclusion: Embodied Imaginings of a 91
  Cyborgic and Cultural Processes in 78
  Enhanced Actor Networks or More

Creolized Objects, as? 84+
Problem, as 70
Question 7, 69
Ethics 84, 87, 181, 209
Ethnography (Fieldwork) 37+, 246, 248
  Analysis in 97
  Anthropological Forms of
    Applied, Professional Politics of
      191
    Critique of within 63, 93
    Distinctive features of 45
    Epistemological Challenges in 62+,
      255
    Locating Cyberspace Ethnography
      within 64
    Versus other forms of 43+
  Backlash against, in Science, Technol-
    ogy, and Society (STS) 38, 60
  Cyberspace, of 2, 41+
    Anthropological 43+
    Applied to Information System De-
      velopment 195
      Policy Implications of 203+
    Communities in 97+
    Defense of 68
    Information System Development
      80+
    Key Issues in 7+
    Knowledge 179+
    Prime Task of 3
    Practice Question in 52,191+
    Proto- , Representativeness of 61
    Reconstructed Techno-science
      Practice, Implications of 225
    Regions 97+
    Rhetorics of, Implications 225
    Work 108
  Ethics of 209
  Information Systems Development, of
    (See ISD)
  Using to Study Cyberspace Versus
    Other Social Formations 67

Versus Natural Science Ways of Know-
  ing 39+
Way of knowing, as a 3.1.1
Ethnological Claims, Ethnology 3, 25,
  249
  Community Computing, in 104
  Those Presented Here 4
Evolution, Evolutionary Approach 25,
  168, 218, 247
  To AIT and social change, an 25+
    Computerization as devolution 32
    CR as "Just Another Technology"
      31
    New stage in the Employment So-
      cial Formation, CR as a 29,
      120+
    Social Revolution 27
    Species Revolution 25
  Cyborgs in 72, 254
  Non-progressivism in 218
Fieldwork (See Ethnography)
Florence Project 196+
Futurism 246
Gender, Gendering
  Cyberspace Organizations, in 118,
    196
  Issue of Technology and 152
  Scandinavia, in 151
Global Factory 170
Globalism 130 163
  Neo-classical Economics and 163
Humans, End of the Age of 25
Identity
  Computer Revolution and 87
  Culture and 90
  Dissolution of Meso-social Relations
    into 107
  Nation and 130
  Self- Issue 7
  Self- in Cyberspace 87+
Imagining 252
  Embodied forms of 91

Grounding Cyberspace in Present
Problems 227
Informatics 13, 41
Information 20–21
Social Formation Type linked to Cy-
berspace, as a 28
Information Society (Critique of Label)
19
Information System Development (ISD)
80, 85
Alternative Cyborgic Model of Cul-
ture, Based on the Ethnography of
80+
Ethnography in 200, 202+
Nordic, Scandinavian Approach to
110, 196+, 255
International Information Infrastructure
(III) 190+
Internet 140
Internet Society 141
Italy 170
Jay County, Indiana 100
Job, end of the Age of the 27, 162
Jobs Study 161, 253
Knowledge, and 180
Knowledge 21, 179
Banking Theory of 80, 180
Constructivism and 181
Cyberspace and the Practice of
Ethnography 179+
Question in Cyberspace 179
Alternative Perspectives 181
Deconstructing 182
Reconstructing 183
Knowledge Society 180
Labor
Cyber- as a Social Activity 121
Cyberfacture as a New Stage in the
Process 30, 120+
Social Formation 28
Theory of Value 218
Language

Archaeology of 81
Creoles in 85
Metaphor and Imagination in 215
Postmodern textualism and 186
Listserv 37
Macro-Social Relations 129+
Management
Organizational "Chain of Command"
as Oxymoron 122
Strategies 118
"Mastering" as a hurdle to doing cyber-
space ethnography 57
Marxism 165+, 253
Mental Activity (See consciousness)
Meso-Social Relations 93+
Micro-Social Relations 87+
Modernism 39, 73+, 129, 89, 182, 219
Multi-User Domain (MUD) 87
Object-oriented (MOO) 87
Myth, Mythinformation 18
Nation 129+
National Information Infrastructure 134,
142
Netiquette: Email and Professionalism at
NR and 108+
New Municipal Socialism in Sheffield
203+
New University Conference 179
Nordic National Computing Project
(NNCP) 49, 143
Basic ethnographic research, as 47+
Course of Work 50
Field experience
Norway 50
Sweden 51
Premises and objectives 47
Procedures Executed 51
Norway
Characteristics of Computing Infra-
structure 147
Fate of the Nation and Nordic Com-
puterization 156

Field aspect of NNCP in 50
National AIT 142, 252
National Policy 147
National Technology Discourses 144
National/Cultural Differences in Constructing Cyberspace 142+
Case Studies of 149
US and Nordic Computing Compared 134+
Professional Politics in 157
Norwegian Computing Center (NorskRegnesentral, NR) 50, 147, 197
Netiquette: Email and Professionalism at 108+
Objects, Cyberspace Entities as 85
Object Orientation 86, 91
Occupational Cultures 115+
Oneida County, New York 52
Organization, Organizational 108+
Continuity of when Cyberspaced 115
Gendering in Cyberspace in 118
Organizational Dynamics in Cyberspace in 118–9
Ethnography of Culture in Cyberspace 115+
External Networks 122
Quality and 121
Race/Ethnicity in cyberspace in 119
Teams, Matrices, and Internal Networks 122
Organization of Economic Cooperation and Development (OECD) 161
Palo Alto Research Center (Xerox PARC) 195, 197+, 249
Participatory Design (PD) 111, 135, 154, 197–8
Philosophy 73+, 249
Place
Decoupling of Space from 86
Meso-Social Relations, in 94
Re-coupling with space via commu-

nity computing? 103
Virtual Work and 119
Policy
Civil Society as an issue 105
Implications of Applied Cyberspace Ethnography for 203+
Reinventing Government outside of Government 125
Textualism and 186
Political Economy 164+
Level of Socio-cultural integration and Cyberspace 10
Political Constructivism 186
Politics 176
Community computing, democracy and 106
Macro-Structurations and 128, 226
Meso-Social Relations and 96
Post-Industrialism 247
Postmodern, Postmodernism 17, 23, 56, 87, 94, 129, 131, 182–3, 250
Practice 61
Cyberspace, in 92
Versus Basic Research 194
"Probleming" as hurdle to doing cyberspace ethnography 55+
Professional, Professionalism
Barrier to Collaboration, as a 201
Communication in relation to 114
Mastery and 57
Netiquette and email 108
"Protecting" as hurdle to doing cyberspace ethnography 60
Race/Ethnicity in cyberspace organizations 119
Realist Actor Network Theory (RANT) 188
Reconstructing Social Service through Advanced Information Technology (RSSAIT) 52
Community computing, as 99
Practice-oriented project, as a 52

Reinventing Government outside of Government 122
Results 216+
  Empirical: What We Can Say about Cyberspace 213+
Region 93+
  Ethnography of Cyberspace Forms of 97+
  Sheffield/South Yorkshire 97+
Representativeness of Cyberspace Data 61
Reproduction 97+
Science 31, 42
  Fiction 227, 256
  Question 220+
  Syncretic 67
  Technology, and Society (STS) 84
"Siting" in Cyberspace Ethnography 58
Scandinavian Approach to Information Systems Development 110, 196, 255
Sheffield/South Yorkshire Region 97, 172
Social
  Capital 95
    Critique of 250–1
  Change and AIT, Evolutionary Approach to 25+
    Initial Empirical Data on 33+
  Constructivism 186
  Formation 1, 245
    Reproduction 159+
    Type of, linked to Information and Cyberspace 28
  Movements and Cyberspace 96
  Networks 94, 250
  Problem, CR as a 17
  Relations
    Close, Intimate, Micro- Level of 8
    In Cyberspace 93
    Intermediate, Mid-range, Meso-Level of 93+
      Conclusions Regarding 126
      Contemporary Issues in 94+

Ethnography of Cyberspace, Issues in 96
  Place in 94
  Politics and 96
Macro Level of 9
  Cyberspace, in 129+
  The Nation: A Declining Form of? 129
  Structure and 131, 252
  Imagination/reproduction of 133
  Social Movements in 251–2
Revolution, CR as a 27
Sociology of Work 30, 108, 247
Space
  Computing and Workspace Cultures 108+
  Virtual Work 119
Species Revolution 25
Structure in Cyberspace 129+. 131
Surfing (e.g., the Internet) in Cyberspace Ethnography 58
Sweden
  Field aspect of NNCP in 51
  National/Cultural Differences in Constructing Cyberspace 142+
  National AIT 142
  National Policy 147
  National Technology Discourses 146
Talking as a Hurdle to Doing Cyberspace Ethnography 61
Technoscience 66
  Non-Modern Conception of 219
  Practice, Reconstructing 217, 220+
Technicism 18–19
Technology, Technological 20, 31, 63+, 185
  Actor Network 23+
    Cyberspace Cyborgs as Actants in? 84
    Entities in Cyberspace, Enhanced? 84+

Social Agency and 23
Anthropological Ambivalence toward 64
Evolutionary Stage #4: Computer Revolution as "Just Another" 31
Forms of 31
General Evolution, in 83
Science Question in Technoscience 220
Transfer 85
Textualism 186
Third Places 103
Trade Unions 126+
Transnational Computer Mediated Communications 140+
Internet 140
The World Wide Web 141
National Information Infrastructures 142
Scandinavia and Differences in 142+
Ubiquitous Computing 121
Unemployment 162
United States
Community Computing in, 99
National Computing Discourse 139
Versus Nordic 134+
User Participation 88, 112, 155
Virtual Reality 90, 183, 254
Work 28, 246
Anthropology of 253
Assessing Culture Correlates of 111
Communication at 114
Culture 115
Cyber-labor as a Social Activity 121
Emergence of Cyberfacture Stage 30, 120+
Meat Cutting 120
Virtual 125–6
Working Class 47, 171, 248
Workspace
Cultures, Computing and 98, 108+
Versus Workplace 109
World System 130
World Wide Web 141
Xerox PARC 122, 197+, 254